Remembering

War

REMEMBERING WAR

The Great War Between
Memory and History in
the Twentieth Century

Jay Winter

Yale University Press
New Haven & London

Published with the assistance of the Frederick W. Hilles Publication Fund of Yale University.
Published with assistance from the Kingsley Trust Association Publication Fund established by the Scroll and Key Society of Yale College.

Set in Minion by Keystone Typesetting, Inc., Orwigsburg, Pennsylvania.
Printed in the United States of America by Sheridan Books, Ann Arbor, Michigan.

Library of Congress Cataloging-in-Publication Data
Winter, J. M.
Remembering war : the Great War between memory and history in the twentieth century / Jay Winter.
p. cm.
Includes bibliographical references and index.
ISBN-13: 978-0-300-11068-5 (hard cover : alk. paper)
ISBN-10: 0-300-11068-5 (hard cover : alk. paper)
1. World War, 1914–1918. 2. Memory—Social aspects. 3. War and society. 4. Civilization, Modern—20th century. I. Title.
D523.W579 2006
940.3'14—dc22

                                                            2005028452

A catalogue record for this book is available from the British Library.

10 9 8 7 6 5 4 3 2 1

Contents

Part Three: *Theaters of Memory*

Part Four: *The Memory Boom and the Twentieth Century*

Acknowledgments

This book is the outcome of a very long engagement with the First World War, both inside and outside the academy. I owe much to my colleagues at the Historial de la grande guerre at Péronne, Somme, and to my friends and students at Cambridge, Columbia, and Yale. All shared my ruminations about war and remembrance, and alongside others who came to lectures, classes, and seminars, they offered valuable leads and invaluable criticisms. Some individuals went even further out of their way to read various drafts of the whole manuscript. My thanks for this major effort go to Jan and Aleida Assmann, Joanne Bourke, Antoine Prost, Diana Sorensen, Ken Inglis, and Harvey Mendelsohn. Responsibility for stubborn interpretations and errors are mine alone.

This book is an extended argument about remembrance and war, a subject which has dominated my private and professional life. Many of these chapters arose under diverse circumstances. The hospitality of colleagues at Indiana University at Bloomington, which welcomed me as Patton lecturer, and at the Royal Irish Academy, Dublin, enabled me to develop some of these arguments. Eight of these chapters have not appeared in print before, and all others have been rewritten to braid together with the others. I am grateful for permission to reproduce images or other material from the

Fortunoff Video Archive at Yale, Leo Baeck Institute, KCET television, the Historial de la grande guerre, and the *American Historical Review*. I am happy to acknowledge support from the Hilles Fund at Yale University.

Remembering

War

_____

Introduction
War, Memory, Remembrance

In this book, I offer an interpretation of what I call the "memory boom" of the twentieth century—the efflorescence of interest in the subject of memory inside the academy and beyond it—in terms of a wide array of collective meditations on war and on the victims of war. This is a partial account of a subject whose sources are very disparate, but many of them, I believe, return time and again to the theme of warfare and its consequences. The initial impulse behind this varied and ubiquitous cultural project emerged during the 1914–18 war. The images, languages, and practices which appeared during and in the aftermath of the Great War shaped the ways in which future conflicts were imagined and remembered. It is in this sense that I refer to the survivors of the Great War as the first (though not the last) "generation of memory" in the twentieth century.

The structure of this study follows its central argument. Two programmatic essays sketch out the varied fields in which the memory boom has appeared in the period since the Great War. I offer some thoughts about its overdetermined trajectory. No one cause can be isolated as decisive, but—so this book argues—the need to attend to, to acknowledge the victims of war and the ravages it causes is at the heart of the memory boom in contemporary cultural life.

Drawing on earlier work on the concept of "remembrance,"[1] the second part of the book presents a variety of signifying practices which have linked history and memory, in particular for those who lived through the upheavals of the first half of the twentieth century. What were their modes of collective remembrance, understood as activities shared by collectives, groups of people in the public domain? Through what means did they trigger their own memories and convey them to those who weren't there? Photography did so; so did the publications of soldiers' letters, so did poetry, war novels, and plays. These forms of remembrance are discussed alongside commemorative projects more directly associated with war losses—the construction of war memorials of various kinds and the braiding together of family history and national history. And imperial history as well, since imperial populations went to war, and imperial families were tied together for a time by shared patterns of remembrance.

In the third part of this book, titled "Theatres of memory," I discuss film, television, museums, and war crimes trials as sites where, at times, long after the cessation of hostilities, groups and individuals negotiate the distance between history and memory in their representations of war. These are spaces where those who were not there see the past not in terms of their own personal memories, but rather in terms of public representations of the memories of those who came before. In a concluding essay, I try to offer some thoughts on the significance for the cultural history of the twentieth century of these practices and discursive engagements with the subject of history and memory in the context of war.

The balance of evidence cited in this book concerns the First World War. That is necessarily the case, since outside the United States it is a commonplace that the Great War set in motion the forces producing both the later world war and the forms in which contemporaries understood its meaning. That is what I read into the term the "Great War." Indeed, one of the arguments of this book is that it is in the Great War that we can see some of the most powerful impulses and sources of the later memory boom, a set of concerns with which we still live, and—given the violent landscape of contemporary life—of which our children and grandchildren are unlikely to be free.

In the twentieth century, there were many generations of memory. I start with pre–1914 explorations of the landscape of memory, and then in the first part of the book I explore remembrance as a multiform social project during and after the First World War. To offer a full account of remembrance in the twentieth century as a whole is beyond the scope of this book. The Second World War and the Holocaust drew upon and transformed the iconographic and programmatic character of remembrance in striking and enduring ways. Other scholars have explored this subject in powerful and sophisticated ways.[2] Nevertheless, it is important to recognize the extent to which in Europe and elsewhere the shadow of the Great War has been cast over later commemorative forms and cadences.[3]

Memory and Remembrance

Anyone who ventures into this field must take a stand on some of the key concepts and linguistic terms which dominate discussions of remembrance. First the contested term "memory." Elsewhere, Emmanuel Sivan and I urged the shift from the term "memory" to the term "remembrance" as a strategy to avoid the trivialization of the term "memory" through inclusion of any and every facet of our contact with the past, personal or collective.[4] To privilege "remembrance" is to insist on specifying agency, on answering the question who remembers, when, where, and how? And on being aware of the transience of remembrance, so dependent on the frailties and commitments of the men and women who take the time and effort to engage in it.

The work of cognitive psychologists reinforces the notion that the act of recalling the past is a dynamic, shifting process, dependent on notions of the future as much as on images of the past.[5] A key element in this work is the view that memory is the product of a multitude of impulses, drawn together in the form of a collage, or approximation of a past event. Schacter notes that our memories are not photographic, producing snapshots of the past. Instead "we recreate or reconstruct our experiences rather than retrieve copies of them. Sometimes in the process of reconstructing we add feelings, beliefs, or even knowledge we obtained after the experience. In other words, we bias our memories of the past by attributing to them emotions or knowledge we acquired after the event."[6] This approach to the notion of memory as unstable, plastic, synthetic, and repeatedly reshaped is the fundamental premise on which this study rests.

Collective Memory and the Memory of Collectives

If individual memory is more process than product, then it is essential for us to insist on process—and the evidence of process—when confronting the traces of groups of people trying to recall or retrieve facets of the past. Most of the time, collective memory—a term the cavalier use of which I criticize in this book—is not the memory of large groups. States do not remember; individuals do, in association with other people. If the term "collective memory" has any meaning at all, it is the process through which different collectives, from groups of two to groups in their thousands, engage in acts of remembrance together. When such people lose interest, or time, or for any other reason cease to act; when they move away, or die, then the collective dissolves, and so do collective acts of remembrance. This is what Maurice Halbwachs meant when he wrote his seminal work on *Les cadres sociaux de la mémoire* in 1925.[7]

The loose usage of the term "collective memory"—framed to mean virtually anything at all—in every corner of the arts and humanities, has persuaded me to abandon the term whenever possible.

Collective remembrance is another matter entirely: it points to time and place and above all, to evidence, to traces enabling us to understand what groups of people try to do when they act in public to conjure up the past.

To be sure, there are exceptions. Some events are so startling or searing that individuals compare stories about them, note where they were when they happened. Everyone, it seems, has a "collective memory" of the day John Kennedy was assassinated, or of the San Francisco earthquake of 1987, or of the attack of 11 September 2001. But aside from these hallmark dates, ones which become iconic virtually at once and reach very large populations through the media, there are other moments of great importance to groups of people which have no meaning at all to their neighbors. Armenians recall the genocide of 1915 in late April, when the mass killings and deportations began, but the date 24 April has little significance to most of those among whom they live; Australians celebrate it as Anzac day; Anglicans as the feast of St George. Where, then, is the "collective memory" of that date? It lies in the acts of remembrance, small and large, of different collectives at different times.

History and Memory

Some of these acts are the work of professional historians; most are not. History is a profession with rules about evidence, about publication, about peer review. Memory is a process distinct from history, though not isolated from it. All historians leave traces in their work of their own pasts, their own memories. And many laymen and women who engage in acts of remembrance read history and care about it. Sometimes they reshape their own memories to fit with history; at other times, they are certain that they have the story right, and historians who say otherwise—whatever the evidence they produce—are wrong. History and memory overlap, infuse each other, and create vigorous and occasionally fruitful incompatibilities. In this book I take the writing and teaching of history to be an act of collective remembrance, of a different order than other such acts, because of the rules which govern it. History is not simply memory with footnotes; and memory is not simply history without footnotes. In virtually all acts of remembrance, history and memory are braided together in the public domain, jointly informing our shifting and contested understandings of the past.

Witnesses and the Victims of War

The subject of war has dominated the memory boom for a host of reasons. It is not just the injuries of war, but its drama, its earthquake-like character, which has fueled the memory boom. The story of war has been narrated by a host of institutions and media whose audiences have never been larger nor more varied. War museums attract very large populations in France, Britain, Australia, and elsewhere. Television series on war have reached millions. Internet sites abound. So have biographies and other publications on war, many written by authors outside the academy. In this part of the memory boom, as in all others, historians are fellow travelers and not pacesetters.

Narratives of war have changed during the memory boom itself in ways which help to account for its spread. It is no longer the generals and admirals, or even soldiers and sailors, who dominate the story of war. It is the victims, more and more of whom have been civilians. If initially the memory boom focused on serving or fallen men, it no longer does.

Women are now at the heart of acts of remembrance because war has moved out of the battlefield and into every corner of civilian life. War brings family history and world history together in long-lasting and frequently devastating ways. That is why women as well as men now construct the story, disseminate it, and consume it. Women join men in forming a new class of historical actors—what we now term "witnesses," people who were there, people who have seen war at close range, people whose memories are part of the historical record. Their testimony documents crimes they have seen, but their stories and their telling of them in public are historical events in their own right.

I try to attend to the varying meanings of the notion of the "witness" in this book. Witnesses were there before war crimes trials gave them a chance to tell their story, but the proliferation of such tribunals since the Second World War has legitimated them. Together with prosecutors and judges, they have created a new theater of historical remembrance—the tribunal. These proceedings have gone beyond the framework of military justice, through which soldiers continue to be prosecuted for violating regulations or the laws of war. Not only have innovations been made in the form in which such trials have taken place, but in some cases—the South African Truth and Reconciliation Commission for instance—testimony by perpetrators of crimes has absolved them from the penalties those crimes would have incurred in a court of law. In a literal sense derived from religious traditions, the truth has set them free. Memory, if honestly recalled in public, has been defined in this special case as the path to repentance, to reconciliation, and perhaps even to forgiveness.

Even more than the perpetrators, the victims needed to find a kind of solace, a way to live with their memories. It is for this reason that there is a very broad and varied therapeutic community at work today in the field of memory. Psychological and psychiatric practices and cultures have many sources, but one in particular is related to the memory of war. Many of the witnesses, victims of war and repression, bear traces of their injuries in subliminal ways. Some psychologists and cultural workers refer to these wounds as "traumatic memory." In the Great War, army physicians termed such disabilities "shell shock"; their successors in the 1939–45 war termed them "combat fatigue." After the Vietnam war, the syndrome was officially recognized as post-traumatic stress disorder. The population affected by these injuries has grown: first it was frontline troops under artillery bombardment, then it included anyone in combat; then it reached anyone afflicted by traumatic events of a life-threatening kind, whether or not they were soldiers.

Whatever their condition is termed, the victims of traumatic memory are "witnesses" of a special kind. Some are trapped in the past, condemned to reenact it when something trivial—smell, heat, sound—triggers something terrifying, buried in their memories. Their historical remembrance is involuntary, and their injuries are now treated by physicians and others who have made major advances in understanding the nature of this kind of remembrance.

It is unlikely that the memory boom will fade in the foreseeable future. Since 1945 wars have been transformed from conflicts between states into conflicts within states or between groups which do not operate at the level of the state. The proliferation of these new forms of conflict has brought warfare into every part of the world. Remembering its victims—in Northern Ireland or in Palestine or at the World Trade Center—is everybody's business.

It is primarily for this reason that the field of memory is such a crowded one. There is a lot to commemorate, and much to do to help the victims of war who are all around us. Viewed from this angle, it becomes apparent that what I have termed the memory boom is a broad and eclectic set of signifying practices, ways of understanding the violent world in which we live and the past out of which it has emerged.

Remembrance: Historical, Familial, Liturgical

It may be useful to add a word or two about the phenomenon I have termed historical remembrance. In the environment of international conflict in which we live today, historians still write about war and all kinds of people still speak of their personal memories of war. Increasingly, though, the space between history and memory has been reconfigured. In between is a varied set of cultural practices that may be described as forms of historical remembrance. It is a field originally formed to commemorate the Great War, but which has been enlarged decade after decade to take account of the upheavals which have followed it, and the millions of men and women who have been injured in wars between nations, civil wars, and insurrections. These are the witnesses—veterans, Holocaust survivors, Guatemalan Indians—whose presence among us we cannot ignore.

To do full justice to this array of cultural activity would require a library rather than a book. But to help sketch out a map of the territory covered by the memory boom, I offer the term "historical remembrance" to help us understand the special features of many of these practices. Historical remembrance overlaps with personal or family remembrance on the one hand and religious remembrance, so central to sacred practices, on the other. But the overlap is only partial. Historical remembrance is a way of interpreting the past which draws on both history and memory, on documented narratives about the past and on the statements of those who lived through them. Many people are active in this field. Historians are by no means in the majority.

Why introduce a new category, historical remembrance? Because the two defining concepts we normally use, history and memory, are insufficient guides to this field. Commemoration requires reference to history, but then the contestation begins. Whose history, written for whose benefit, and on which records? The memory boom is about history, to be sure, but historians are not its sole or even its central proprietors. Witnesses demand the right to be heard, whatever historians say. When the Enola Gay exhibition at the Smithsonian

Institution in Washington, "The Last Act: The Atomic Bomb and the End of World War II," was constructed painstakingly as history in 1995, it was attacked and rejected by people—ex-servicemen—who had their own history. And the "witnesses" won. The exhibition was reorganized. This was no simple tale of sordid political pressure. Here was a real collision between "history" and "memory," a collision arising out of the different subject positions of those involved in the exhibition. The outcome was a kind of historical remembrance which made space for the claims both of historians and of those whose lives as soldiers they were describing.

If "history" has difficulty in withstanding the challenges of "memory," the opposite case can be just as problematic. Over three decades ago I interviewed Leonard Woolf about his part in the re-construction of the Labour party in Britain in 1918. He was at the key meetings, and participated in all the discussions, records of which I had just read. I asked him about what happened, and the tale he told me was completely mistaken: wrong dates, wrong places, wrong people, wrong decisions. The errors were not even interesting ones, covering up alternative narratives. He had just forgotten, as we all do. To be sure, this was fifty years after the fact, and he was much more interested in talking about his wife, Virginia Woolf, as—after a brief interval—was I. I did not challenge his memory, but could use none of it in writing up the history in which I was engaged. In this context, memory alone would have made the rendering of history impossible.

Historians do matter, but not as much as they think they do. Those who try to reconstruct their "memory" of past events need historians to establish the boundary conditions of possibility. We can establish with much greater firmness what did not take place than what did, and historians have access to records which—at times—prevent people from either misconstruing or lying about the past. In the case of Leonard Woolf, misconstruction was the problem; in many other instances, willful distortion is the name of the game.

But even if we assume honorable intentions in all parties, the problems associated with remembering the past are greater still. "Memory" is a category with its own history, and its own mysteries. Cognitive psychologists and neuroscientists have taken huge strides in understanding how individuals remember, but leaders in the field admit that there is a vast amount of fundamental work still to be done. How much harder is it to construct a model or set of pathways to describe how groups of people remember together.

And yet these traces are all around us. Historical remembrance is a discursive field, extending from ritual to cultural work of many different kinds. It differs from family remembrance by its capacity to unite people who have no other bonds drawing them together. It is distinctive from liturgical remembrance in being freed from a preordained religious calendar and sanctified ritual forms. And yet historical remembrance has something of the familial and something of the sacred in it. When all three are fused, as in some powerful war memorials—Maya Lin's Vietnam memorial in Washington comes to mind—historical remembrance is a phenomenon of enduring power.

Adopting the term "historical remembrance" has other advantages as well. Using it helps us avoid the pitfalls of referring to memory as some vague cloud which exists without agency, and to history as an objective story which exists outside of the people whose lives it describes. Historians have memories too, and their choice of subject is rarely accidental. They are part of the memory boom, though not its leading part. When they join other men and women who come together in public to remember the past—their past—they construct a narrative which is not just "history" and not just "memory," but a story which partakes of them both. Historical remembrance is what they do, and how they contribute to a memory boom which extends well beyond the historical profession.

Commemorative moments, alongside acts of witnessing and healing, are the most public features of the memory boom. But it is important to note too that in virtually every facet of the arts, the subject of memory is ubiquitous. It is hardly surprising that this is so. Cultural studies have long since dispensed with the outmoded division between politics and the arts. Both form part of a public conversation on themes of importance in contemporary life. Picasso's *Guernica* was painted in the privacy of his atelier on the Left Bank in Paris, but it was almost immediately transferred to the Spanish pavilion of the 1937 Paris international exhibition of the arts and technique of daily life. Was it a private statement or a political statement? Why not both? The same is true for Benjamin Britten's War Requiem, in which Wilfred Owen's poetry is set to music composed to mark the reconsecration of Coventry Cathedral in 1962. Private or public? Certainly both.

In the exploration of aspects of cultural work that deal with representations of war in the second part of this book, one fundamental theme recurs. It is the struggle against forgetting, mediated in a host of ways in social practices, in literature and the arts. It is not only that much of the violent history of the twentieth century is intrinsically worth remembering, but rather that those who died or who were injured can so easily be forgotten. A painting or a poem may defer oblivion a bit, but most of those whose works we survey were well aware of the quixotic nature of their enterprise. What photographs, or plays, or poems, or letters provide are traces of a world that has almost vanished from both memory and history. The memory boom, therefore, may be understood as an act of defiance, an attempt to keep alive at least the names and the images of the millions whose lives have been truncated or disfigured by war.

To be sure, there are many other sources of the memory boom. This book deals with but one, and does so by and large from the perspective of European history. The focus is on the long shadow of the First World War; that of the Holocaust and the Second World War requires a study of its own, well beyond the limitations of this book. The story of historical remembrance in the twentieth century is much broader than the one told here, but to emphasize one (and only one) facet of it, related to the Great War, should draw attention to the commemorative impulses which refer to other events and in other ways. What this study hopes to do is simply to open the door for others to pass through to their different destinations.

Part One

War and Remembrance

CHAPTER 1

The Setting
The Great War in the Memory Boom of the Twentieth Century

Memory is in the ascendancy these days. In virtually every corner of intellectual life, there is evidence of a major change in focus, a movement toward the analysis of memory as the organizing principle of scholarly or artistic work. Whereas race, gender, and social class were foci of early waves of scholarship in cultural studies, now the emphasis is on a set of issues at the intersection of cultural history, literary studies, architecture, cognitive psychology, psychoanalysis, and many other disciplines besides. What they have in common is a focus on memory.

Part of the force and logic of this cultural movement is academic, and I will turn to this matter later in this chapter. But part of it is largely independent of the world of scholarship. We historians are swimming in a stream of memory studies, but our current is but one of many which have become a torrent both inside and outside of the academy.

This chapter explores the setting in which the activity I term historical remembrance has unfolded. It is a complex, multifaceted environment, reaching issues related to the economic, political, and intellectual history of diverse groups in many different parts of the world. The previous chapter provides a synopsis of the argument of this book, and some of its fundamental claims and assumptions.

This chapter offers some remarks of a general nature on the origins and contours of our contemporary fascination with "memory," however defined.

It is important to insist upon the fact that we are by no means the first generation to be drawn almost magnetically to memory. We have inherited and are working through an earlier generation's fascination with, indeed obsession with, memory. What I would term the first generation of memory in the modern period spanned the years from the 1890s to the 1920s. Its focus was on memory as the key to the formation of identities, in particular national identities, although social, cultural, and personal identities were also in mind. Remembering the fallen of the Great War was a very significant part of this movement. The second "memory boom," which emerged in the 1960s and 1970s, was in large part a form of remembrance of the Second World War and the Holocaust. There are other issues at stake here too. In recent years many people have come to see in memory a way out of the confusion bred by the fragmentation of the very identities forged by and during the first "memory boom." The term "memory" has become a metaphor for ways of casting about in the ruins of earlier identities and finding elements of what has been called a "usable past,"[1] or what the French historian Pierre Nora calls *lieux de mémoire*.[2] But what the contemporary fascination with memory seeks is not the same past or set of sites which, for example, James Joyce sifted through in his *Portrait of the Artist as a Young Man*, published in 1916. We are in another world. Who today would try to "forge in the smithy of my soul the uncreated conscience of my race"?[3] The tortured history of Ireland—a fragmented identity if there ever was one—simply cannot be constituted in this way. The Second World War and the Holocaust broke many of the narratives at the heart of the first "memory boom."

Instead, today we confront subjectivities, hybridities, multiple subject positions which we all occupy at different times and places in our lives. A century ago, the concept of memory was harnessed by a host of men and women as a means to constitute or fortify identities, in particular national identities in an imperial age. That age has gone, and so has its unities and its certainties. In its place memory still stands, but as a source of fractured national, ideological, and cultural forms, forms which are resistant to linear reconstruction; the onward march of progress is a thing of the past.[4]

To be sure, memory was a term used to define history, ethics, and art well before the late nineteenth century. The arts of memory were highly developed in the Renaissance,[5] and there is little we would add to ancient Egyptian commentaries on the plight of those "without a yesterday," without memory understood as a sense of obligations and duties to those around us.[6] What modern commentators offer is less a set of new ideas than new configurations of old ones.

Today those drawn to memory adopt widely varying styles and inflections in their work. For some the memory boom is nostalgic, a yearning for a vanished or rapidly vanishing world. For others it is a language of protest, seeking out solidarities based on common narratives and traditions to resist the pressures and seductions of globalization. For others still it is a means of moving away from politics, and of re-sacralizing the world, or of preserving the voice of victims of the multiple catastrophes of the last century.[7] And for some, it is a way of confronting the Holocaust at the very moment which the survivors are steadily passing away. To capture their voices, their faces, and, through them, to establish a bridge to the world of European Jewry which the Nazis succeeded in destroying, is a major agenda fueling the contemporary memory boom.

We are clearly dealing with a dissonant chorus of voices here, and the sheer variety of work on memory in contemporary culture precludes any easy analysis of its origin or quality. Above all, it is the overdetermined character of the memory boom which is its most striking characteristic. There are so many sources of it that it is hard to identify the marginal from the crucial, the transitory from the long-lasting. The superficial and the profound are both in evidence in our contemporary obsession with memory. In this highly charged and rapidly changing field, there is one certainty on which we can all agree. It is that no two people invoking the term "memory" seem to use it in the same way. And yet, its resonance and near ubiquity suggest that it discloses a quest we simply cannot do without.

The First Generation of Memory

Part of the aim of this book is to isolate one particular vector in this broad set of cultural movements. Later in this book we shall turn time and again to the subject of war and the victims of war. In the first quarter of the twentieth century, the need to acknowledge the men who died in the Great War lay behind a very widespread search for appropriate commemorative forms. But as in every other aspect of the cultural history of the war, the way contemporaries understood the upheaval through which they had lived was marked by notions developed before, and to a large degree independent of, the war.

The fascination with memory was one such prewar form which expanded exponentially during, and as a result of, the Great War. The war did not create the first memory boom of the twentieth century, but it transformed it in enduring ways. One way to put the point is to say that there is a cohort of men and women born approximately between the 1860s and 1880s who came into academic, literary, professional, or public prominence in the period 1890 to 1920 through their writings on or about memory.[8] Much of this work appeared in the period 1895–1914. Much of it is very familiar. Sigmund Freud, born in 1856, was at the older end of this cohort, alongside the French philosopher Henri Bergson, born in 1859 and author of *Matter and Memory*, published in 1896.[9] A bit younger was the German art historian Aby Warburg, born in 1866, creator of a whole school of memory studies embodied to this day by the Warburg Institute in London.[10]

One of the most interesting figures in the transmission of ideas about memory in the Anglo-Saxon world was W. H. R. Rivers—physiologist, social anthropologist, and psychiatrist at the Craiglockhart hospital, where he treated shell shock victims of the Great War, among them the poet Siegfried Sassoon. Rivers was born in 1864 and died in 1922.[11] Also dying that year was Marcel Proust, whose name is inextricably linked with the multiple pathways of memory, at the age of fifty-one.[12] The novelist Thomas Mann was born into a well-to-do Lübeck family in 1875; a year later, the French sociologist of memory Maurice Halbwachs was born.[13] His pathbreaking work *Les cadres sociaux de la mémoire* was published in 1925, at the end of our period of interest.[14] Both Halbwachs and Proust were a bit older than that master storyteller, James Joyce, born in Dublin in 1882, and whose *Portrait of the Artist* was published in 1916, in the midst of the appearance of Proust's masterpiece *A la recherche du temps perdu*. Its first volume was published in 1913, and six subsequent volumes appeared over the next decade and a half. Virginia Woolf was born in the same year as Joyce, 1882, and her representations of time and what we now term "traumatic memory" appeared at the end of our period in many novels, including *Mrs Dalloway* (1925) and *To the Lighthouse* (1927).

There is no reason to believe that these people self-consciously wrote as part of a generation, but it is striking that their outlook and sensibilities all intersected with the subject of memory and that they did so at a very unusual time in European history. Try to throw your mind back to a period when the French Republic was just decades old, when the German state was in its infancy, and when British imperial power was both at its zenith and beginning to take on the distinctive aroma of an overripe fruit, and you will see some of the ways in which cultural explorations of memory intersected with political and social interrogations of the subject.

In both the late nineteenth and the late twentieth centuries there occurred a rush toward memory in which at least three processes were of great importance—which we may term construction, adaptation, and circulation. Let me try to unpack these notions. The first was formed by independently generated work within the arts, science, the academy, and the free professions. The memory work of Proust or Freud cannot be reduced to a set of quasi-Pavlovian responses to political or social stimuli; they lived very much in their social worlds, but their writing had its own internal dynamic and creative sources. The second development emerged out of cultural activity surrounding the construction of what Halbwachs came to call social memory—the memory of the people who form social groups, and whose recall gives those groups coherence and form. A word or two on what collective memory is may be useful here.

Halbwachs's position is a straightforward one. Collective memory, he argued, is constructed through the action of groups and individuals in the light of day. Passive memory—understood as the personal recollections of a silent individual—is not collective memory, though the way we talk about our own memories is socially bounded. When people enter the public domain, and comment about or commemorate the past—their own personal past, their family past, their national past, and so on—they bring with them images and gestures derived from their broader social experience. As Halbwachs put it, their memory is "socially framed."[15] When people come together to remember, they enter a domain beyond that of individual memory.

That work of collective remembrance was everywhere in evidence in Europe between 1890 and 1920, and its multiple agendas were transparent and widely circulated. Such transmission of narratives of memory were not at all restricted to Europe. South American Republics all had centenaries of their independence to celebrate in the early twentieth century. But in France, Germany, Italy, and elsewhere, new political regimes had to invent or unearth an illustrious past to justify and stabilize their nascent political forms. Collective narratives of state formation, performed in public and understood as an artifact, a construct, a kind of Potemkin village of the mind, constituted a significant part of that unifying force. It was expressed in many ways, from the celebration of days on the calendar, to what Maurice Agulhon calls "statue-mania,"[16] to the highly visible veneration of newly found ancient traditions, to the constructions of historical narratives (some well-documented, some mythical) written, published, and recited in schools and other public venues.

In Britain, there were parallels, though their origins were different. Imperial power under threat also cast a long shadow into a semifictional past, reconfigured in traditions invented for the purpose, as Hobsbawm and Ranger remind us.[17] The cult of the British monarchy was not based on practices observed time out of mind; this cult and the supposedly ancient ceremonial practice attached to it were constructed between 1870 and 1914. To some they reflected grandeur; to many others—Kipling among them—they reflected the beginning of the end of hegemony, the time when "the captains and the kings depart."[18]

As for the landed gentry, the birth of the National Trust in Britain in 1895 showed a direct link between their penury and preservation. Many landowners, some recently ennobled, some of the ancient families of England, passed through the agricultural depression of the 1870s and 1880s with an eye on escape. To preserve their stately homes was both a national mission and a private parachute for those who wanted out of the bucolic world of landed estates.[19] Here economic decline merged with a kind of antiurban sentiment, never far from the surface in Britain, which invested country homes with the

cultural capital of centuries of British history.[20] For those depressed
by the very rapid urbanization of the country after 1851, a physical site
evoking a world which no longer existed was a symbol of a very comforting kind. And so it remains to this day. E. M. Forster's *Howard's
End*, published in 1910, located the struggle to preserve a vulnerable way of life in one country home, remote from the motorcar-
dominated city. The National Trust extended the cultural politics of
nostalgia to the countryside as a whole.[21]

Economic motives were evident in the first memory boom, but
political agendas are probably of greater importance in our understanding of their genesis. The best-known contemporary formulation of this vision of memory as political glue was provided by
Ernest Renan. In a series of lectures in Paris in 1882, entitled "What Is
a Nation," he noted that

> A nation is a soul, a spiritual principle. Two things, which, in
> truth, are really one, constitute this soul, this spiritual principle.
> One is in the past, the other in the present. One is the possession
> in common of a rich legacy of memories; the other is the present
> day consent, the desire to live together, the will to continue to
> value the undivided heritage one has received. . . . To have the
> glory of the past in common, a shared will in the present; to
> have done great deeds together, and want to do more of them,
> are the essential conditions for the constitution of a people. . . .
> One loves the house which one has built and passes on.[22]

Such ideas and images were commonplace in late-nineteenth-
century Europe. What was much newer were powerful means to
disseminate them—the third vector of the first "memory boom."
Writers on memory reached a much wider audience than ever before. The expansion of the print trade, the art market, the leisure
industry, and the mass circulation press, allied to developments first
in photography and then in cinematography, created powerful con-
duits for the dissemination of texts, images, and narratives of the
past in every part of Europe and beyond.

Some of these means of capturing the past revealed a considerable degree of nostalgia about a vanished or vanishing world. In Britain and elsewhere, the use of photography to reach areas which were on the edge of absorption into the modern world was a late Victorian and Edwardian industry. The French banker Albert Kahn sent out scores of photographers to capture something about the entire world, and took especial interest in those areas like China or equatorial Africa where what he considered to be indigenous ways of life were being eroded by contact with the imperial gaze.[23] Photography could celebrate imperialism or expose its ravages.[24] Photography of the wilderness—in America or Mongolia—had a similar purpose: to reach the pristine before the philistines got there, or sometimes to record their arrival. Nostalgia was engraved onto nitrate plates, and, whenever possible, onto the new practices of cinematography.

War and the Cult of Memory

Warfare in this period moved the cult of memory onto the level of mass production and consumption. After the Franco-Prussian war, *Souvenir Français* emerged as an association within civil society to preserve the memory of the men who died in France's lost war of 1870–71. As Madeleine Rébérioux has shown, other lost causes were captured in stone. The *Mur des Fédérées* in the Père Lachaise cemetery in Paris—more a secular shrine than a memorial—was preserved as the site where the last of the Communards—the diehards of the first communist revolution in history—were shot among the gravestones on 28 May 1871.[25] Bills of exchange, stamps, and coins all took on the imprint of national nobility expressed through historical or mythical notation, much of it martial in character.[26]

This commemorative moment was powerful, but after 1914 it was eclipsed by the avalanches of images and words surrounding the dead of the Great War. And here the cult of memory became a universal phenomenon. War memorials were constructed in every French commune and in almost every British village. German, Austrian, and Italian churches and village crossroads had them too. Their message was to remember the sacrifice, the suffering, the slaughter, the names of the fallen. And in a host of paintings and books and films, this cult of memory became a cult of mourning.[27] Thus the pioneers of the first generation of memory—Freud, Mann, Proust, Rivers, Bergson among them, all prewar figures—joined the memory boom of their generation after 1914 in the collective work of commemorating the lost generation of the Great War. That collective effort is the subject of the later chapters of this book.

The Second Generation of Memory

Now to the second generation of memory. It emerged in the 1970s and 1980s, but many of its sources lay clearly in the Second World War. War and mourning for those who suffered in war are also at its core, but its trajectory differed sharply from that of the first memory boom. For many reasons, the balance of creation, adaptation, and circulation in producing the second wave of concern about memory was entirely different from the earlier case.

The first and most significant point about the second memory boom is that while the Second World War is central to it, there was a time lag before it emerged. Fully three decades had to pass before the new obsession with memory took on its full features. Why the delay? In the 1940s and 1950s, collective stories about the war focused on heroic narratives of resistance to the Nazis and their allies. Even when such stories were true, they took on mythical proportions. The notion of a noble and ecumenical Resistance mixed accounts which were valid with claims which were not. The Resistance was not popular until late in the war; it did not shorten the war; and on balance, it did not liberate oppressed people from the night of Nazi rule.

Why did this kind of idealizing remembrance flourish? Because intrepid chronicles of Resistance were more useful in the revival of the political culture of countries humiliated by occupation and collaboration.[28] But by the 1960s and 1970s, that narrative work had done its job; the transition to postwar political stability was complete. The European community was up and running.

There is an element of generational conflict here too. Student movements, culminating in the events of 1968, aimed to expose the hypocrisy of their parents' generation. Time and again they asserted that the rebirth of Europe after 1945 occluded the complicity of millions of prominent and prosperous men and women in the crimes of the Nazis and their allies.

The Age of the Witness

This was the time when the victims of the concentration camps could come forward. And come forward they did. The "memory boom" of the late twentieth century took on momentum and major cultural significance when the victims of the Holocaust came out of the shadows, and when a wide public was finally, belatedly prepared to see them, honor them, and hear what they had to say. When Primo Levi published his first book, *Se questo è un uomo (If This Be a Man)*, in 1947, its reception was polite but very restrained. It was only in the 1970s and 1980s that he became an international figure of the first order, and his books were reissued and sold in very substantial numbers in a score of languages. *Il sistema periodico (The Periodic Table)*, published in 1975, and *I sommersi e i salvati (The Drowned and the Saved)*, which appeared eleven years later, have become iconic accounts of the Holocaust and the astonishing power of one man to retain his quiet dignity and powers of sympathetic observation in its midst. What matters in this context is that they took thirty years to find an international audience and international acclaim.[29]

Collective remembrance is a matter of activity. Someone carries a message, a memory, and needs to find a way to transmit it to others. The second memory boom privileged a new group of people and their memories. No longer would one group of carriers of memory— the heroes and heroines of resistance—eclipse another group. Before the 1970s, as Annette Wieviorka has put it, Buchenwald (the camp for political prisoners) occluded Auschwitz (the camp for racial prisoners).[30] By the 1970s, new voices emerged with new memories. These were the new "remembrancers,"[31] the new carriers of memory; they form a new singular collective which we term the witness.

Paralleling this shift in speakers and in audiences was a shift in the means of circulating their message. By the 1970s developments in audio- and videocassette recording meant that survivors could now testify before a camera, sometimes in private, one on one, sometimes for more general viewing. Both sets of images could be easily preserved. This was a development which seemed to validate their stories. "For many of us," noted Levi, "to be interviewed was a unique and memorable occasion, the event for which one had waited since liberation, and which even gave meaning to our liberation."[32] In the 1940s and 1950s, many survivors feared that no one would ever believe what they had to say. Three decades later, their fears were laid to rest, and the interviews they gave were there, an enduring record for posterity.

In other ways, too, filming the voices and faces of the survivors of the Second World War played a decisive role in the creation of the postwar memory boom. Here were preserved the testimony of those who struggled with the Nazis or who aided their victims outside the system of concentration and extermination camps. In 1969, Marcel Ophuls completed a four-hour documentary on French life under Nazi occupation. It was entitled "the Sorrow and the Pity," and took the city of Clermont-Ferrand as a microcosm of the Second World War in France.[33] The film obliterated the myth of heroic resistance, a myth symbolized, indeed completely embodied, by Charles de Gaulle, president of the French Republic from 1958 until April 1969.

His passing from the political scene was significant in a number of ways relevant to the postwar memory boom. The first was that with the departure of a figure totally identified with the romantic view of the Resistance as the nation in arms, the force of that myth began to fade. And when the myth evaporated, behind it emerged a nest of embarrassing issues pointing to the culpability of Frenchmen for crimes committed against Jews who, though full citizens of the Republic, had been deported from France. Of a prewar population of 170,000, 52,000 were sent to their deaths by French bureaucrats in French trains through French transit camps.

After the mid–1960s, these French collaborators in mass murder were vulnerable to arrest and trial in France. This was an entirely unintentional effect of a change in the statute of limitations for war crimes in 1964, which was supposed to stop retired Germans who had done nasty things in the war from holidaying on the Riviera. What was aimed at Germans could be used against Frenchmen. And so it was in three famous trials. The first was against the Nazi officer Klaus Barbie, who had tortured to death the leader of the Resistance, Jean Moulin, and who had been deported to France from Bolivia in 1983. He was convicted and sentenced to life imprisonment four years later. Then came the trial of Paul Touvier, a French subordinate of Barbie in Lyons who had executed seven Jews in 1944 as a reprisal for the assassination of a prominent collaborator. Touvier was convicted in 1994 and died in prison two years later. In 1998 it was the turn of the distinguished civil servant Maurice Papon, who had held many high posts in the Fourth and Fifth Republics but who had efficiently administered the deportation of Jews from the Bordeaux region during the Vichy regime. He too was convicted of crimes against humanity, and, after a brief period on the run, he was returned to prison to face a ten-year sentence for his complicity in murder.[34]

These trials brought out two critical features of the second generation of memory. The first was the way they disseminated very widely the notion that discussions of the Second World War could not be separated from discussions of the Holocaust. And the second was the way they brought out vividly the notion that memory was moral in character, and that the chief carriers of that message were the victims themselves. These points had emerged in part during the Nuremberg trials of 1946 and the Eichmann trial of 1961, but the first had focused on the perpetrators. The memory boom of the 1970s and 1980s was based on a different optic: its gaze was increasingly turned to the victim.

Thus a new form of collective remembrance was born, that of the witness, understood in both senses of the term. The witness was a survivor, a truth-teller, sworn under oath to tell the whole truth, but he was also a visitor from another planet, as the Israeli poet Ka-Tchetnik put it in the Eichmann trial. These people spoke of things we could see only through a glass, darkly, but through their voices we might be able to reach out to those who did not return from the camps.

Holocaust witnesses took on therefore a liminal, mediating, semisacred role since the 1970s. They spoke of the dead, and for the dead, whose voices could somehow be retrieved in the telling of these terrifying stories. Their words, their acts of remembrance, gave them a quasi-religious tone, and listening to survivors appeared to be a kind of laying on of hands, an acceptance of the witness in the early Christian sense of the term, as a person who testifies to her faith, even while in danger of dying for it.

Commemorations of War and Holocaust

Once more we return to the linkage between memory and mourning. But in this contest, the problem which emerged in the 1970s, and which continues to bedevil commentators, witnesses, and politicians alike, is how to link the new culture of the witness to commemorations of the Second World War. In the Soviet Union, which suffered by far the heaviest toll in terms of loss of life in the war, this issue hardly came up. Critical works like Vasily Grossman's *Life and Fate,* an account of Stalingrad and of anti-Semitism in wartime Russia, were suppressed, appearing only after the author's death.[35] But in the West, it became increasingly difficult to separate the war from the Holocaust.

Here is where official commemorations—publicly performed acts of remembrance defined by a politically sanctioned script—became problematic. As in all forms of collective memory, the character of the event changed over time. V-E Day and V-J Day came to jostle with D-Day as moments of solemn recounting of the Second World War. In Israel Yom Hashoah comes a week before Independence Day, and is clearly intended to link the catastrophe of the Holocaust with the birth of the State of Israel. These commemorative moments were well established in the 1970s. Now they have been joined by 27 January, the day Auschwitz was liberated by the Red army. But this linkage of the commemoration of war and Holocaust brings us to another way in which the Holocaust has informed the second "memory boom" of the twentieth century and increased the tensions imbedded in it.

The decision of the German government to build a Holocaust memorial near the Brandenburg gate in Berlin set off a massive argument. The monument, a stone's throw from the new Reichstag and from Hitler's bunker, is unavoidably part of the story of Germany reborn. Some believe the monument is an essential and properly placed part of the story; others opposed the location of a commemorative monument to victims of the Holocaust within such a narrative. Placing the monument in the heart of the national capital, geographically and metaphorically, and focusing on the national level of notation, locate the Holocaust within a political framework—that of Germany debased by the Nazis and of Germany reborn today.

The difficulties were multiple, but among them was the use of a form of political culture developed in the first "memory boom" to mark a set of events of an entirely different political and moral order. In the first "memory boom," commemorative projects had transparent political agendas, central to which was the stabilization of new or older nations and empires in the wake of war. The problem is that the Holocaust resists this kind of stable encapsulation, or in fact any encapsulation within a particular system of meaning. To paraphrase Primo Levi, a set of events about which one cannot in any recognizable manner pose the question of "why?" is also an event about which it is impossible in any straightforward sense to pose the questions of historical context or meaning within twentieth-century history.[36]

After the First World War, commemorative efforts aimed to offer a message that loss of life in the conflict had a meaning, that these sacrifices were redemptive, that they prepared the ground for a better world, one in which such staggering loss of life would not recur. Two decades later those hopes were dashed. The problem of meaning only got worse after the emergence of the Holocaust witness in the 1970s. What did their testimony tell us about the question as to whether the Holocaust had any "meaning"? Their voices, while poignant and indelible, did not offer any firm answers. Increasingly, the Holocaust appeared to be an event without a meaning. It was a giant black hole in the midst of our universe of reason.[37]

History, Post-Modernism, and the New Political Order

If the Holocaust had no "meaning" in any conventional sense of the term, was it possible that theories of Enlightenment or of progress were void of sense as well? Here was a point at which the second "memory boom" and philosophical inquiry intersected. Through the works of the French scholars Jean François Lyotard[38] and Emmanuel Levinas, a student of the German philosopher Heidegger,[39] and the Romanian-born poet Paul Celan,[40] a radically subversive view of reason and rationality emerged in the postwar decades. It is a perspective which offers a critique of earlier linear views of history and grand narratives of the progress of the human spirit. As Benjamin put it in his seventh thesis on the philosophy of history, etched on the gravestone erected in his memory in Port Bo, "there is no document of civilization which is not at the same time a document of barbarism." To mediate on the dialectic between the two was a preoccupation of many of those who broke with the Enlightenment project and its grand narratives, rooted in a belief in progress and reason.[41]

In parallel, a set of political changes seemed to prove these critics right. The grand narrative of nation-building, out of which the first memory boom had emerged, bore little resemblance to the political fault lines of the later twentieth century. Here too we turn from what I have termed "construction" to the "adaptation" of messages about memory in political and social discourse. And once more we can see how new technologies, in particular those associated with computer technology and the Internet, circulated these ideas in new and powerful ways.

The second memory boom coincided with what Charles Maier has called the "end of territoriality."[42] His point is that the process of state-building in Europe spanned the century between 1860 and 1960, after which different political forms were redrawn or more porous boundaries began to dominate international political life. The emergence of the European Union is one such development; the erosion and collapse of the Warsaw pact and the Soviet Union was another. The replacement of war between states in Europe and beyond by organized violence within states or across their boundaries is a third. Corporate globalization further perforated (though did not eliminate) state borders constructed strenuously over the course of a century.

With the demise of a certain kind of nationalism in Europe, symbolized by de Gaulle, and a certain kind of socialism, symbolized by Gorbachev, the pole stars of the political firmament in Europe and elsewhere began to fade from view. This led a number of observers to try to escape from their disorientation through a search for the elements of national identities that were now in question. This was the origin of the powerfully original and influential project of Pierre Nora to provide an inventory of the French *lieux de mémoire*. In seven learned tomes, he collected the work of over one hundred leading scholars who catalogued the ways French men and women constructed their multiple identities. Now we have parallel ventures in Germany, Italy, and Portugal, with more promised for the future.[43]

Identity Politics and Testimony

This interrogation of identities coincided with other facets of the memory boom rooted in what we now call identity politics. Here is a story with European origins but which must be distinguished from facets of the memory boom elsewhere, and in particular in the United States. The distinction must be made because Nora's project rests on the assumption that identity politics is incompatible with the French definition of citizenship. In law, and in academic discourse, there are no Arab-Frenchmen or African-Frenchwomen. They are simply French men or women whose origins do not enter their (singular) political identity. Nora's exploration of *les lieux de mémoire* is not about ethnic or racial groups within France, but about Frenchness *tout court*.

Elsewhere, what Latin-American scholars term "living on the hyphen" is not only tolerated, but celebrated.[44] Ethnic identities are defined by narratives of the past, and in part by narratives of suffering and survival of subordinate groups within a national polity. Here is yet another powerful source of the contemporary memory boom. State-bounded narratives increasingly compete with others of a regional or ethnic kind. On both sides of the Atlantic, in the developed "north" and the developing "south," many ethnic groups and disenfranchised minorities have demanded their own right to speak, to act, and to achieve liberation or self-determination. And those struggles almost always entail the construction of their own stories, their own usable past. Collective memory is a term which can no longer be collapsed into a set of stories formed by or about the state or about nations as a whole.

Each collective constructs its own narratives of collective remembrance. In North America, this phenomenon is at the heart of identity politics.[45] One clear example is the placement of the National Holocaust Memorial on the Mall in Washington. It is, in this sacred space, both a statement of universal truths, and an expression of Jewish-American pride. The museum speaks in a grammar living on the hyphen, the hyphen of ethnic identity. The framework cannot escape from its location. The redemptive elements in the story surround it on the Mall. They tell us of the wider struggle for tolerance, for freedom of religion, for freedom from persecution; they locate the Holocaust within the American narrative, itself configured as a universal.[46] Here we have arrived at the right-hand side of the hyphen "Jewish-American." The museum is the bridge between the two.

There have been many other instances of commemoration as an expression of the tragic history of persecuted minorities. The AIDS quilt is one;[47] monuments to the struggle for African-American freedom raise the same point. Recent attempts to represent the imprisonment of Japanese-Americans during the Second World War express the same set of issues, both unique and universal. Again the hyphen of identity is strengthened by commemoration.[48]

As I have already noted, in Latin America and elsewhere, identity politics takes on other forms, in particular, the cadences of persecuted minorities or political victims. Testimonial literature rescues histories trampled on by military dictatorships. The stories of cruelty and oppression once retold constitute acts of defiance; through the narrator, the voices of the dead and the mutilated can still be heard. The Truth and Reconciliation Commission in South Africa has been a focus for the release of imprisoned memory, in this case the stories of a majority imprisoned by a minority.

At times, the boundaries between truth and fiction become blurred in such storytelling, whether its setting is a public forum or an individual memoir. As Doris Sommer has put it, the boundaries between informing and performing are porous.[49] But even when the storyteller goes beyond what can be verified through other sources, or even when the witness distorts the past, her voice in Guatemala or Chile still stands for a generalized sense of oppression. Here is "memory" understood as a set of narratives, a "counterhistory that challenges the false generalizations in exclusionary 'History,' " penned by those trapped in a Eurocentric and imperialist sense of what constitutes the past.[50] This dimension of the "memory boom" has little purchase with respect to Holocaust testimonies, but it tells us much about other narratives of oppression.

Affluence and Remembrance

I have tried to emphasise the multifaceted and eclectic nature of the two "memory booms." There have been political, technological, and philosophical impulses toward privileging the subject of memory in many discursive fields. But there is yet another dimension to this story to which we must attend. It is more about audiences than about origins, and while not of fundamental significance, it still is part of the story of why so many people are talking about "memory" today. In the West, one important precondition of the "memory boom" has been affluence. In a nutshell, rising real incomes and increased expenditure on education since the Second World War have helped shift to the right the demand curve for cultural commodities.

In the history of this rising demand, higher education has played a central role. Since the 1960s there has been a rapid expansion in the population of university-trained people, whose education provided them with access to and a desire for cultural activities of varying kinds. In Britain the number of university students expanded very rapidly after the Robbins report of 1963, granting the right to free higher education to all who could pass entrance requirements. There were at least three times as many people studying in institutions of higher education in 1990 as there were attending thirty years before. The same upward trend in the size of the tertiary sector of education may be detected across Europe and in the United States after 1960. Part of the increase is demographic: the baby boom generation was coming of age; but there was more at work here than the shadow of postwar fertility. Systems of higher education differ markedly, but even with a host of qualifications, the international trend is evident. There were eight times the number of students in higher education in Germany in 1990 as compared with 1960; in France, six times more over the same period; in Italy, Belgium, and Denmark, and the United States, five times more. Taken together, the 15 member states of the European Union had 12 million students in higher education in 1990; there were about 13.5 million such students in the United States. And the numbers continued to grow throughout the last decade of the twentieth century.

The student revolt of 1968 was an effect, not a cause, of this trend. In France, student numbers grew more rapidly in 1966–67 than in

1969–70; German growth was about the same before and after the "troubles," precipitated in part by rising numbers and insufficient resources devoted to them. Changes in higher education had fundamental effects not only on the skill composition of the labor force, but also on the stock of cultural capital circulating in society as a whole.[51] By the 1990s there was a larger population of university-educated people than ever before. Their demand for cultural products of many different kinds was evident. What might be described as the industry of culture was in an ideal position for massive growth. The market was evident. The target population for cultural products was there; and after two decades of retrenchment, state support for "heritage" or *le patrimoine* was there, with greater or lesser degrees of generosity.[52]

The British economic historian Alan Milward has pointed to the material echoes of these two cultural bywords, "heritage" and "patrimony." The "memory boom," he rightly notes, has happened in part because both the public and the state have the disposable income to pay for it. This is how Milward put it in a review of books on memory and history in Europe in *The Times Literary Supplement:*

> The media are the hypermarket outlet for the consumption of memory. Stern moral and methodological rejection of earlier historical fashions does not alter the reality that this latest fashion, like the earlier ones, is driven by the all-too-positivist forces of the growth of wealth and incomes. The history of memory represents that stage of consumption in which the latest product, ego-history, is the image of the self not only marketed but also consumed by the self.[53]

There are differences among European countries, which may require us to qualify or modify Milward's sardonic interpretation. But in the British and French cases, there is a symmetry between economic trends and cultural trends which we ignore at our peril.

Dwelling on memory is a matter of both disposable income and leisure time. Milward has a telling point: affluence has helped turn identity into a commodity, to be consumed by everyone in her (increasingly ample) leisure time. A "common" identity is one sharing a set of narratives about the past. Many of these take the form of bricks and mortar—fixed cultural capital. Exploiting their attractiveness, as in Britain's National Trust stately homes and gardens, the patrimony or heritage trades became a profitable industry, with market niches and target consumers. The marketing of memory has paid off, in a huge consumer boom in images of the past—in films, books, and articles, and more recently on the Internet and television. There is an entire industry devoted to "blockbuster exhibitions" in museums, whose visitors seem to respond more and more to spectacular shows. History sells, especially as biography or autobiography, or in Milward's (and Pierre Nora's phrase) ego-history.[54]

The British satirical writer Julian Barnes produced a marvelous *reductio ad absurdum* of this phenomenon in his futuristic spoof *England, England,* published in 1998.[55] Why should tourists have to travel to consume the icons of British history? Surely it makes more sense to bring or imitate the lot on the Isle of Wight? But whatever its potential for humor, the history business has never been more profitable. It would be important, though, to have more precise information of the choices cultural consumers make. My hunch is that over the last two decades, the growth rate in attendance at the Imperial War Museum, the British Museum, and Madame Tussaud's in London, for instance, has been greater than the increase in attendance at sporting events or rock concerts. This is a conjecture, but one worth pursuing in a more rigorous manner.

Affluence has had another by now commonplace by-product. One vector of the circulation and dissemination of the "memory boom" may also be the exteriorization, or expression in public space, of the interior discourse of psychoanalysis. Just as Woody Allen has popularized therapy as an addictive way of life, so the nearly universal spread of therapy cultures has made memory a light consumer durable good for those—yet again—with the cash to afford it.

History and Family History: Vectors of Transmission

So far I have tried to sketch some of the political and economic preconditions for the contemporary "memory boom." But there is another level of significance in this story, one which is more demographic than political, more about families than about nations. In our profession, we should be grateful that history sells; one reason that it is such a popular and money-making trade is because it locates family stories in bigger, more universal, narratives. One way to understand the huge growth and financial viability of museums and fiction set in the wars of the twentieth century is to see them as places where family stories are set in a wider, at times universal context. Some grandparents knew the Blitz; now they can bring their grandchildren to the "Blitz experience" of the Imperial War Museum in London. Such imaginings of war are attractive because they rest on the contemporary link between generations, and in particular between the old and the young, between grandparents and grandchildren, at times over the heads of the troublesome generation of parents in the middle. In the 1960s and 1970s, this link pointed back to the First World War; later on, to the Second.

Many best-selling novels set in the two world wars take family stories as their form. Examples abound: like Jean Rouaud's *Champs d'honneur,* winner of the Prix Goncourt in 1991,[56] or Sébastian Japrisot's moving *Un long dimanche de fiançaille,*[57] or Pat Barker's fictional trilogy on the Great War,[58] or Sebastian Faulks's powerful *Birdsong.*[59] Barker has written a sequel whose central figure is a one-hundred-year old veteran and father of the narrator.[60] Faulks has placed within a later novel about the Second World War a story of the transmission of traumatic memory between father and daughter.[61] There are deep traces here of the history of several cohorts, moving through time, across this fictional landscape. Today's grandparents were children after the 1914–18 war, and their stories—family stories—are now imbedded in history, and fiction, and exhibitions, and museums, and pilgrimage, in all the stuff of ritual which deepens the "memory boom." The linkage between the young and the old—now extended substantially with the increase in life expectancy—is so central to the concept of memory that its significance may have simply passed us by.

Let me take a moment to describe a personal experience which illustrates this point. Chapter 10 of this book has a further discussion of this set of issues. I have been privileged to work as one of the creators of an international museum of the First World War, located at Péronne, in the Department of the Somme, an hour north of Paris. Péronne was German headquarters during the Battle of the Somme in 1916. This museum was the product of a specific and fleeting generational moment in the 1980s, when history became family history, and therefore could include scripts not yet inscribed by the French in their national narrative of the war. Because of family memories, and traumatic memories at that, we were able to find a way to justify a major French investment in a story very few Frenchmen had acknowledged as of fundamental importance to them and to their sense of the past. Verdun, that other great disaster of 1916, had occluded the Somme in France, despite the fact that the French lost 200,000 men in the battle there. The man who saw this opportunity was Max Lejeune, president of the Conseil Général and a former Defense Minister at the time of Suez. He was a characteristic Fourth Republic politician, skilled in the byways of Parisian infighting, but whose power rested on a personal fiefdom and following in his own Department of the Somme. Tourism mattered to him, but so did the memory of his father, an *ancien combattant* of the

Battle of the Somme, who had returned from the war a troubled man. The childhood Lejeune recalled was not a happy one; the war had broken his father, and a lifetime later, in the 1980s, his son Max Lejeune wanted to find a way to put those memories to rest.

For Lejeune, the idea of a museum originated in family history, his family history. But his insight was in seeing that such a museum was a means of turning national narratives into family narratives, resonant to a very wide public of several nationalities. In this way, this venture could bring French children at the end of the twentieth century into contact with the world of his childhood, in the 1920s and 1930s, shadowed as it was by the Great War. It could also describe the dis-integration of Europe in 1914–18 in a way which highlighted the urgent tasks of European integration eighty years later. It could combine nostalgia, ever-present in family narratives, with a civics lesson in the future of the new Europe.

With the support of a *notable* of the eminence and power of Lejeune, it was possible to secure the financial investment necessary for the creation of a museum. Ultimately, the project cost one hundred million francs. Lejeune also embraced the argument, and inserted it in the budget where it has remained to this day (2006), that a museum without a research center would atrophy over time. Placing historical debate permanently within the museum, and funding postgraduate studies for people anywhere in the world working on the Great War, are steps which have invigorated the enterprise and ensured its survival. Without family history (and French cash), none of this would have been possible.

This positive story should not obscure other, more difficult, ways in which memories of war continue to linger even now, more than half a century after 1945. The "memory boom" has enabled some people to hide one set of memories behind another. In France and elsewhere, some narratives of the First World War help people evade both personal and national stories about the Second World War.

This is by no means true everywhere; in Russia, for example, the First World War simply vanished as a subject of public discourse, eclipsed by the Revolutions of 1917 and the civil war which followed it. But where collaboration raised uncomfortable questions in the aftermath of the Second World War, many people were happy to sing along with the French troubadour Georges Brassens, "Qu'est-ce que c'est la guerre que je préfère, c'est la guerre de '14–'18."

Family Memory, Traumatic Memory, and War

Here the diversion of the narrative from one war to another was deliberate. Other people were not so fortunate. When we encounter family stories about war in this century, we frequently confront another kind of storytelling, one we have come to call "traumatic memory." The recognition of the significance of this kind of memory is one of the salient features of the contemporary "memory boom." I take the term "traumatic memory" to signify an underground river of recollection, present in the aftermath of the First World War, but a subject of increasing attention in the 1980s and 1990s, when post-traumatic stress disorder became the umbrella term for those (as it were) stuck in the past. The "memory boom" of the later twentieth century arrived in part because of our belated but real acceptance that among us, within our families, there are men and women overwhelmed by traumatic recollection. The second chapter of this book returns to the origins of this term in the history of shell shock in the Great War.

War veterans bore the scars of such memories even when they did not have a scratch on them. The imagery of the shell-shocked soldier became generalized after the Second World War.[62] In 1939–45, the new notation for psychological casualty was "combat fatigue," an unavoidable wearing out of one of the components of the military machine. Holocaust victims had a very different story to tell, but the earlier vocabulary of trauma was there to be seized. And seized again. This was true in commemorative art as much as in medical care. The notation of Maya Lin's Vietnam Veterans Memorial is that of Sir Edwin Lutyens's monument to the missing of the Battle of the Somme at Thiepval, inaugurated in 1932, but commemorating the engagement of 1916. The Great War created categories which have framed much of the language we use to describe the traumatic memories of victims of the Second World War, the Vietnam war, and other conflicts.

This is also the case in the field of psychiatry, where the notion of post-traumatic stress disorder—previously termed "shell shock" or a host of other terms—was accepted as a recognized medical diagnostic classification only in 1980, a few years after the end of the Vietnam war. Once accepted as a syndrome, PTSD validated entitlements—to pensions, to medical care, to public sympathy. It also "naturalized" the status of Vietnam veterans. The mental scars of Vietnam vets, once legitimated, could be treated alongside other victims of urban violence, or sexual or family trauma.[63] In all these cases, violence seemed to leave an imprint we now call "traumatic memory."

In this area, enormous progress has been made over the last thirty years in the field of neuroscience. The biochemistry of traumatic memory is now a field of active research, and various pathways have been identified which help us distinguish between different kinds of memory traces. There is now a biochemistry of traumatic memories, memories which are first buried and then involuntarily released when triggered by certain external stimuli. The world of neurology has had its own "memory boom," which in turn has helped establish the scientific character and credentials of the notion of "trauma."[64]

Fiction and fictionalized memoirs have also been important vectors for the dissemination of notions of traumatic memory. This has been true since the Great War, and the appearance in print of the poems of Wilfred Owen, who did not survive the war, and Ivor Gurney, who did but who spent the rest of his life in a lunatic asylum. Some veterans may have retreated into silence, but there were many storytellers among them, and among their contemporaries, who to this day continue to teach us much about what "trauma" means. Virginia Woolf's *Mrs Dalloway* of 1925 is one poignant example. The figure of Septimus Smith was drawn from her encounter with her brother-in-law and his condition. It is essential to acknowledge the role of storytellers in the public understanding of traumatic memory as a fact of twentieth-century family life. Two recent books, David Grossman's *See under Love* and Peter Balakian's *The Black Dog of Fate,* are powerful evocations of this setting of remembrance.

The "Cultural Turn" in Historical Studies

The memory boom of the late twentieth century is a reflection of a complex matrix of war damage, of political activity, of claims for entitlement, of scientific research, of philosophical reflection, and of art. In conclusion, it may be useful to add a few words about the intersection of these broad trends with a number of narrower movements within the historical profession itself. The first may be described under the heading of "the cultural turn" in historical studies. When I was an undergraduate at Columbia, forty years ago, cultural history was a form of *Geistesgeschichte,* a rich tradition in which German intellectual history was of central importance. Just emerging in the mid–1960s was an exciting mixture of disciplines to challenge the prevailing consensus; it came in many forms, but probably is best summarized as social scientific history. Over the next two decades historical demography and other forms of sociologically or anthropologically inspired historical study proliferated. Alongside them was a politically committed variation of Marxist thinking which created labor history. The now essential historical journal *Past & Present* was initially subtitled "a journal of scientific history." The subtitle was discarded; the journal thrived. These strands of historiographical innovation produced work of outstanding and enduring quality. But as broad programs of historical interpretation, both of these schools failed to deliver the goods they had promised. There was no new paradigm like that of the *Annales* school of the 1920s and 1930s, promising total history. Instead, the positivist assumptions of social scientific history, and the heroic narratives of the making of the working class, began to fade by the 1970s and 1980s.

Even in Paris, where the phrase "nous les Annales" still echoed magisterially, the hold of the old ways of thinking began to loosen. Part of the challenge came from postmodernists, unconvinced by the grand narratives of industrialization or other forms of linear progress, or unprepared to go on charting the history of militancy, or the transformation of a "class in itself" to a "class for itself." As I have already noted, the inspiration behind *Les lieux de mémoire* was political. After the collapse of the twin stars in the French firmament, Gaullism and communism, many scholars of contemporary history, including Pierre Nora, sought a reorientation of their outlook through a reflection on what being French entails. And that meant seeking out the multiple sites of what he termed French "memory."

In North America, part of the "cultural turn" reflected the way the neighbors began to colonize history. We should note in particular the increasing significance within historical study of literary scholarship, offering fundamental contributions to the cultural history of the First World War, at least in the Anglo-Saxon world. Feminist scholars have brought to this subject and to many others powerful new perspectives. No one today writes about the cultural history of imperialism without some meditation on the work of

Edward Said and some reflection on that protean concept "Orientalism." And one need not agree with everything Steven Greenblatt has had to say in order to appreciate the excitement of his ideas and those of his former colleagues at Berkeley who edit the journal *Representations.* There were as many panels on subjects in cultural history at the 1999 Modern Languages Association meeting in San Francisco as there were at the American Historical Association meeting in Chicago the following year.

Where once French or French-inspired historians had sought out clues concerning the features of the unchanging mental furniture of a society, loosely defined as *mentalité*, by the late 1980s many were looking at language and representations. Roger Chartier has helped bury the outmoded distinction in cultural history between "superstructure" and "substructure" by insisting that "the representations of the social world themselves are the constituents of social reality."[65] Gareth Stedman Jones echoed the same point in his influential study *Languages of Class,* published in 1983.[66] German scholars, following first Reinhard Koselleck, in the study of *Begriffsgeschichte,* or historical semantics,[67] or following the work of Jan Assmann and Aleida Assmann, have created an entire literature in the field of cultural memory.[68] And these seminal works are but the core of a much wider circle of scholarship they have inspired and informed.

Globalization is evident in the spread of these approaches to the study of memory. Saul Friedlander and his students in Israel, Germany, and America helped launch the successful journal *History & Memory* in 1987. Oral historians in many countries have added their voices, and have helped ensure that the study of "memory" is informed by a sensitivity to issues of gender.[69] In much of this broad field of work, Foucault and Lacan have been the inspiration;[70] other scholars have found much in the reflections of Lyotard or Kristeva about the ruins of symbolic language in the aftermath of the

Holocaust.[71] Post-modernist interventions have returned time and again to memory,[72] as a site of nostalgia. Some favor turning to the individual's stories as the cornerstone for the recovery of the subject, whose position is always in question.

Others in the field of critical theory are skeptical about all the talk about memory. I will return to this theme in the final chapter of this book. To Kerwin Klein, the memory boom is a betrayal of the radical credentials of critical theory, for it "marries hip new linguistic practices with some of the oldest senses of memory as a union of divine presence and material object." In some hands, Klein argues, the evocation of memory becomes a kind of "cultural religiosity," a "re-enchantment" of our sense of the past.[73]

By the 1990s these critical standpoints and innovative approaches clearly occupied an influential, though certainly not hegemonic, position in the discipline. Some style the sum of these contributions as the "linguistic turn," simply meaning the general acceptance that there are no historical "facts" separate from the language in which they are expressed in time and place. Others call it the "cultural turn," meaning the concentration on signifying practices in the past as a major focus of current historical research. Whatever it is termed, and whatever its origins, the tide has indeed turned, and cultural history is now all around us. It has benefited from the influx of refugees from Marxist or *marxisant* history, who watched their historical paradigm disintegrate well before the Berlin Wall was breached. At times, cultural history has taken an entirely idealist turn, in the sense of suggesting that representations constitute the only reality. This is an extreme position, but it does exist. However configured, the "cultural turn" in historical study describes an agenda of real popularity and potential. Students are voting with their feet here: economic, demographic, and labor history have not kept their audiences; to a degree, cultural history has drawn them away, and in the field of cultural history, the subject of memory is ubiquitous.

Witnesses and Historical Remembrance

I have noted the overdetermined character of the contemporary memory boom. Returning to some of the same concerns of the early-twentieth-century memory boom, many people inside and (perhaps more importantly) outside the academy have made of memory a critical focus of cultural life. The second memory boom of the twentieth century presupposes and builds on the first.

The phenomenon of the "witness," discussed in chapter 11, shows how this is so. There have been three levels in which witnessing has been central to narratives of remembrance. The first is legal. Witnesses in war crimes trials, trials of those accused of crimes against humanity, or in tribunals of reconciliation have provided the material testimony central to judicial acts which could not have occurred fifty years ago. In 1948 who could have foreseen that the Universal Declaration of Human Rights would support a structure of international law reaching out to those who violate human rights in Yugoslavia or Chile? Witnesses are central to this process.

The second level on which the "witness" has emerged is moral. Those who have testified about genocide, terrorism—state-sponsored or not—or persecution speak of particular grievances associated with the tragic history of specific populations. Here survivors of the Holocaust have been prominent, but it is important to note that narratives of Nazi persecution have served to frame, perhaps even to legitimate, other narratives. The very word "genocide" was invented by Rafael Lemkin in the context of Nazi persecution, but once adopted it moved back in time to inform discussions of the Armenian genocide of 1915 and forward to characterize massacres in Cambodia, Bosnia, and Rwanda. Those who tell of these crimes have a standing which goes beyond the specific testimony they can offer. They speak of absolute evil, and thus touch issues of moral significance which place them in a category different from that of other survivors of twentieth-century violence. They seem to come from another world, one we ignore at our moral peril.

This leads to the third level of witnessing, one of universal significance. For beyond the war crimes trials, and beyond narratives of persecution or genocide, there stands the witness as a spokesman for humanity as a whole. Witnessing has thus come to take on a kind of categorical imperative which Kant wrote about two centuries ago. They tell us of events which, whatever their origin, seem to make moral thinking, indeed moral living, impossible. Thus listening to witnesses, aiding them, respecting them, appears to be a precondition of moral life as a whole. "The duty to remember" is a phrase which captures the multifaceted meaning of witnessing in our times. This is part of the story of the memory boom, but by no means its only source.

There were witnesses of many kinds who emerged from the Great War to tell their stories and to make their moral claims on the survivors. War crimes trials were held after the war in Germany and in Turkey, but they were relatively limited in their scope, and they were soon forgotten. But if the witnesses were not in courtrooms, they were everywhere else. The two memory booms of the twentieth century share this focus on the authority of direct experience, on the words and images we have of those who went through *la boucherie,* the slaughterhouse of the Great War, or through the concentration and extermination camps of the Second World War.

One of the challenges of the next decades is to try to draw together some of these disparate strands of interest and enthusiasm through a more rigorous and tightly argued set of propositions about what exactly memory is, and what it has been in the past. The only fixed point at this moment is the near ubiquity of the term. No one should delude herself into thinking we all use it the same way. Our concern with memory has grown exponentially, and at a pace much more rapid than the development of the conceptual tools we need to understand it. But just as we use words like love and hate without ever knowing their full or shared significance, so we are bound to go on using the term "memory," the historical signature of our own generation.

With this set of cultural developments in mind, the rest of this book dwells on one crucial element in the linkage between history and memory. The primary focus of this study is on the ways groups of people, particularly in Europe since 1914, have imagined and remembered war and the victims of war in the twentieth century. While the subject of war by no means reaches all the protean features of the "memory boom," we cannot ignore war and memories of war as central to the activity I term historical remembrance. The rest of this book aims to show how this is so.

CHAPTER 2

Shell Shock, Memory, and Identity

In one particular way, the Great War reconfigured popular and medical notions about memory. In 1915, the British psychiatrist Charles Myers introduced the term "shell shock" to describe a set of disabling injuries suffered by men at the front. The medical history of this term has been ably explored; less well documented is the way the appearance of thousands of men with psychological injuries has come to frame what we now term "traumatic memory." Shellshocked soldiers were the first carriers of post-traumatic stress disorder in the twentieth century. To appreciate how we, nearly a century later, understand the memories of those who survive overwhelming violence, we must return to the Great War and to the history and representation of shell shock. Those representations took many forms—medical, poetic, fictional, visual. We need to attend to them all to be able to comprehend why this phenomenon, arising in the 1914–18 conflict, has come to symbolize traumatic injury and traumatic memory throughout the twentieth century.

Shell Shock

First, what did the term mean to those who saw it during the Great War and after? Shell shock is a condition in which the link between an individual's memory and his identity is severed. A set of unassimilable images and experiences, arising from war service, either in combat or near it, radically disturbs the narrative, the life story, of individuals, the stories people tell themselves and others about their lives. Through such stories, we know who we are, or at least we think we do.[1] Shell shock undermines that orientation, that point of reference from which an individual's sense of self unfolds. His integrity, in the sense of his having an integral personality, one with a then and a now which flowed together, becomes uncertain because of what he has felt and seen and what he continues to feel and see. In many cases the visual imagination is central to this condition. Before the eyes of a shell-shocked man were images frequently of an uncanny, life-threatening, and terrifying kind, and they endure. Their meaning, that is, their location alongside other images and experiences, is unclear or bizarre. These visualized or felt traces of war experience can tend to live a life of their own, a life at times so vivid and powerful as to eclipse all others. They can paralyze; in extreme cases, they can kill. Suicide is the ultimate escape from them.

Fortunately, most of the men who fought did not suffer from this condition, and most of those who did were able to find a way to live with it or move beyond it. Their recovery was independent of most medical care, since the pathways of causality in this area of neuropsychology were unknown and patterns of care were unsettled and highly subjective. Many doctors made informed guesses, but the initial presumption of a purely organic cause of psychological disturbances had to be discarded over time. What would replace the initial, purely physical model of psychiatric illness was an open question; it remains open today.

Whatever the state of medical knowledge, physicians still had a task to do. They had thousands of psychologically damaged soldiers to care for. By 1917, perhaps one quarter of all men sent down the line in British forces were unfit because of psychological stress of one kind or another. The breakdown rate was no lower in the German and Austrian armies, but the recovery rate of such men was higher, in part because of the assembly-line treatment of these men. Recovery rates of 90 percent were reported,[2] but surely these results simply meant that damaged men were declared healthy, then sent back to the front, where they broke down again. Shell shock was the same in all armies, though medical nomenclature and policy differed between and among them.[3] In every army doctors did what they could, mostly through listening, caring, and counseling. In this way they played a real, though sometimes minor, role in the rehabilitation of these men. When discharged, shell-shocked men found much less sympathy from war pension officials, whose job primarily was to reduce the charge on the public purse rather than to meet the state's obligation to men suffering war-related injury.[4] Self help, camaraderie, and family support were the most common path to recovery for those not severely disabled.

Whatever the degree of disability they suffered, and however they were cared for, the presence in towns and villages, in cities and on the land, of thousands of shell-shocked men raises important issues for our understanding of the aftermath of war, and of the way the Great War configured different notions of memory at the time. Thinking about the term and the men whose lives it describes offers a framework within which to claim yet again that the survivors of the Great War constituted a "generation of memory." In this case the memories in question were disabling, disturbing, unassimilable.

In the later twentieth century, this form of troubled remembrance has been reconfigured in different ways, as combat fatigue or post-traumatic stress disorder. But all discussions of the notion of traumatic memory sooner or later return to the scene of the crime, the site of combat in which the term "shell shock" was invented and circulated.

In this chapter, I want to offer a number of reflections on shell shock. Contemporaries had enormous trouble in comprehending a set of conditions which did not fit normative categories of behavior under fire. At one pole of rectitude stood duty and stoical endurance. At the other stood deceit—feigned psychological injury. There were many good examples of both. But between the two was a vast array of men whose condition barred them from duty through no fault of their own, and through no effort to deceive. The predicament of these men and those who treated them is at the heart of the history of shell shock.

Embodied Memory

One way to open this discussion is to visualize it (figs. 1–3). Early in the war, army physicians began to handle cases of psychological breakdown, paralysis, and disturbingly uncontrolled physical behavior among men who had been in combat. From these cases, C. S. Myers and others coined the term "shell shock," assuming that some physical damage like concussion arose from exposure to artillery fire and the like.[5] Though these physicians were later to distance themselves from this nomenclature, it stuck.[6] It is important to try to see the phenomenon with their eyes. What was it that these physicians saw? We know something about this question from physician training films made in the war. The disturbing character of these images, I believe, lay both in the body of the sufferer and in the gaze of the onlooker. Together they (and we) share embodied memory.[7] In almost every instance, the conversion of emotional states to physical ones is apparent. The involuntary movement of the jaw of a man who had bayoneted another locates the incident in his own body. His body is telling the story of what he had done. There are war stories too in the unsuccessful efforts of a man trying to stand up or in the tremors of the man whose walking is not under control, and whose walk has a curious resemblance to Charlie Chaplin's. More of that below. We can simply ask, where had their legs taken them?

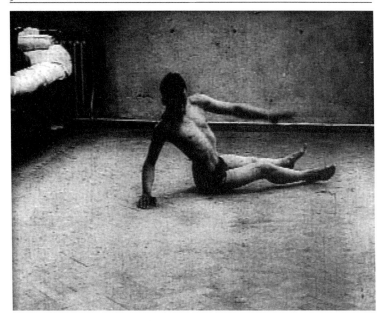

Fig. 1. Shell-shocked British soldier in rehabilitation to regain the use of his limbs. (KCET, Los Angeles)

Their bodies bore the traces of combat. There is embodied memory too in the case of a man who responds to nothing other than the word "bomb," which (when heard) sends him scurrying under the bed; and in the terrified response of a French soldier triggered by the sight of an officer's hat. These soldiers have internalized memory; it is inside them, and when touched, their bodies respond as if they were sprung coils.

Here we can see and feel one kind of embodied memory. It is *written on* the men who fought, or inscribed in them in a way which is not subject to their direct or premeditated control. In all instances, images and memories seem to live both imbedded in these people and curiously detached from them; memory itself, or images of overwhelming events, appear to be free-floating powerful agents

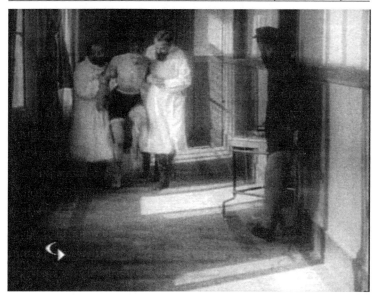

Fig. 2. Shell-shocked French soldier relearning the use of his legs. (KCET, Los Angeles)

which somehow control the jaw of a man, or his leg, or all his movements.

In effect, these men's bodies *perform* something about their war experience. As we shall consider in the conclusion to this book, shell shock is a theater of memory out of control. The bodies of these soldiers hold traces of memory; they are speaking to us, though not in a way which we usually encounter. Here stories become flesh; physical movements occur without end or direction, or there is no movement at all.

If memories tell us who we are, then what did these powerful memory traces of combat tell these men about who they were? These images, feelings, and memories didn't fit; they could not be interpolated in a story of before and after. They challenged and sometimes even fragmented identity, and one of the fragments overwhelmed all

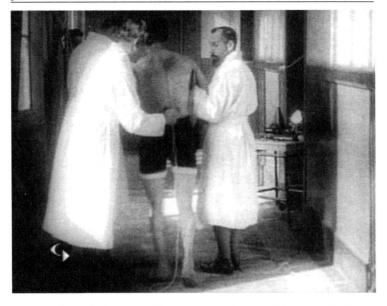

Fig. 3. Shell-shocked French soldier recovering the use of his limbs with the aid of electric-shock treatment. (KCET, Los Angeles)

others. It is this kind of frozen moment which we see in these images; a few gestures concentrate those events and memories of them. Sometimes soldiers (with or without the aid of physicians) could specify what these memories were. It may have been an incident in combat; at other times, crucial events were more difficult to locate. But in all these cases, bodies seem to remember something, they engage in a kind of unwitting reenactment[8] which tended to defy both verbal expression and the urge to forget.

I want to turn now to the second sense of embodied memory, that related to those who viewed these images, or who saw these men or thousands like them. The films of these images were made to train physicians how to treat psychologically damaged soldiers. Most army doctors were at a loss as to how to help these men; Freud was similarly puzzled and uncertain.[9] We know that other physicians—

the Austrian physician and future Nobel prize winner Julius Wagner-Jauregg, for instance—used electroconvulsive shock treatment to discourage malingering. In Figure 3 we see a rare photograph of the use of electricity to stimulate recalcitrant muscles to help do their job, and to help a man clearly struggling to walk again. No malingering here. We know that other physicians used electroconvulsive shock treatment in even more radical ways, though these celebrated cases were exceptional.[10] What were the lessons learned by the original viewers of these images, the medical men whose job it was to try to make them better? It is hard to say precisely; such evidence as we have indicates that these images were used to help separate the malingerer from the legitimate sufferer of shell shock. The movements of these men are not conjured up; the men can't repeat them on request, because they are automatic or uncontrolled. Charlie Chaplin can walk with an awkward gait, and make us feel he is about to fall; everyone knows it is an act, he can start it or stop it at will; but these men are not acting. Wartime film footage was there to better enable physicians to tell who was really sick and who was simply trying it on. How to separate the two was a virtually impossible task, but visual evidence was there to help.

The therapeutic context was only one site where such images appeared. Other soldiers saw such men, and so did civilians, when the soldiers were sent back from casualty clearing stations to base hospitals or home, or when they returned to the front and broke down again, a far from uncommon occurrence. These injured men were there, an integral part of the community of soldiers, not so much a nation as a brotherhood, the "génération de feu," "ceux de '14." And yet their illnesses were so odd, so frightening, that their presence was always a problem. The stigma of mental illness did not vanish just because it was registered in the service of one's country. To see such men was to encounter a side of war no one wanted to confront.

Shell-shocked men were not the only people hard to face in the postwar world. The *gueules cassées,* or disfigured men, were there too. So were the amputees and those with prosthetic arms and legs. Otto Dix painted them on street corners in Germany, or playing cards in a harsh satiric reconfiguration of Cezanne's *Cardplayers* of 1893–96.

My fundamental point is that these men challenged contemporary understandings of memory. The images these men had in their minds did not fade when they left the field of battle. Conventional notions of masculinity or stoicism did not hold when men of unquestionable courage broke down under the weight of their memories. Those who saw these medical training films were viewing memories which had taken over the lives of the men who had them. These people were walking arguments against the view that demobilization came to an end when the last serving soldier in a combat unit left the service. Mental illness—as much as physical disabilities—told another story, one which lingered.

There is a third concentric circle we need to examine—beyond the sufferers and their comrades. What do *we* see when we gaze at these images? We see men who suffer; men like us. We see their embodied memory, and link it to what we think we know about war and its aftermath. How this happens is a complicated and lengthy story, but my guess is that for several generations, in some countries and not in others, such images have been fundamental in establishing what Samuel Hynes calls a "war-in-the-head," mental furniture about war and what it does to people. It challenges our understanding of what memory is.

It is important to note the culturally differentiated nature of this argument. In Britain (but not to the same degree or in the same way in France or Germany), as a result of stories, poems, and especially images, successive generations have inherited a set of icons or metaphors about the war. Shell shock is one such metaphor. Metaphors are always open to interpretation. But they have truths in them to which their survival attests. One of them is that battle does not end when the firing stops; it goes on in the minds of many of those who returned intact, or apparently unscathed, and in the suffering of those whose memories are embodied, enacted, repeated, performed.

Memory and Identities

I have tried to suggest that the phenomenon of shell shock raised fundamental questions about the linkage between memory and identity. This subject has a vast literature in the field of cognitive psychology.[11] What historians of the Great War can contribute to this discussion is documentary evidence as to how in the past this link was broken in some cases and fortified in others in particular by the telling of stories, the creation of narratives, which may have helped some men to withstand memories of combat. There can be no firm rules applied to this process, which varied according to a host of factors related to a soldier's age, education, profession, temperament, the nature and duration of the particular ordeal he had to endure, as well as the speed and kind of medical care and other assistance he received when injured. Physical injury had psychological sequelae, a complication which almost certainly makes all statistics about the number of men who suffered from something like shell shock a serious underestimate. What we can rely on, though, are contemporary representations of shell shock. I will try in a handful of cases to illustrate this subject, both with respect to those who suffered disabling psychological injury and to those who apparently did not. In both cases, we can offer some documentation about the ways soldiers represented or explained terrifying experiences to themselves and to those around them. When such accounts were made to fit into a life history, into the story of a man who had a before- and an after-the-war, then the pathways from memory to identity and back again remained intact. When the images and feelings did not fit, when they continued to have no location in a soldier's sense of who he was and where he was, then a kind of disorientation, lasting for varying periods of time, was inevitable. Why this complex framing of memories in a broader temporal context succeeded in some cases and not in others is, of course, impossible to explain. Healing has its mysteries too, and even when we admit the obscurity of its workings, we should never lose sight of its power.

In this context, I would like to offer some instances of these narrative arts of healing before turning to those men whose disabilities (and stories) were of an entirely different order. Once more, I am interested in what Hynes has called "the soldiers' tale,"[12] rather than the particular mix of factors which led some to resume their lives and others to be unable to do so. Then I would like to relate some of the broader questions about the significance of the phenomenon of shell shock to our discussion of configurations of memory in the century of total war.

Soldiers' Tales: Memories and Identities

Duty, deceit, disorientation, and disability: these terms were intertwined with the subject of shell shock from the very beginning of the war. Disentangling them proved an arduous task. One reason is that shell shock is a continuum of conditions rather than a stable category. In no sense should shell shock be approached as a single entity, separable from other states of mind we call "healthy." Most soldiers who went through significant encounters with the enemy during the war were put under stress which we may find difficult to imagine. What is surprising is not that some men broke down, but that so many did not. I want to tell the story of two of these un-shell-shocked men before returning to the narratives of men less fortunate than they. I will use both stories to locate shell shock within a constellation of narratives of war which brought memories and identities together.

Cassin

First, duty. Consider the case of René Cassin, later the author of the Universal Declaration of Human Rights. He was a soldier of the Great War. On 12 October 1914, he was severely wounded near St Mihiel. He was hit in his side, abdomen, and left arm. He knew that a stomach wound was almost always fatal.[13] Somehow, he got through the night and was handed over to the French army medical services.

There he was treated with bureaucratic stupidity of the highest order. I have told this story elsewhere.[14] Cassin could be treated—regulations insisted—only in the medical facilities of his regiment, which was six hundred kilometers away. So, his stomach wound unattended, he left on a ten-day journey to meet up with his regiment. When he arrived and the doctors saw his condition, they decided to operate immediately—without anesthetic. This too he survived.

The narrative Cassin constructed out of this ordeal was that of a conventional French patriot and a Jew. The horrors of his experience were palpable, but somehow he managed to frame his part in it without doubting that it undermined his own identity. In fact, his commitment to securing justice for *les mutilé de guerre* and for their offspring formed part of his subsequent career, first as a leader of the veterans' movement, and then as a founder of the international human rights movement. What matters in this context is the extent to which he was able—stoically, powerfully, unmistakably—to bring his prewar identity and his wartime memories into line.[15]

The story of Cassin and his operation is about more than a narrative. It is about suffering of a kind hard to imagine. So are accounts of shell shock. Palpable suffering is at the heart of all these stories, but no two men reacted to it, or understood it, in the same way.

Céline

The contrasting case I want to present is that of a man who could not have been more different from Cassin. During the Second World War, Cassin was one of the leaders of Free France in London, de Gaulle's trusted legal adviser and minister in exile. By then, Louis-Ferdinand Destouches had become a world-famous novelist and anti-Semite, writing under the pen name of Céline. He was living in Paris, where he had been born, and said much both before and during the war about the need to get rid of the Jews. *Bagatelles pour un massacre* is the title of his 1937 meditation on this theme.[16] On Hitler's birthday in 1941, he shocked his German hosts (including Ernst Jünger) by calling them "pas sérieux" about killing the Jews. He, Céline, a veteran of the trenches, would know what to do if the task would come to him. He could (perhaps should) have been shot as a collaborator but hid in Denmark long enough to avoid the *Épuration*. He made his return to France when reconciliation was the theme of the day, received a slap on his wrists for his nastiness, and died in his bed in 1961.[17]

What makes it useful to bring the names of Cassin and Céline together is not the Second but rather the First World War. Nothing could be more remote from Cassin's stoical tale of suffering and reinforced patriotism than that of Céline. Still Destouches in 1914, and six years younger than Cassin, the man who later became Céline was deep in his apprenticeship as a master of misanthropy and deceit.

He entered the cavalry in 1912 and soon discovered that he hated the army. When war broke out in 1914, Destouches's unit moved east, facing Metz and Nancy, and then moved into German territory. The cavalry were used to cover the massive French retreat after the bloody Battle of the Frontiers. Though they didn't suffer many casualties, they saw them and the detritus of war all around them.

When this part of the front stabilized in early October, Destouches's unit was sent north and west to Flanders. This time, near the river Lys, the cavalry were deployed to guard the flanks of the British Expeditionary Force. By mid-October, they were near Poelkappelle on the outskirts of Ypres. There Destouches, sent at night to find another isolated post, was hit in the arm by a ricocheting bullet. He was evacuated on 26 October. Instead of going to a military hospital, the wounded man found his way to a Red Cross ambulance, and was treated in one of their hospitals in Hazebrouck. Bullet fragments were still in his arm. Destouches refused morphine or an anesthetic, fearing amputation. A civilian doctor removed the bullet without anesthetic and sutured the wound.

From his Red Cross hospital, he proceeded to the military hospital in Paris at Val-de-Grâce. There he was awarded the Military Medal. His exploits were immortalized in the patriotic journal *L'Illustré national.* In its issue of November 1914 it saluted Destouches, of the 12th Cavalry Regiment, who had "spontaneously volunteered . . . to deliver an order under heavy fire. After having delivered the order, he was seriously wounded on returning from his mission." The truth was more mundane: he had not volunteered; he had been hit accidentally, and then wandered around in the darkness.

That was the full extent of his active military service, but Destouches invented an entirely different set of events. He was, he proudly asserted, a victim of shell shock. There is absolutely no evidence to support this claim. He simply made it up. He liked to show off a photograph of himself and some other soldiers at Val de Grâce, where he was wearing a cloth secured under his chin and covering his head. Treatment for shell shock, was how he described it. The reality was that he suffered from a toothache.[18] What a perfect incarnation of the army's worst fears! A man who was prone to violent denunciations of the authorities, women, Africans, Jews, just about anybody, hid behind shell shock as the reason for his "delirium of words." What a marvelous cover for whatever toxic pollution he chose to exude.

Ironically, Destouches, a man who reveled in filth, sought out a home after the war in the medical profession. But he really hit the jackpot in 1932 when his war novel *Voyage au bout de la nuit* was published. It is an astonishing tale, a barroom rant of two old soldiers, based on the story one of them tells about the war, about his brush with shell shock, and an unlikely postwar career as the director of a lunatic asylum. Céline himself conjured up the tale that his (fabricated) experience of shell shock in the war was the source of this novel, now a classic of twentieth-century French literature. Its truth value is of no great interest, since war novels are never documentary, even though they may pretend to be so. What is intriguing is the way Céline defined shell shock in his novel as a convenient cover for malingering and misanthropy.

Cassin and Céline: in their words we have the two poles of storytelling about war service. At one extreme was Cassin's endurance, with no apparent psychological damage; this was the ideal of all armies. At the other was Céline's malingering, fake psychological injury, and a mockery of the real suffering, both physical and emotional, which war service entailed. This was the nightmare of all armies—to confront masses of men who invented nonexistent illnesses and shirked their share of the burdens of war. The two cases I have cited are emblematic: one presented courage and fortitude without psychiatric injury. The other feigned psychiatric injury without courage. The real victims of shell shock shown in the medical training films are somewhere between the two.

The narratives of Céline and Cassin, though, do share one important element. In their very different "soldiers' tales," both men were engaged in a kind of self-fashioning. They were young, just starting out in the world, and aimed at creating a kind of self which drew their prewar lives, their wartime memories, and their identities together. The way they talked about the war was central to who they were. Their memories of war (even false ones) were built into their identities.

Shell Shock, Memory, and Identity

Point—counterpoint. These two cases are no more than that, but they do enable us to frame the history of shell shock in terms of contemporary categories of normative behavior, which Cassin fit to a tee and against which Céline spent his life in revolt. The men they became were the product of their own efforts to locate the war in their personal narrative.

Shell-shocked men were not so fortunate. In a host of ways, their stories were disruptive of the linkage between memory and identity. This approach enables us to see too that shell shock is not one category but a myriad of cases, in all of which some degree of disorientation occurs. For example, Siegfried Sassoon had nightmares of the dead staring at him in his bed, but his physician, W. H. R. Rivers, found no evidence of shell shock in what he said, just an "anti-war fixation." Was he shaken? Yes; was he shell-shocked? No. Many other men were similarly on the fringes of this category of disability, which we must treat as a continuum rather than as a fixed label.[19]

Others still were entirely disoriented by what had happened to them in war. I will now discuss a mere handful of such men, but will do so with the full recognition that no one instance can stand for the rest. Once again, the issue of memory and identity helps us see what ties together these stories and the suffering they disclose.

One of the most sensitive students of this set of disorders was E. E. Southard, professor at the Harvard Medical School and director of the United States Army Neuropsychiatric Training School in Boston in 1917–18. In 1919 he compiled the most complete and up-to-date casebook of shell shock cases and treatments from all combatant armies.[20] His fundamental approach was to refuse to separate those ailments which were of organic origin from those which were functional. The overlap between the two was considerable. Still, a substantial number of cases were much more functional than organic. Shell shock, Southard argued, reflects the inability of a person's mind to integrate into his life story the sense experience of combat. This disorientation, which may have physical causes too, converts shell shock from an event which happened into a condition. The purpose of medical treatment, Southard argued, was to reverse this process, and turn a condition into an event which could then be aligned with other events in a person's life. This could not be done in all cases, but it could in many: "A shock is not a smash, a crush, a breach. A shock literally shakes. The shaken thing stays, for a time at least. Shaken up or down, the victim of shock is not at first thought of as done for. The spirit of the language is against the thought of shock as destruction or even as permanent irritation. . . . Shell-shock . . . is or ought to be, as a pathological event, reversible."[21]

Southard's collection of nearly one thousand case histories is very instructive in the context of my argument, since it shows how some physicians operated on the assumption that shell shock had many sources, but its essence was a kind of cognitive dissonance. Something didn't fit in a man's sense of who he was and where he was. Southard and others tried to point out how natural, how normal, it was for men to feel this way in wartime. He understood his job as a guide, a map reader of dark places, bringing men back to their senses, back to themselves. It is no accident that he used phrases from Dante's *Inferno*, throughout the book, concluding with the hope that patients and doctors, like Dante and Virgil, could one day "issue out again to see the stars."[22]

Consider but a few of the case histories he presented in his pioneering text. His book is a record of suffering and (to a varying degree) recovery not just from the results of artillery but from generalized fear and exhaustion. Strain could break a man's sense of self like a matchstick. De Massary and du Sonich reported the case of a French soldier who was captured in Belgium in 1914, and then succeeded "under great strain in escaping." He endured heavy bombardment at Verdun, during which time he was bowled over and buried alive temporarily. By January 1916 he had to be evacuated from the front due to depression and exhaustion. After convalescence, he returned to the front, but soon developed involuntary movements, which made him appear to "dance." Slowly, he regained control of his body. What he had seen and endured was simply too much for any man; his body rebelled, it moved to its own rhythms. Once out of the line, and after a period of rest, he returned "to himself." Another French soldier under their care was sure that the Germans were kind and the French cruel; he forgot which side he was on. This reversal of loyalties also faded over time.

The French physicians Mairet and Piéron reported on the case of a shell-shocked soldier, aged forty, who woke up in a hospital in Tunis with the feeling that he had been "born again." In time, he became depressed "due to despair at not being able to know who he was" and what he was doing. Nine months later, his old memories came back suddenly, with a gap of about twenty-five days following the explosion which had incapacitated him in the first place. With this caesura, this soldier resumed his life and returned to the front. Gilles reported on the case of another French soldier who endured the Battle of the Marne phlegmatically, but a week later, on the Aisne, he was paralyzed by dreams of the horrors he had seen. At those moments he lost track of where he was. We do not know the outcome of his treatment.

This kind of repressed imagery in the memories of shell-shocked men was noted repeatedly by Rivers in his account of work in Craiglockhart and elsewhere. An army private he treated had been found "wandering in a village, in shirt and socks, unable to give name, regiment, or number."[23] Who he was came to him slowly but surely under hypnosis. Others recovered through their own efforts of conscious retrieval of memories. Another of Rivers's patients had been buried alive in a collapsed trench and then wounded as soon as he had extracted himself. He could not evade insomnia or the battle dreams which haunted him. Rivers tried to get this man to bring the story to the surface; repression, he argued, was crippling. Only by narration could the story be located in a continuum. He realized, of course, that in some cases, the retrieval of these moments brought the initial feelings of horror to the surface as well. But he remained convinced that subliminal memories were worse, since they never let go.

The German neurologist Max Nonne, who treated many such men in Hamburg, told of one soldier who was totally paralyzed from the waist down. When he received word that he had been promoted to lieutenant and had received a decoration, "he fell forthwith into . . . convulsions, in the midst of which the hitherto paralyzed legs worked perfectly well." Here a message about what he had done enabled him to place his story (and his fears) in a socially sanctioned narrative. Not all the case histories ended so successfully. Binswanger told of a German soldier whose arm wound appeared to be unrelated to a generalized tremor, which he tried to hide. Even when treated and after extended leave, the tremor returned periodically; his body was remembering something his mind had tried to set aside.[24]

I cite these instances not to make a systematic statement about shell shock. All I hope to do is to show how physicians were sensitive to the ways these narratives, these medical histories, circled around questions of identity and the role of memory in stabilizing or destabilizing. The strain of combat led many men to wonder who they had been before battle, and who they had become as a result. Few were fortunate enough to follow Cassin into an unbroken heroic meta-narrative of stoical heroism. Few were venal (or clever) enough to follow Destouches/Céline into his imaginary condition and his splenetic contempt for humanity. Most tried their best to survive between the two, and to retrieve some sense of fit, some way of squaring memory and identity. Some failed in that effort; what is surprising is that so many others found a way out of the labyrinth, and, as Southard had hoped, did manage to see the stars again.

One final example may help to illustrate my claim that shell shock was a condition in which the link between memory and identity was weakened or severed. Those who suffered long-term psychological damage as a result of their war service saw action in many theatres of operation. Many never had to endure artillery fire, which was initially identified as the source of the trouble, and many such men did not evidence their disturbances until well after their military years were over. Shell shock quickly escaped from its descriptive origins to become a metaphor, something suggesting the plight of men who could not come home again, who had lost the threads of their prewar lives and who could not pick them up again.

The life of one such individual, a celebrated man to be sure, can make this more general point, of relevance to many, more obscure, ex-soldiers. T. E. Lawrence, known to posterity as Lawrence of Arabia, was the leader of the Arab revolt of 1916–18. After the war, Lawrence spent his life in search of a name, an identity which could bring him peace. He never found it. Perhaps this would have been his fate, war or no war, but his story is not unique. For many, war memories were so indelible that they could not be integrated into a postwar life. For such people, recollections are reenactments, crushing burdens, never losing their grip.

Part of the sense of alienation with which Lawrence had to live was directly related to his war service; but part derived from his sense of the betrayal by the British delegation at Versailles in 1919 of promises made to the Arabs during the war. Parts of the story are unclear, and likely to remain so. The story, though, is instructive, in that it shows yet again how memories of wartime injury prepared the way for a later fragmentation of personal identities.

Some parts of the story are certain. In November 1917 Lawrence was the British liaison officer between British forces in Egypt and Palestine and Arab tribes in revolt against Turkey. He was arrested while in disguise, scouting out the defenses of the Syrian town of Deraa. He tried to pass himself off as a Circassian, but the ruse failed: fluent Arabic couldn't hide his European features. He was then severely beaten and raped. Like many victims of rape, Lawrence felt the violation of his integrity, his physical wholeness, for years after the war.[25] Some account for his aversion to physical contact of any kind by reference to this sexual assault. Marriage was unthinkable; loneliness unavoidable.[26]

Severe bouts of depression dogged Lawrence for the rest of his life. Some occurred before the incident at Deraa, but many more seemed related to the shame, guilt, and pain of the rape. But such shadows were but a specific form of a more general inability to forget. This is what he had in mind when he wrote to Robert Graves about their failure to get away from the terrors of the war. They could never say "Goodbye to all that," in the title of Graves's later war memoir; already in 1922, Lawrence wrote Graves: "What's the cause that you, and Siegfried Sassoon, and I . . . can't get away from the war? Here are you riddled with thought like any old table-leg with worms; [Sassoon] yawing about like a ship aback; me . . . finding squalor and maltreatment the only permitted existence; what's the matter with us all? It's like the malarial bugs in the blood, coming out months and years after in recurrent attacks."[27]

The second source of Lawrence's alienation from whom he had been and what he had done in the war comes from the peace conference of 1919. Lawrence had accompanied King Feisal to France to take part in the deliberations. But from the beginning, it was apparent that allies in war were now to be reordered as dominant and subordinate peoples. So much for Woodrow Wilson's principle of self-determination. The Arabs (like Lawrence himself) were pawns again, and were to remain so. His sense of humiliation was overwhelming. Lawrence had been used again; his integrity was once more broken. Even after a spell in 1921 as adviser on Arab affairs to Winston Churchill, then Colonial Secretary, he never lost sight of the promises broken, the faith not kept.

Here his war experience and his early life came together. He learned as a teenager that he was illegitimate, as indeed was his mother. Having "no name," in the Victorian sense of the term, he was free to shed the one by which the public knew him. He took a new name and built a new life, in the Royal Air Force, as Airman First Class John Hume Ross. It didn't take long for the press to find out who he was.[28] The leak put the RAF in a difficult position: Lawrence was a decorated colonel: what the devil was he doing taking orders from junior officers in the RAF base at Farnbrough? The solution was simple: Lawrence was discharged.

The search for anonymity was far from over. This time he enlisted in the tank corps as a private soldier, under the name T. E. Shaw, found at random in the *Army List*.[29] Once more, he went through the humiliations and rigors of basic training. Once more he tried to bury himself alive. To one Oxford friend, he confided that "reason proves there is no hope"; anyone who hopes does so "so to speak, on one leg of our minds"; "perhaps," he wondered, "there's a solution to be found in multiple personality."[30]

Another solution was in speed. He was an aficionado of danger, and sought it out in many ways. One was on his motorbike. He told Curtis this: "When my mood gets too hot and I find myself wandering beyond control I pull out my motor-bike and hurl it at top-speed through these unfit roads for hour after hour. My nerves are jaded and gone near dead, so that nothing less than hours of voluntary danger will prick them into life."[31] This was written by the author of

The Seven Pillars of Wisdom, the classic account of the revolt in the desert during the Great War. The book was written during 1920–22, then revised and published in 1926. It became a best-seller in America and in Britain.

The greater the celebrity status, the greater the wish to evade it, to fade into the background. Every time someone praised him to the skies, Lawrence shrank further into self-loathing. Why? Because "I know the reverse of that medal, and hate its false face so utterly that I struggle like a trapped rabbit to be it no longer," or at least to "shun pleasures," a partial "alleviation of the necessary penalty of living on."[32] Living on after the war; living on after his rape.

After the tank corps came literary work, followed by reentry into the Royal Air Force. This time he tested speedboats, and found some modicum of quiet in the service. He even went so far as to change his name by deed poll to Shaw.[33] After twelve years in the RAF in Britain and India, hounded by the press to the end, he tried to find solace in Devon, in a country house built to his specifications. But journalists still dogged his steps and stripped him of the tranquility he so desperately sought. Lawrence still overshadowed Shaw. On 11 May 1935, he got on his motorbike and headed down a country road to send a telegram to another Great War veteran and writer, Henry Williamson. He never sent it: he swerved off the road to avoid hitting two cyclists. They were uninjured. He crashed, suffered brain damage, went into a coma, and died on 19 May 1935, aged forty-six.

A broken life, and an unusual one undoubtedly, but one which described much about the profound difficulties of living with memories of war. Lawrence, the maverick, the individualist, the artist who had created his own persona, constantly sought to escape the romantic legend he embodied. The memories of the dark side of the war, of his own traumatic past, exploded the legend he refused to embody. Instead he became a wanderer, a man who shed identities like a chameleon.

Was he afflicted with what we now call "traumatic memory"? Perhaps. Would he have performed his multiple identities without the war? Perhaps. But his story does throw light on the central issues of this chapter. Lawrence was much closer to Cassin than to Céline in his commitment to the cause, but the rape Lawrence endured may have made it impossible for him to bring wartime memories and postwar identities together. This is what shell shock is all about.

Conclusion

One way in which to frame the history of shell shock is to examine the phenomenon as a kind of syntax about the war, an ordering of stories and events elaborated by men who served. In this narrative, some men never demobilized; they were frozen in time, not out of choice, but out of injury, internal injury known only to them. The suffering of these men, so resistant to medical treatment, was both a reminder and a reproach. It disrupted heroic narratives of the war, and challenged conventional interpretations of its meaning. It made everyone—patriots as well as ordinary onlookers—uncomfortable. Shell shock placed alongside one line of temporality, in which there was antebellum and postbellum, another sense of time, what some scholars call "traumatic time."[34] It is circular or fixed rather than linear. Here the clock doesn't move in a familiar way; at times its hands are set at a particular moment in wartime, a moment which may fade away, or may return, unintentionally triggered by a seemingly innocuous set of circumstances. When that happens, a past identity hijacks or obliterates present identity; and the war resumes again.

This kind of arrested demobilization is embedded in "traumatic memory," and much of the way we understand the concept today, and its relevance to the victims of current conflicts, rests on a reading of this aspect of the history of the Great War.[35] That this phenomenon is only part of the legacy of the war needs emphasis. The subject of "traumatic memory" is of fundamental importance, but it must not replicate its referent and eclipse other narratives of war. The years after the Armistice were a time when competing and contradictory narratives were elaborated, at times by different people, at times by the same person, at different stages of his or her life. Duty, deceit, and disturbance were there in abundance. The messy, unstable, unsettled character of demobilization derives from this war of narratives, a war which has gone on and on, and still can be heard now, nearly a century after the Great War began. By bequeathing to us these narratives of imprisoning memories, of broken identities and of identities restored, the survivors of the Great War fashioned themselves as central figures in the first, though not the only, "generation of memory" in the twentieth century.

Part Two

Practices of Remembrance

CHAPTER 3

All Quiet on the Eastern Front
Photography and Remembrance

The power of photography to act as a trigger of memory is familiar to us all. Family albums are filled with scenes enabling us to conjure up a now-vanished world of encounters and gestures, which, taken together, describe the stories families tell about themselves. Much of this rhetoric is nostalgic, and tends to offer a sepia-tinged view of the past.

But what of photography of another kind, that produced by soldiers in wartime? Here too the camera captures incidents in life histories, though the moments preserved form part of a highly unusual set of personal encounters. In many cases, the exotic and the bizarre attract photographers in uniform, men and women who never dreamed that they would be armed and uniformed tourists in very foreign lands.

No one knows how many collections of photographs still exist which arose out of the photographer's military service. The number must be legion, and it would be foolish to try to develop a typology of this collection of memory banks. What matters is to appreciate the significance of photography as offering a bridge between history and memory.

And a very problematic bridge it is. Today the phenomenon of fraudulent photography abounds, due to the ease with which digitized images are changed. But a century ago, the notion of photography as a record of truth was equally suspect, if not more so. Spirit photography made fortunes for those shrewd enough to convince the vulnerable that their loved ones, departed from this world, had left shadowy traces on negative prints. These "cloud chambers" of the dead probably provided some solace to the bereaved, but they did nothing to enhance the documentary credentials of the photographer.[1]

If we bypass the issue of the truth value of photography, we can see how important collections of photographs have been in the reconstruction of wartime experience in later years. Old soldiers may fade away, but many of their photographs do not. That is one reason why war museums and archives have collections of photographs which, in sheer volume, equal or exceed their printed or written holdings. And for every public collection of such materials, there are dozens which remain within family circles, mostly unnoticed by the younger generation. But in their time, they had evocative power, the power to return the photographer to where he was and who he was in wartime.

One such collection, fortunately preserved in the Leo Baeck Institute in New York, discloses this mass of images which once linked history and memory. It is an extraordinary record of an ordinary soldier—a physician who served in the Austrian army on the Eastern Front in the Great War. In the story of the war in which he served, and of the corner of it he captured in photographs, we can get a glimpse of the power of photography to narrate and shape memory.

The Unknown War

Before turning to the photographer and to the photographs themselves, it is essential to describe the war in which they were taken. For it was a war about which we know relatively little. The ten million men in uniform who fought the First World War on the Eastern Front constituted the largest group of unknown soldiers in the twentieth century. Though much of this conflict was fought on the territory of the Russian Empire, the Great War has been largely a non-event in Russian historical literature. The two revolutions of 1917 simply occluded these events, or turned them into a prelude to the Bolshevik seizure of power. In Western historiography, the Eastern Front has also been neglected, though for other reasons. In part, historians have interpreted the war as a giant contest between Britain and Germany for domination of north–western Europe. This view, which I share, tended to draw the eyes of all observers—and subsequently of most historians—away from the east. Consequently, there is a massive imbalance between the voluminous historical literature and visual evidence available on the war in the west and the relative paucity of material concerning the war in the east.

It is first and foremost for this reason that we are indebted to the Leo Baeck Institute for preserving a window into this hitherto neglected world at war. And a world it was. If you took a line on a map which presented the Eastern Front in the 1914–18 conflict and transferred it to the west, it would describe a space from Scotland to Morocco. It would stretch from Königsberg (now Kaliningrad) in Russia to Kosovo and beyond. It would encompass sophisticated urban populations and rural settlements whose rhythms and poverty hardly showed traces of change since the Middle Ages. And it would cover the major concentrations of Jewish life, in the great centers of learning in Lithuania to the sources of Hassidic inspiration and fervor in what is now Poland, Byelorussia, Russia, and Rumania.

This is the vast expanse that soldiers in the German, Austrian, Bulgarian, Serbian, Rumanian, and Russian armies traversed for four years. In a way, this theatre of operations was worse than that in the west. This was a twentieth-century war fought with twentieth-century weapons and on a twentieth-century scale, but in a rural landscape which was home to a large population remote from the industrialized west.

This was a war of movement, huge movement, over vast areas. This movement was horse-drawn or on foot. Given the primitive conditions of logistics and maneuvers, and given the firepower of the combatants and the protracted nature of the conflict, it is not surprising that the war on the Eastern Front was more lethal than the war in the west. Epidemic and endemic diseases took their toll on these armies in the east in a way that the sanitary authorities and medical services in the west managed to prevent. The major exception to this contrast was the outbreak of influenza in 1918, which was ecumenical in the toll in took on young people, both soldiers and civilians alike. But on the Eastern Front, the epidemic of the Spanish flu, as it was called, was one of many: cholera, dysentery, typhus were killers in the east in a way they never were in the west.

The second reason why it is justified to claim that the war on the Eastern Front was worse than the war in the west is that the bloodletting did not end on 11 November 1918. Because of the intersection of war and revolution, armed conflict in Poland and Russia continued until 1921. Some German soldiers simply moved from one conflict to another. *Freikorps* operated in the east, made up of some men who wanted to stop the Bolshevik tide and of others who simply liked killing. For a number, the war never ended.

The late George Mosse wrote about a process of brutalization, of the progressive erosion of the limits on cruelty and violence, which the 1914–18 war brought about.[2] The origins of such behavior antedate the conflict: witness the treatment of Africans at the turn of the century, by the Germans in southwest Africa, and by the Belgians in the Congo. In 1914, such commonplace brutality returned to the European continent.

This confrontation with mass death is a powerful antidote to those who argue that nineteenth-century hatreds led in a linear fashion to twentieth-century crimes.[3] The First World War stands between them. It changed what was thinkable, what was imaginable, about human brutality and violence. It opened a door through which others passed a brief two decades later.

German and Austrian Jews in the Great War

The Great War was a precondition, necessary but certainly not sufficient, of the Holocaust. Those who fought in the 1914–18 conflict, though, had no idea that this was so. Millions of men served honorably and with the conviction that to do so was simply a matter of moral responsibility and duty. In this respect, German Jews were entirely representative of the nation as a whole. The same was true among Austrian Jews. Liberal, conservative, and even most socialist Jews supported the war effort in 1914. They accepted the view that Germany and Austria were fighting a defensive war, a conflict not of their own making, forced upon them by other powers jealous of German dynamism and her potential for world leadership. Now, in light of documentation unavailable to them, this belief is hard to justify, but at the time, it made sense—the same sense that it made to citizens in other combatant countries who also believed that they were fighting a defensive war and that to serve in it was an honorable course of action.

As the war went on, that initial sense of solidarity was progressively eroded. As a consequence, patriotic Jews were caught in a terrible predicament. A war of unity had become a war of disunity and polarization, one in which the enemies at the front were not the only enemies vilified at home. It mattered little that prominent Jews like Walter Rathenau had virtually singlehandedly shifted the German economy onto a wartime footing, or that other Jews like Fritz Haber had provided the German army with a massive advantage in what was increasingly becoming science-based warfare. Haber's genius in fixing nitrogen from the air helped Germany compensate for a massive shortage in essential chemicals. Jews worked for the

German war effort in every corner of the country; the same was true in Austria.

As the war dragged on, though, and as casualty lists lengthened seemingly without end, older prejudices took on new forms. One such form was the 1916 census of Jewish participation in the German war effort. On 11 October 1916, in the midst of the murderous battles of Verdun and the Somme, where over one million men were killed and the Western Front moved not at all, the Prussian war minister sent an order to all German units to ascertain whether there were any grounds to complaints the Ministry was "continually receiving . . . from the population at large that large numbers of men of the Israelitic faith who are fit for military service are either exempt from military duties or are evading their obligation to serve . . . or have obtained assignments in administration or clerical posts far away from the front line."[4]

This order, coming just weeks after the accession of Ludendorff and Hindenburg to the command of the German General Staff, was one of a number of indications that the way the war had been conducted was going to change. Now was the time to introduce total mobilization, according to what was termed the "Hindenburg plan," an elaborate effort at maximizing military participation of the population as a whole. There would be no room in this plan for shirkers, who would be stamped out wherever they were.

In November 1916, the news of this census got out, and Jewish groups mobilized to counter the scarcely veiled slur in this inquiry. The Verband der Deutschen Jüden, and its chairman, Oskar Cassel, organized a reply. His representations had some effect. On 11 November a further directive went to the army from the War Ministry, stating that the census was going forward to examine charges raised against Jewish soldiers, and not to justify the removal of Jewish soldiers from their posts. But the underlying insult stood, and despite remonstrations from Max Warburg and other prominent Jews, the inquiry apparently went on. I say "apparently" because the information collected and the statistics gathered appear to have vanished, perhaps in aerial bombardment during the Second World War. But there is still a lingering doubt that when the data were processed, and the German high command saw that Jews were bearing their share of the burdens of the war and more, they simply destroyed the evidence.

The slander stuck, though, especially in the minds of those convinced from the outset that the Jews were draft-dodgers and shirkers. No evidence would budge such a view, which found a natural home in the emerging brew of notions distilled into the legend of the stab in the back, a legend which was formed while the war was still going on.

It is clear, therefore, that the earlier claim about Jewish shirking of military service helped prepare the ground for a wider attack on the responsibility Jews bore for German defeat in the First World War. We all know Hitler's version of this calumny, but it is important to register how widely shared it was.

After the war, sufficient statistical information on German war losses was collected and published to enable us to unpack this claim. It shows that the proportion of the Jewish population enlisting in the 1914–18 war was about the same as that of the rest of the nation. About one in six of the relevant age cohorts were in uniform. A rough estimate would indicate that of the one hundred thousand German Jewish men who served in uniform, approximately twelve thousand died on active service. Statistics are sketchy, but approximately three hundred thousand Austrian Jews served and roughly forty thousand lost their lives.[5] These figures are provisional; no fully documented total of Jewish casualties in the Great War exists, for any combatant country.

Jewish men came forward and were killed from the first months of the conflict. The first Reichstag Deputy to be killed in the war was the socialist Ludwig Frank. There were approximately ten thousand Jewish volunteers like Frank in 1914, and their actions formed part of a moment of patriotic unity which, if it fell short of a general "war enthusiasm," did describe a space of patriotic solidarity occupied by Jews and non-Jews alike.

There is a small difference to account for when comparing aggregate German casualty rates of 15.4 percent of all enlisted men killed or who died in action, and Jewish death rates of 12 percent killed of those who served. We must treat such statistical differences with caution, but if Jewish casualty rates are indeed a bit below the national average, such a disparity may be accounted for, ironically enough, by anti-Semitism. Until 1914, Jewish soldiers had been barred from serving as officers; after the outbreak of hostilities, such barriers persisted in many units. Since officer casualty rates were approximately twice those of men in the ranks, such prejudice probably saved the lives of many loyal German Jewish soldiers.

In sum, Jewish participation in the German war effort was by and large indistinguishable from that of their non-Jewish neighbors. Among prominent antiwar activists there were some Jewish figures. But alongside Rosa Luxemburg was Karl Liebknecht, and Rosa simply denied that her Jewishness mattered one bit in her political outlook. Those working for the war effort on the home front found a way to do so, be it in Jewish or Christian voluntary organizations.[6]

Rabbis followed their clerical brethren in finding biblical parallels to wartime travails. And they were engaged as much as pastors and priests in the arts of consolation. Jewish families knew the bitterness of bereavement all too well during the war. When the anti-Semitic weekly *Auf gut Deutsch* offered a prize for evidence that a single Jewish family had sent three sons to the army for a period of more than three weeks, Rabbi Freund of Hannover provided a list of twenty such households. Legal action ensued which forced the editor to pay the prize to a Jewish charity.[7]

But such setbacks did little to erase the popular image of Jews as shirkers and cowards. A right-wing veterans' organization spread this piece of soi-disant humor, in 1925, in its journal *Der Schild:* "A field hospital for Jews was established near the front lines, beautifully equipped with the latest medical gear and an all-Jewish staff. After waiting for eight weeks it treated its first patient, who arrived shrieking with pain because a typewriter had fallen on his foot."[8] This well-known stereotype of Jewish weakness and an unmasculine aversion to combat was trotted out time and again in the postwar years.

It was only after the Second World War that the federal government of Germany acknowledged the scale of Jewish sacrifice for their country in the First World War. But at such a distance of time, and with the Holocaust unavoidably in mind, it has been extremely difficult to move back to a period when Jewish men were proud of wearing a German or Austrian uniform.

Bernhard Bardach and Images of the Eastern Front

Bernhard Bardach was one of them, and his collection of photographs, preserved in the archives of the Leo Baeck Institute in New York, describe that world of service and sacrifice. Bardach was forty-eight years old when the Great War began. He was born in Lemberg (now Lwow), had a Jewish education, and, after gymnasium, studied medicine in Vienna and Graz. He served in the Austrian army in Galicia in the 1890s, before marrying the daughter of a Jewish landowner. She gave birth to two girls but then died of pneumonia. Bardach remarried in 1910, and two more daughters joined the family in 1912 and 1916. By then he was on active service on the Eastern Front as a career officer. He was a loyal soldier, with few illusions about war. In his diary he wrote that it was bound to lead to "mass murder and the annihilation of innumerable souls."[9] The mud and the difficult conditions of everyday life preoccupied him, but he found time too to rejoice over Austrian gains against the Russian army. By the end of the war, he had moved to the Italian front. In 1920 he left the army and worked as a physician in Vienna, specializing in dermatology and venereal medicine. After *Kristallnacht*, Bardach and his wife left Vienna, and via Italy and Portugal they reached the United States in 1941. He became an American citizen in 1946 and died the following year. Three of his four daughters also emigrated to the United States.

Bardach's collection of papers and photographs on his war service at the Eastern Front is valuable on a number of levels. It is palpable evidence of the Jewish contribution to the war effort of the Central Powers and, while unquantifiable, provides a host of ripostes to the half-formulated slurs of the *Judenzählung* and the *Dolchstosslegende*. But it also introduces us to themes central to our understanding of the linkage between war and memory, themes which these photographs help relocate in an entirely new geography.

The war in the east was a landscape for the encounter, even the collision, between the old and the new. In these photographs, we see a Viennese doctor, with the training and outlook of modern medicine, enter a world remote from its tools, its outlook, its scientific method. The view of the other gained by physicians like Bernhard Bardach reflected the isolation, the poverty, the traditional character of rural settlements throughout the combat zone which linked the borderlands of the Austrian, German, and Russian empires.

Many of the photographs he took were of non-Jewish communities and subjects. Christian religious observance is privileged, as are the faces of Polish and Russian peasants, caught up unfortunately in the maelstrom of war. But alongside these portraits of Christian life disrupted by war are glimpses of the world of eastern European Jewry. Some of the portraits of Jewish figures are striking and attractive; comparisons immediately suggest themselves with the faces in Roman Vishniac's work.[10] Others are less noteworthy. But however we evaluate them, these faces illustrate the profoundly important encounter between western Europeans and eastern European Jews in the First World War.

The literature on German and Austrian reactions to the Ostjuden is vast. But much of it considers the uneasy reception of immigrants from the east who sought safety and security in the Kaiserreich. But here, in these photographs, the movement is in the other direction. When educated and sophisticated German and Austrian Jews arrived in the small shtetls of eastern Europe, they were turning the clock back two hundred years. We can only speculate on the range of reactions this encounter elicited. Curiosity, puzzlement, distaste, affection, even solidarity are there in the photographs. The mix varied with the viewer and the viewed.

I wonder too about the reaction of eastern European Jews to their co-religionists in uniform. Isaac Bashevis Singer told the Nobel Prize ceremony attendees that Yiddish has many virtues. Among them is the fact that it "possesses no words for weapons, ammunition, military exercises, war tactics."[11] The religious communities of eastern Europe which feared the appearance of armies as the prelude to impressment or pogrom had little reason to expect to find Jews in uniform. My guess is that many simply saw such behavior as part of the madness of assimilation.

Occupiers and Occupied

Who knows if a conversation along these lines ever took place. But Bardach and his fellow soldiers were in a position which made understanding or fraternization very difficult, if not impossible. They were, after all, occupiers. Both in the east and in the west, the German and Austrian armies of 1914–18 turned from the tasks of an army of defense to those of an army of occupation. This was true in virtually all of Belgium and of northeastern France. But it was even more evident in the huge swath of the former Russian Empire occupied by the German army after the expulsion of Russian invaders in eastern Prussia following the rout at Tannenberg in August 1914. There were reversals—and the Brusilov offensive of 1916 threatened to move the front west. But most of the time, the front stayed in the east.

A Russian wartime joke caught the essentials of the military balance—or rather imbalance—of power on the Eastern Front. In this apocryphal story, a cease-fire has enabled two patriotic soldiers, one Russian, one German, to exchange views as to who was wiser, nobler, and braver, the Kaiser or the Tsar. The German soldier proudly salutes his Kaiser, who, each time there is an offensive on the Eastern Front, puts on his uniform, and rushes from Berlin directly to the front to salute the army. The Russian soldier is prouder still. "Our Tsar is even wiser. Every time there is an offensive, he sits in his palace and lets the front come to him."[12]

After the last major and disastrous Russian offensive of the war, in July 1917, it was not only the front which moved east, but the bulk of the Russian army, who, as Trotsky put it, voted with their feet against the war. And then, after the second Russian Revolution of 1917, the new regime under the Bolsheviks sued for peace.

Russians soon discovered that German terms were very harsh, amounting to the creation of a vast satellite empire, either directly or indirectly controlled by Germany. The intention was that the Russian and Ukrainian "breadbasket" would produce a cornucopia of goods to compensate the hard-pressed German home front for the material sacrifices they had made during the war. In response, Trotsky tried to stall and to negotiate a space of "no war—no peace," and thereby to bypass these harsh German demands. After the breakdown of talks at Brest-Litovsk, the German army simply moved farther east, into the heartland of Russia, and the old Pale of Settlement. By March 1918, when the Treaty of Brest-Litovsk was signed, ending the war in Russia, the German army was in occupation of much of European Russia. And even after the war in the east had formally ended, in March 1918, and two million soldiers moved west to support the vast offensive aimed at breaking the Allies on the Western Front, there were still one million German and Austrian soldiers stationed in the territory of what had formerly been the Russian Empire. Bardach was one of them.

The army's role in that occupation was complex. Some of it was purely administrative; some of it was repressive. There is a wealth of documentation about this aspect of the war in the Bibliothek für Zeitgeschichte in Stuttgart. Among the documents in that collection is a fly sheet in five languages—German, Yiddish, Polish, White Russian, and Russian—announcing the penalties the local populace faced if they did not license their dogs. Much more important edicts faced the same linguistic maze. The German army was responsible for order and sanitation, both extremely difficult to maintain in wartime. The control of a displaced civilian population was a virtually impossible task. The numbers were overwhelming. One estimate has it that one in five residents of European Russia was a refugee by 1916.[13] It is this ambulant population, as well as those desperately trying to stick to their villages, their families, their livelihood, that German soldiers like Bernhard Bardach encountered during the war.

Many of the photographs taken by this extraordinary doctor show some of the face of this vast corner of the conflict. There are photographs of hospital work alongside some images of prostitutes, who were screened by the army medical corps to limit the spread of venereal disease and prevent it from crippling the whole of the German army (fig. 4). There are images of typhus wards, and the constant effort of washing and cleaning to prevent the outbreak of epidemic disease and to repair its ravages. There are also scenes of the army at rest, or hunting game with hounds, or putting on a concert for the local population. There is a field cinema to bring to

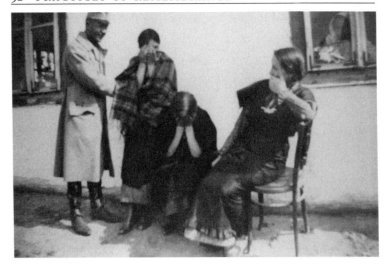

Fig. 4. Prostitutes shielding their faces. (Courtesy of the Leo Baeck Institute, New York)

the east the latest in the doings of the film industry, beleaguered as it was by the shortage of Western films. And there are a number of photographs of Bardach the artist, drawing and painting in his spare time some of the rural scenes which had managed to withstand the ravages of war (fig. 5).

Other photographs are more somber. He captured images of villages on fire, villages destroyed, spies strung up (figs. 6–8). He recorded sights of carnage, with bodies strewn haphazardly across the landscape. And time and again, the photographs return to the tension between a modern war in a very unmodern environment. Flame throwers operate in a vast hinterland untouched by the sources of such new weaponry (fig. 9). Airplanes appear, and then, to make a point, the more familiar mode of transport—horses—tow them to their hangars (fig. 10). The army too was loathe to shed some of the vestiges of older forms of combat. Uhlans, Bardach's camera shows us, strode across the Eastern Front months, even

Fig. 5. Bardach the artist at work. (Courtesy of the Leo Baeck Institute, New York)

Fig. 6. Village burning on the Eastern Front. (Courtesy of the Leo Baeck Institute, New York)

Fig. 7. Village destroyed on the Eastern Front. (Courtesy of the Leo Baeck Institute, New York)

Fig. 8. Spy strung up on the Eastern Front. (Courtesy of the
Leo Baeck Institute, New York)

years, after they were blown off the landscape of the battles in the
west. A vanishing world indeed.

The scale and complexity of the Eastern Front defies any attempt
to capture it in the gaze of a single man. But some features of the
old, fixed in photographic images by Bardach, had a specifically Jewish character. He photographed the Great synagogue in Brest, alongside the old cemetery, filled with tombstones at odd angles covering

Fig. 9. Flame throwers on the Eastern Front. (Courtesy of the Leo Baeck Institute, New York)

Fig. 10. Airplane hauled by horses on the Eastern Front. (Courtesy of the Leo Baeck Institute, New York)

Fig. 11. Old man with a sack, at an unspecified location in Volhynia, c. 1916. (Courtesy of the Leo Baeck Institute, New York)

generations of Jewish families in a patchwork blanket of stone. These photographs are poignant in part because they show the features of the old Jewish world in the east of Europe in the first phase of its fragmentation. Bardach was very sensitive to the contours of this world and to the faces of the people who inhabited it. He captured the face of a Jewish pedlar, his back bent by his bag of wares, and the shape of a family—probably refugees—pausing for prayer in a field (figs. 11, 12). He saw the rhythms of daily life in the shtetl, the towns where the bulk of the Jewish population lived, and captured them on film (fig. 13).

Pogroms and hardship had impelled much of this vast population of Jews out of Poland and Tsarist Russia before the 1914–18 war. But the Jews Bardach encountered had also known another series of calamities during the Great War itself. When Russian armies fled east, after the defeats of 1914 and 1915, Jewish villages were torched and looted, and their inhabitants raped and killed. It is no irony to

Fig. 12. A Jewish family, probably refugees, pausing for prayer in a field. (Courtesy of the Leo Baeck Institute, New York)

Fig. 13. Daily life in the shtetl, c. 1916. (Courtesy of the Leo Baeck Institute, New York)

say that advancing German army units were seen as liberators of some Jewish communities, reduced by fire and slaughter to a miserable state.[14]

And yet we must not be too sanguine about the nature of the Germany army's encounter with both the Jewish and non-Jewish population occupied during hostilities. Occupation is never a clean operation. Injustices occur; suffering is inevitable. There is some evidence that Jews were treated more harshly than the rest of the occupied population. There was forced labor, ironically bringing the *Ostjuden* to Germany against their will.[15] And the indigenous population did suffer from a host of diseases, and were reduced to appalling levels of poverty. Bardach's Jewish consciousness, evident in his proud choice of Jewish subjects, was, of course, exceptional. It is not too difficult to imagine what many other German and Austrian soldiers made of this primitive, otherworldly population of poor Jews. It is likely that in some elements of the German and Austrian armies, the encounter with Yiddish-speaking, inward-looking, impoverished Jews was a moment in which curiosity led to contempt, which in turn led to racial hatred. Anti-Semitism grew in Germany and Austria because of the war. It grew too out of the encounter between German soldiers and *Ostjuden* during the long years of occupation in the east.

It is thus apparent why this particular occupation was a terrible portent. The vast territories in the east, encountered for the first time by millions of ordinary Germans and Austrians, were indeed a field of conquest between 1914 and 1918. There and only there the Germans won the war. In contrast, no matter what the architects of the *Dolchstosslegende* said, the war in the west was lost on the battlefield. Not so in the east. Nationalists in the 1920s and 1930s saw that if German power were ever to expand again, the record of warfare in the east suggests clearly where that role would be worked out. It would be in *Ostland,* in the vast hinterland of Poland and

Russia, where the German army ruled between 1914 and 1918 and where, in a terrifying recapitulation, another, very different German army would come again two decades later.[16] Bardach's photographs, taken before the Holocaust, tell us of that first twentieth-century encounter of west and east, of Jewish modernity and Jewish tradition, of occupier and occupied, of German and Slav, a multifaceted encounter preserved in these photographs of lasting historical value.

It is tempting to think of Bardach, in his later years, opening this scrapbook and reconstructing his recollections of military service (fig. 14). No doubt millions of men who had served did so, and thereby contributed to one of the most ubiquitous kinds of memory work—the review and revision of the soldier's memories of war. "The true picture of the past flits by," wrote Walter Benjamin. "The past can be seized only as an image which flashes up at the instant when it can be recognized and is never seen again."[17] We cannot help seeing in these images today a view of a world on the brink of a terrible precipice. Such was the landscape of Jewish life in eastern Europe, soon to be hit by even worse pogroms in 1919 and 1920 and by a terrible famine accompanying the Russian Civil War in 1921. Following were the ravages of forced collectivization, the purges, and then war again. What happened to the Jews whose paths crossed that of Bardach we will never know. Their survival chances were, to say the least, precarious.

This landscape, human and physical, was captured by a man whose temperament and whose Jewishness gave him a special sensitivity to the Jewish world he stumbled upon during his military service. He did his duty as a physician in a cause which must be distinguished from that of the Third Reich. One of his photographs captured the graves of Jewish physicians, who perished while on active duty on the Eastern Front; so much for the Jewish census and its implicit message of hatred. These Jewish soldiers fought and died alongside their fellow Christian soldiers, and Bardach was proud to

Fig. 14. Bardach photograph album. (Courtesy of the Leo Baeck Institute, New York)

have been among them. His patriotism may have been troubled, but it was not misplaced. To appreciate the meaning of the war to the approximately half-million German and Austrian Jews who served in the Great War, we must see it through their own eyes. These photographs enable us to begin to do so. They were proud of being Jews and proud of their country, and the dignity of that hard-won and soon to be lost identity is unmistakable in the face of one Jewish physician, Bernhard Bardach, who, while stationed at the Eastern Front, paused for breath, as it were, and then breathed life into a world which was soon to vanish forever. To get a sense of the Eastern Front, its contours, and its confrontations, photography of the kind Bernard Bardach took and preserved is an invaluable guide (fig. 15).

Images of the kind Bardach captured also triggered remembrance, albeit in selective and frequently nostalgic ways. But the

Fig. 15. All quiet on the Eastern Front, c. 1916. (Courtesy of the Leo Baeck Institute, New York)

photographs reveal more than just the angle of vision of the man who took them. The work of people like this one Austrian physician-soldier captured encounters between men and women thrown together haphazardly by the fortunes of war, people who gaze at each other with a host of emotions and gestures. The traces of these chance meetings are all that remains of them. But they happened. A man with a camera once decided to freeze time by capturing the scene, and by doing so, he engaged in the difficult art of bringing memory and history together. To be sure the photograph is an image, full of distortions and misleading elements. But once located within the life of the photographer, such images tell us much about the visual world of remembrance in the twentieth century.

CHAPTER 4

War Letters
Cultural Memory and the "Soldiers' Tale" of the Great War

There has been a burst of interest in recent years in "war literature," understood as a genre of writing in which soldiers display the authority of direct experience in telling their "truth" about war and combat. In the process, they offer reflections on much else besides— on comradeship and masculinity, on the image of the enemy, on national sentiment, on the burden of survival when so many others failed to come back, and on the "lies" that those who were not there told about those who were.

Much of this discussion centers on memoirs written long after the Armistice of 1918, but it also refers directly to a vast body of evidence derived from soldiers' letters—in particular those written by men who died in the war—which were published during and after the war. To Samuel Hynes, these letters were "war memoirs of the dead."[1] This massive body of correspondence is an essential but relatively unexplored part of the cultural legacy of the Great War.

Never before did soldiers create such an avalanche of letters and postcards. Estimates vary, but the number of items sent by soldiers to their families in wartime must be calculated in the tens of million. Most such items were ephemeral; indeed, the British army had a standardized form for soldiers to tick off boxes corresponding to their physical and mental well-being and so on.[2] Censorship lay behind this effort to restrict soldiers' comments to the absolutely anodyne; officers were obliged to read handwritten missives and eliminate any information potentially of value to the enemy.

Soldiers' letters have rarely been examined systematically[3] or in comparative perspective.[4] One way to begin this task is to consider them in terms of the shaping of what Jan and Aleida Assmann have termed "cultural memory." To the Assmanns cultural memory is a set of codes in which educated men and women place their personal recollections of the past in a literary, aesthetic, and philosophical framework. Those codes are frequently defined as national in character, with deep resonances in the literary and religious life of a people. They therefore are intensely political, though in a very broad sense.[5]

To uncover cultural memory we must explore the construction, adaptation, and circulation of these codes which frequently take the form of texts about significant historical events, initially produced by those directly engaged in them, but codified in an archive of words, sounds, and images accessible to later generations. Soldiers' letters clearly form one such archive of cultural memory.

Here is a useful framework for the analysis of the publication of soldiers' letters. On the one hand, they commemorate the dead through their own words. On the other hand, they use the language of dead soldiers to fortify a view of the war as noble and uplifting. Thus it is apparent from the outset that what soldiers wrote about the war must be separated from what was done with their words. The "soldiers' memory" of the war is not at all the same as the "cultural memory" of the war.

The War Letters of Fallen German Soldiers

Let us consider this distinction in terms of one celebrated collection of the letters of fallen German soldiers, edited by the literary scholar Philipp Witkop and revised and published five times between 1916 and 1941.[6] This book was one of the foundational texts of the myth of "war enthusiasm," the *Augusterlebnis,* the experience of national exhilaration during which all political parties rallied around the flag in the first weeks of the Great War. Here was the essence of the German people, revealed in a flood of light at the outset of the war.

This story about public opinion is both time-honored and false.[7] This popular mood was neither homogenous nor enduring. Panic, anxiety, and stoicism matched patriotic fervor in Germany as it did in all other combatant countries. Photos of student rallies or urban crowds in the capital reinforce the myth, but they are misleading; these orchestrated events, duly recorded in newsreel film, tended to naturalize what was artfully and systematically constructed for political purposes. And what was seen in Berlin tells us little about what happened in other towns, with large working-class populations, or in the countryside, where the harvest was under way. Exhilarated patriotism in August 1914 as a collective phenomenon is a myth.

How did this story about German national identity in 1914 become part of the archive of German cultural memory? One source was the publication of soldiers' letters. During the war, the German army was favorably disposed to this kind of publication, and in the Weimar Republic successive state Ministries of Education continued to cultivate (and subsidize) such works.[8] The Nazis too had their reasons for disseminating this story, though their motives for doing so were entirely different.

Witkop, whose project we examine here, was professor of modern literature at Freiburg, a friend of Thomas Mann, and an expert on German lyric poetry.[9] He was a poet in his own right, a distinction which did not find favor in the hearts of some of his Freiburg colleagues of a more "scientific" disposition. Of direct relevance to his later work, though, was his parallel interest in workers' education, on which subject he published his first book. As Wolfgang Natter has shown, here in this early work are the seeds of Witkop's anthologies, which also took as their function the elevation of a reading public to a higher cultural and spiritual level of existence.[10] Nurturing *Bildung* is one way to describe his lifetime mission. Another way of putting it is to say that his business was the dissemination of texts disclosing (while constructing) German cultural memory.

First in 1916, in a collection of German soldiers' letters, of both those who had died and those who were still alive, and in 1918 in a collection of fallen soldiers' letters, Witkop made selections which constructed a highly idealized portrait of the German soldier. By choosing student letters, he projected onto the mass of German soldiers the taste for philosophical prose and poetry he spent his own professional life exploring. He believed that soldiers in 1914 were reaching out for some spiritual guidance, and had found in the Bible, in Goethe, and in Nietzsche—in particular in *Thus spake Zarathustra*—the stuff of which stoicism and sacrifice had been made. Such a claim about soldiers' sensibilities was not original, and drew on celebrated cases of artists who volunteered early in the war, like Otto Dix[11] and Franz Marc, among others.[12] The problem was that Witkop's project suggested that these unrepresentative soldiers stood for the army as a whole. The fact that both Dix and Marc, among others, shed their early idealism in the mud and detritus of the trenches was never fully acknowledged.

Witkop's Hegelian sleight of hand—taking elites as representative of the nation as a whole—was an intrinsic part of the project of constructing a specifically German cultural memory out of the up-heaval of the Great War. If spiritually minded soldiers carried the *Geist*—the spirit of the German *Volk,* or people—then an explora-tion of their letters would take on the features of cultural anthropol-ogy: Germany—the true Germany, the ideal Germany—was in es-sence what these soldiers said and did. In other words, those who expressed their Germanness in an idealistic form, either in writing or in military deeds, were to Witkop and people like him "seers," visionaries who could conjure up the outlines of the life and pulse of a nation in a way no materialist could do. They pointed the way to a better future, one worthy of the sacrifices of so many idealistic young men.

Witkop worked to bring together these spiritual "leaders" of the German nation and the rest of the army in two ways. The first was by organizing courses in higher education within the army itself; soldiers were granted two weeks' furlough to attend.[13] The second was by providing articles and commentary in one of the army's official newspapers, the *Kriegzeitung der 7 Armee,* which he helped edit. This publication must be distinguished from trench journals, cyclostyled or mimeographed by soldiers at the front, frequently using "borrowed" equipment and whatever paper was not nailed down. The cost of these newspapers was minimal, but it was paid by small groups of men who knew each other and who shared the same sense of humor and grievances. The life expectancy of the newspapers was even shorter than that of the editors and readers. They came and went and sometimes came again.[14] In contrast glossy periodicals were published at the army's expense for separate army groups. These bore no resemblance to the bottom-up journalism produced not only in the German army but in other combatant forces too. They were dirigiste in character, presenting to soldiers what the army high command believed they should think about the war.[15]

Witkop's war service was within the cultural apparatus of the German army. He was a patriot and a liberal intellectual. His commitment to collecting soldiers' letters in wartime was intended to honor all those who had fought. But his goal was also to preserve and perpetuate what he saw as the idealism of those who had volunteered for duty during the first days and weeks of the war, and to show how deeply ingrained in the German nation as a whole were the values of these young men, many of whom were students. These young men were subject to conscription, but could come forward to serve even before they had been called. About three hundred thousand men did so.[16] To understand fully the nobility of these men, Witkop urged us to turn to their letters.

In 1916, Witkop brought out the first of his edited anthologies under the title *Kriegsbriefe deutscher Studenten* (War letters of German students). In 1918, he published a slightly longer edition—this time 153 rather than the 114 pages in the 1916 collection—with the new title *Kriegsbriefe gefallener Studenten* (War letters of fallen students). Ten years later, at the tenth anniversary of the Armistice, Witkop published a much-expanded collection of letters, from which an English translation was made. This 1928 German edition was reprinted and, after the Nazis came to power, weeded to remove some Jewish and pacifist voices among the letter-writers anthologized in it. Witkop never joined the Nazi Party and tried unsuccessfully to resist these efforts to "cleanse" his book. He died of natural causes in 1942. Estimates of circulation of the war letters project are hard to pin down, but the figure of two hundred thousand sales in the interwar years appears to be approximately reliable.[17]

CONSOLATION

Now that we have some idea as to why these volumes were produced, and what political and cultural issues surrounded their initial and later publication, we can turn to the question of their intended audience. This project was clearly aimed at a population in mourning. Witkop got permission during the war from the army to write to the families of men who had died on active service and to ask them to contribute letters to a book. He received thousands of replies. We can imagine the difficulty parents or wives had in sifting through the papers of a son or a husband, and making a gift of the letter to Witkop and, through him, to the nation.

Here we reach the intersection of politics and bereavement. The entries in the book resemble gravestones, in a general way. There is the name and, instead of military rank, there is an academic affiliation. Then follows the date and place of birth and death. So far the parallel with a gravesite is clear and is similar to that used in other similar ventures, for instance, Laurence Housman's *War letters of fallen Englishmen.*[18] Housman's identification also includes the service arm and rank, which Witkop's book avoids. Still, the similarity to a cemetery stone is clear.

What both editions add, of course, is a letter or several letters.[19] This practice helps establish the individuality of the soldier who died; without such special individuation, he would fade into an army of the dead, and therefore into oblivion. Thus these books offer two services to bereaved families. For those whose sons or husbands or brothers had no known grave, these pages provide a kind of surrogate resting place his remains never had. And secondly, the text of the letters does more than just list a name, date of birth, and date of death. It is a kind of portrait, like those found in eastern European cemeteries. The letters construct a snapshot of the mind of the fallen soldier. The prose comes to stand for the man himself, his nobility, his beliefs, his aspirations. It is as if he wrote his own epitaph.

The parents of Friedrich Steinbrecher wrote to Witkop on precisely this point. They thanked him for having "erected a memorial" for their son. "We cannot have his grave decorated," they noted, "since his last resting place is unknown." As Natter has shown, Witkop's mission was to give his book the character of "a cemetery of honor, a monument of honor that these young fallen have built for themselves; a national book of edification, to which we, to which our grandchildren, will return over and over again, touched, with respect, love, and gratitude."[20]

The task of producing such a book as Witkop's or Housman's

was clearly a tribute of an older generation to a younger one. The editors did not fight, and they recognized a debt to those who did, to make something better in the world after the war. These collections of letters were therefore moral promissory notes, statements of an indebtedness which could never be fully discharged. These men had given everything; how small, though real, a tribute it was to gather together the letters of such men in a volume of collective mourning and collective remembrance.

There is every indication that Witkop edited the letters for publication, but precisely how this was done is not specified. Censorship operated on several levels. The first was in the initial drafting of the letter. Soldiers were well aware of the army censors' sensibilities, and may have limited their griping or caustic remarks accordingly. In addition, there is the censorship of the men themselves with respect to their families' sensibilities. Here too there is great variation, but as we have already noted, social conventions probably constrained the content of the letters. If we add to these two constraints the editorial hand, invisible to the book's readers at least, then it is clear that we are confronting not "raw evidence," but constructed representations of war and of warriors.

Representations

These representations are framed by a narrative, a story about the war which privileged what was understood to be direct, unvarnished experience. This is what gave this form of cultural memory its power and authority. What do we learn of the "men of 1914" from these letters? First, we see them as fully aware of the evils of war. Indeed, the language many of them use is that of soldier pacifists, people who took up arms in defense of their country, but who—after what they had seen—would willingly take up arms against war itself. One soldier wrote that war is "a very, very evil thing," but one which must be faced out of duty to one's nation. And then, the writer insisted, after peace is restored, "I have firmly resolved, if I do come back, to do everything in my power to prevent such a thing from ever happening again in the future." These sentiments, voiced by Franz Blumenfeld, a student of law killed on the Somme at age twenty-three in 1914, were repeated time and again by the men whose letters Witkop collected. To Karl Josenhans, a student of theology killed in the Argonne in 1915, aged twenty-three, war was "a degrading thing," and though Germans were not to blame for it, its cruelties were "sickening." To Robert Otto Marcus, a medical student from Munich, this was not war at all, but "abominable, cruel, wholesale assassination . . . unworthy of human beings." Richard Schmeider, a student of philosophy in Leipzig, told his parents that "there are moments when even the bravest soldier is so utterly sick of the whole thing that he could cry like a child. When I heard the birds singing at Ripont, I could have crushed the whole world to death in my wrath and fury." Here is the mental world of thoughtful German soldiers, utterly remote from the worship of war.

The second representation of the soldier which emerges out of these letters is deeply romantic and sentimental. Walter Roy, a student of medicine from Jena, wrote his parents a farewell letter before the attack in which he was killed in April 1915, thanking them "for all the sunshine and happiness in my life." Ludwig Franz Meyer wrote a poem to his mother on the Eastern Front, saying that whatever hardships he faced, his mother had most to bear. Willi Bohle wrote home in April 1917: "Darling Mother, darling little Mother, and you too, my brother and sister, I am ready to endure anything for your sakes, so that you may never see what ruined villages and shell-destroyed fields look like; so that you may never learn what the word *war* really means."

The third representation is that of the Christian soldier. Religious sentiment appears regularly in Witkop's collection. Heinz

Pohlmann, a philosophy student from Berlin, said farewell to his parents and urged them not to lament for he felt "safe in the Hands of God." Johannes Haas, a student of theology from Leipzig, actually had the time and presence of mind to write to his parents to thank them for "having led me to the Saviour," and then, upon being fatally wounded on the field of battle, to tell them, "I think I am dying. I am glad to have time to prepare for the heavenly homecoming." In Hungary, Walter Schmidt, visited the Virgin of Timosaora: "Here in the heart of the Mother of God the suffering find comfort and succour and the afflicted a refuge!"

There are letters about Christmas truces, and a kind of Christmas spirit which is laced with nostalgia for home. Martin Müller, killed on the Somme in 1916, described in 1914 how "the Holy Night sank softly down upon the earth." He heard the sounds of "Silent Night" and then enjoyed a Christmas tree in the trenches, decorated by a Coblenz Pioneer with "angel's hair," "little bells and gold and silver threads." Hugo Müller's Christmas in 1915 was more modest, though festive: "Even the rats and mice had a share in the celebration, nibbling the cake crumbs and the eel's skin." Hans Spatzl wrote his parents in December 1916 that "I am looking forward to Christmas even more than I did last year, for I am in hopes that the dear Christ Child may have mercy upon us. . . . We shall not rise without having received a gift."

Peace-loving, sentimental, religious in a kind of ecumenical spirit: these are the facets of the soldiers' temperament described in these letters. In short we are in the world before the war, transposed into a landscape of which no one had even dreamed before 1914. Here is the drama of these letters: decency confronted but not overwhelmed by fire and steel.

What was new and odd about the landscape of industrialized warfare, dominated by machines and metal, is the subject of other soldiers' comments. Here is a world of work, though in an assembly line of human destruction. Helmut Schuppe saw all hell break loose in artillery fire, producing jagged and lethal metal fragments "in a fantastic manner such as no power on earth could devise." Hugo Müller wrote home of uncanny sights, of having confronted "a human hand with a ring on one finger" or of having to use his shovel to scrape away the brains of a comrade, killed the day before by a shell which had decapitated him. Adolf Stürmer couldn't look at a corporal in his unit, killed that very day, and whose face was "so set, pale and covered with blood"; "only that morning we had sat together, chatting and laughing . . ." Friedriche Oehme wrote of villages which looked as if they had emerged from Dante's *Inferno,* and of men "crazy with fear" going into battle. After three days in the line, his men were "frozen, dead-tired, and broken down by shell-fire." Gerhard Gürtler's men hear nothing in the front line but "the drum-fire, the groaning of wounded comrades, the screaming of fallen horses, the wild beating of their own hearts, hour after hour, night after night." And even out of the line, "their exhausted brains are haunted in the weird stillness by recollections of unlimited suffering." Having been awarded the Iron Cross while convalescing in hospital, Helmut Schuppe thought the cross itself was "made of shell-splinters—black blood congealed on a yellowish dead face with open mouth—bandages encrusted with pus—the strangled cries of hoarse voices—flaccid, gangrened flesh on the stump of a leg."

To some soldiers, exposure to extreme violence was "purifying and deepening." This was Hero Hellwich's conclusion; but to others it was a school in disenchantment. "The war which began as a fresh youth is ending as a made-up, boring, antiquated actor" called Death. "When one has seen how brutal, how degrading war can be, any idyllic interval comes like a reprieve from the gallows," wrote Friedrich Georg Steinbrecher in November 1916. And his reprieve was up five months later.

As, at one time or another, was that of every single soldier whose letters were published in later volumes. What we hear are the voices of those whose sole legacy lay in the letters they sent home. Herein resides the poignancy of this collection, and its power. The letters were written not for publication, but to strengthen the ties between a soldier and his family, for the defense of which he had gone to war in the first place.

Experience

These images of war and of the soldiers' temperament were drawn from an unrepresentative sample of the army or the German population as a whole. These are highly educated men, many were officers, and their letters are clustered in the early part of the conflict. But what gave their testimony power and a more general purchase was the sense that they had had access to an experience the rest of the world did not know.

It is in this notion of "war experience" that we can see the most striking legacy of these and other writings about the Great War. These letters were constructed as a window into a special world, an odd world of the familiar and the unfamiliar mixed in equal parts. The letters disclosed the exposure of soldiers to a level of extreme violence and suffering that most of us never approach; their passage through the crucible of war gave their voices reverberations which seemed to come from another world. They represented those who had gone through war as an "inner experience," something extraordinary, something overwhelming, a secret which only they could know. The religious overtones are hard to miss.[21]

For this very reason, the concept of "experience" emerging from soldiers' letters is an essentialist one. That is, experience is a thing—fixed, immutable, separate from the man or woman who had it. The soldier writing home has gathered some fragments of this "experience" and tries to convey it in a kind of prose which would enable his loved ones to grasp where he is and what he is. The quasi-sacred nature of these letters arises out of this externalized sense of what is war experience. That is why proprietary possession of these letters was a matter of political importance in the interwar years. They disclosed what the war "meant" in a way which only those who had fought could know.

It is crucial, though, to see that the publication of such letters introduces a second meaning to "experience," which is central to the ways such collections were mobilized in the decades since they were written. As Joan Scott has argued, experience is not something which individuals have, but something out of which the individual's sense of self emerges. Experience is therefore not "the authoritative (because seen or felt) evidence that grounds what is known," but rather the social construction of knowledge by people who define themselves in terms of what they know.[22] Experience from this point of view is constituted by subjects, and thus highly volatile; it changes when identities change, and has no inert, external, objective existence outside of the people who contemplate it. Experience is thus ascriptive, not descriptive.

This second sense of war experience helps us see how it was that Witkop's project, steeped in German idealism, could just as easily be interpreted and used as an internationalist or even as a pacifist tract, and a few years later be published, with some emendations to be sure, by the Nazis as a paean to the German martial spirit. The text itself went through both stages. First, the letters were published as unvarnished experience. The letter writers were privy to a truth; their experience was something they and they alone had had. But over time, their war experience became the constitutive material out of which new political and social identities emerged. The "experience" did not change; just its location. Subjects do not reach out to grasp experience in the external world; they construct experience internally, as part of their sense of who they are.

The Soldiers' Tale: National Variants

The stories soldiers relate tell us something of what they have been through; but the act of narration tells us who they are at the time of the telling. Later on, the experience changes as the narrator's life changes. Since identities are not fixed, neither is "experience." It is the subject's "history," expressed at a particular moment in the language of the subject.[23] That language is not universal; it is particular, localized, and mostly regional or national in form.

The "soldiers' tale" is the framework within which knowledge about war is constructed by men whose identities were defined for them by what they had seen. Those who write the stories tell us who they were and who they have come to be. This process of change, these personal odysseys, do manifest some universal elements. But in conclusion, it may be useful to show that we must differentiate between and among national and other forms of the soldiers' tale. The German soldiers' tale stands alongside other similar national narratives, but it is not identical to them.

For this reason, we need to qualify some interpretations of soldiers' language as essentially universal in character. Here is Samuel Hynes's opening description of what he means by the soldiers' tale:

> In the title of this book, *Soldiers'* is plural and *Tale* is singular. I have imagined that if all the personal recollections of all the soldiers of the world's wars were gathered together, they would tell one huge story of men at war—changing, as armies and weapons and battlefields changed, but still a whole coherent story. Such an entire tale can never exist: the men who could tell it are mostly dead, and while they lived they were inarticulate, or unlettered, or simply distracted by life, so that their wars were left unrecorded. Nevertheless, that notional tale is my subject: what happened in war, one man at a time; who the men were who told war's separate stories and what their stories tell us (and don't tell us) about war; and how the experience of war has changed in our century, as one war has followed another.[24]

Even a cursory glance at Witkop's edition of German students' letters is sufficient to expose the need to nuance this claim about a universal soldiers tale. The particular inflections and references imbedded in these letters disclose a cultural memory, a national archive of meanings which are not the same as those linked to other national groups. The language of spirituality is distinctive; so are codes of emotional expression. Anyone who has written a poem for a German family birthday party will know how different it is from a French or British or American occasion of the same kind.

There are two premises essential for interpreting this kind of evidence. The first is that experience, refracted through memory, helps constitute identities. The second is that experience changes as subject positions shift over time. Given these two assumptions, then no one soldiers' tale, no one meta-narrative of war experience can be said to encompass them all. Accepting the idea that experience is not external to the storyteller, something he has as a property, but rather is a part of his or her subjectivity, has other advantages as well. It will allow us to incorporate the voices of women into the narrative of war; as it stands Hynes's soldiers' tale is irredeemably masculine. The soldiers' tale is about war experience, to be sure. But in the dual sense of the term used here, the notion of war experience cannot be restricted to those who bore arms. Women told "truths" about war of no less value or significance than the "truths" imbedded in collections such as Witkop's.[25]

Even if we restrict our gaze to the writings of men in uniform, it is evident that we need a much more multivocal approach to soldiers' tales in order to register the ways in which different cultural archives inform storytelling, and how storytelling becomes part of different cultural archives. Only then will the many forms of the soldiers' tale emerge as poignant, distinctive, and powerful elements of national cultural histories.

CHAPTER 5

Ironies of War
Intellectual Styles and Responses to the Great War in Britain and France

Irony, Paul Fussell tells us, is a complex trope of remembrance. It is, among other things, a style of thinking and writing in which those trapped in a world threatening to destroy them convey a sense of who they were then and, having managed to survive, who they are now. Irony, he argues, is at the core of war literature, described in his terms as the carrier of "modern memory." In a book on the multiple intersections of history and memory, this approach is of great interest.

In this chapter, I want to interrogate the claim Fussell has made in terms of a comparison. For only by taking his point of view outside of the British world he knows best can we see what is of general interest in his influential and powerful argument. I intend, therefore, to address a problem in comparative intellectual history: why is it that the imaginative language in which most British intellectuals, writers, and artists addressed the Great War was fundamentally different from that used by their French counterparts? I will summarize these differences and provide a sketch of some of their origins. The basic argument is that Fussell is right: British intellectuals did indeed privilege irony in a way which has informed the construction of a canon of war literature. This emphasis on irony is emphatically at the heart of war poetry and the war memoirs of the two postwar decades.

While irony is in no sense uniquely British in origin or nuance, it is nonetheless the dominant style of British thinking about the war, informing a set of attitudes which has been passed down to later generations. Nothing of the kind exists in France. This contrast is evident in the simple fact that the poetry of Wilfred Owen was translated into French only in the late 1990s.[1] The first translation of Siegfried Sassoon's poetry was rendered in French in 1987,[2] though a French edition of *Memoirs of a fox-hunting man* was published in 1937.[3]

The absence of French versions of canonical British imaginative works on the war has led to a further deepening of the conceptual distance between later British and French versions of the cultural history of the conflict. It is hardly surprising that a country whose publishing industry found no place for the poetry of Owen and Sassoon would find no place for translations of the pathbreaking works of Fussell himself on *The Great War and modern memory*,[4] or of Samuel Hynes on *A war imagined*,[5] both of which deal at length with the ironies of British war writing.

Another Anglo-Saxon work of scholarship has made it across the channel. Modris Ekstein's *Rites of spring* was translated into French a few years after its publication in English.[6] But this fact reinforces my overall argument, for Ekstein's book is primarily about the avant-garde. Think about Stravinsky's music to "Rites of Spring" or Diaghilev's choreography, or the uproar they created in Paris. No irony here.

In sum, I want to explore the landscape of a kind of cognitive dissonance between British and French imaginings of the Great War, imaginings whose differences persist to this day, but whose origins can be traced to the beginning of the twentieth century. Layer upon layer of ironic meaning has been placed on the Great War, a war endured but not quite shared imaginatively by these two allies. It is through an understanding of this aspect of what Raymond Williams called structures of feeling[7] that we can begin to appreciate how in very different ways the 1914–18 war became a crucial part of the

distinctive cultural histories of Britain and France in the twentieth
century.

The Ironic Temperament

The literature on the subject of irony is vast. I want to focus on two
levels on which the scholarly literature operates. The first deals with
textual strategies which impart a tone to a conversation or a text; the
second uses a more generalized sense of the term as suggesting a
temperament or a form of reflection. Another way of putting the
point is to suggest that one location of irony is within literary history
as a device central to certain representational practices, certain narrative strategies in prose or poetry. But in addition, the notion of
irony implies an attitude, a stance, what Samuel Hynes calls a "turn
of mind."[8]

Literary scholars have produced rich and learned works on the
forms of ironic prose—the juxtaposition of anticipation and outcome, the existence of more than one meaning of a phrase or action,
and the implicit bond between author and reader over the head of
the characters as to what those meanings are. There is much of
importance here in the study of comparative intellectual history.[9]

I would like to focus on the second usage of the term *irony,* one
which suggests its disruptive and disturbing playfulness. This inter-
pretive strategy in no sense reduces irony to but one level of meaning
or power; highlighting one facet of the subject simply helps frame a
necessarily complicated set of issues in cultural history. Hutchens
has put the point well regarding the kind of irony I would like to
trace: irony as a certain kind of play. She urges us "to see it as a sport,
a game played for its own sake," but a game in which the ironist
exhibits a "curious detached enjoyment, even in the midst of making
a serious case."[10]

Irony, though it may be directed toward an end, is in itself a
sport—a sport the neat trickiness of which is felt to be enjoyed
by the ironist for its own sake, quite apart from his purpose in
employing it. (Here, incidentally, may be the reason why detachment is generally held to be a necessary element of irony,
even though the ironist may be quite evidently making a case.)
   Irony may therefore be seen as basically *the sport of bringing
about a conclusion by indicating its opposite*.[11]

The difference between irony and deception is that the ironist has no
advantage to gain by saying one thing and meaning another. The
gain, so to speak, in her pose, is that she avoids seeing the world as a
site of action where justice reigns, or could operate. Irony is an
antidote to zealotry, to chauvinism, or even to moral certainty. No
categorical imperatives here. On the contrary; *pace* Kant, lying is
entirely justifiable. Why? Because something or someone is making
a sport of human existence, and the language appropriate to that
sport is irony.

   This notion of irony is not merely verbal. Understood as a temperament, irony is always the work of an agent; someone expresses
it, breathes it, lives it. It is both a grammar and a condition of
existence. It is a way of representing both the self and the world, at
some distance from each.

The Importance of Being Earnest About the War: British Responses

How did this sense of destiny as a sport, a game played for its own
sake, translate into a stance central to many British representations
of the Great War? Partly through the world of sociability that British
men enjoyed in football leagues and the like in the prewar period. It
was to defend that world of clubs and pubs and small solidarities
that many of them joined up in the first place.

It is, therefore, hardly surprising that sporting metaphors litter soldiers' correspondence. After all, even though the football league suspended its schedule in 1915, football continued on the other side of the Channel. A civilian army brought its civilian entertainments with it to the Western Front. Football leagues mushroomed in the base areas behind the lines, and offered some semblance of normalcy and physical exertion without the risk to life and limb soldiers faced further up the line. The conceit of turning war into sport and sport into war turned darker as the war went on. The 1st Battalion of the 18th London Regiment literally kicked off the Battle of Loos with a football in 1915. A year later it was the 8th East Surreys turn to "play the game." Each of the four platoons of the company, commanded by Captain W. P. Nevill, went over the top with a football. He offered a prize to the first unit to reach the German lines. A neighboring battalion witnessed what happened. "As the gun-fire died away," recalled Private L. S. Price, "I saw an infantryman climb onto the parapet into No Man's Land, beckoning others to follow. As he did so he kicked off a football; a good kick, the ball rose and traveled well towards the German line. That seemed to be the signal to advance." Captain Nevill never got to hand over the prize; he was killed, but two of the footballs made it. One is in the National Army Museum in London; the other at the Queen's Regiment Museum in Canterbury.[12]

Even a cursory glance at British intellectuals' responses to the war indicates how deeply colored by such sporting images were literary accounts of the conflict. Sport created a familiar space in which the incongruities of war could be imagined. "Have you forgotten yet," Siegfried Sassoon asked, "that war's a bloody game?" Just the sort of thing for "a fox-hunting man" turned into another kind of hunter by the outbreak of war. Irony riddles his account of the incident which won him the Military Cross, an honor he was later to hurl into the Mersey in protest at the never-ending character of the war. He encountered a squad of German infantrymen in a trench, hurled his grenades at them, and mused over the fact that they never knew they were fleeing from "a single fool." This kind of physical prowess and deception would not have been out of place on a playing field, but it became odd and even alarming when the stakes were dismemberment or mutilation. Irony here explodes heroic pretensions and the prose (and honors) which conventionally accompany them.

Further ironies in Sassoon's war emerged directly out of his celebrated protest against it. Here the game pitted one well-connected junior officer against the entire General Staff. Once more the "single, solitary fool," Sassoon kicked off with a letter to his superior, explaining why he couldn't return to his unit at the end of his leave. The war was insane and its continuation a crime. The letter was printed in *The Times* and read into *Hansard*. The army parried by declaring him mad. When he was posted to Craiglockhart, he fought another duel, this time against a more sympathetic adversary, his attendant physician and psychologist, W. H. R. Rivers. Rivers tried to convince Sassoon that his duty lay in France, not in futile protest in Britain. To refuse to go back was selfish, not selfless; it was too close to cowardice for comfort. This got to Sassoon, who finally saw that the only way for him to protest further against the war was to go back to it, to stand alongside the men he led, "and in their tortured eyes / To find forgiveness."

Consider the irony of Rivers's double bind. A physician, honor-bound to do the sick no harm, was entrusted with the task of curing shell-shocked men and thereby returning them to the site of their injuries, where they were almost certain to face the horrors which had broken them in the first place. By healing men he was killing them. What kind of sport is that? Rivers is neither a fool nor a charlatan. He is trapped in a game not of his making. And together with Sassoon—who refers to Rivers by his real name in *Memoirs of an infantry office*—Rivers is forced to confront the fact that someone or something is making a sport of their lives, their sense of honor, their common decencies, and those of the millions of men with whom they served or against whom they fought.

Sassoon's and Rivers's different dilemmas share one crucial feature. They share a deep sense of irony, which enables Sassoon to frame dissent, and Rivers to contain it. When all is said and done, they both play by the rules of the game. A game after all is a stylized encounter after which nothing happens; it is self-contained.

Other kinds of gamesmanship mark the irony in Robert Graves's approach to reality in his celebrated war memoir, *Goodbye to all that.* "In 1916, when on leave in England after being wounded, I began an account of my first few months in France. Having stupidly written it as a novel, I have now to re-translate it into history."[13] Real documents jostle with imaginary ones in the book in such a way as to mock anyone who tries to read it to find out "what the war was really like," in a phrase which would have been perfectly at home in the language of his great uncle, the German historian Leopold van Ranke. Captain Robert von Ranke Graves, proud British warrior against the Hun, is an irony in and of himself. Surely this lies behind his famous epigram that "the memoirs of a man who went through some of the worst experiences of trench warfare are not truthful if they do not contain a high proportion of falsities"; only those who tell lies about the war can actually tell the truth. His ironic detachment, his status as a "trickster," subverts the notion that any kind of history can be written about the war.[14] It might be useful to pause at this point and to note the irony of my writing a history of the effort to subvert the writing of history. Wheels within wheels indeed.

There is irony and much more in these scattered instances of gallows' humor, of laughter from the graveyards, which are repeated in many other British accounts of the war. It is their ironic tone which gives so many of them their detached and ambivalent character. The men who wrote them were soldier pacifists, men who told tales of war with pride, but did so in order to eviscerate the lies of those who had no idea how ugly war is. Robert Graves was proud of the regimental traditions of the Royal Welsh Fusiliers; but his memoir is hardly a celebration of its fate. By saying *Goodbye to all that,* he was stating the opposite, and insisting that echoes of "the game" would never vanish from their lives. Charles Carrington called this attitude "the 1916 fixation."[15] If anyone wrote memoirs for the purpose of putting memory to rest, he was in for a surprise. The war just wouldn't let you go. "Once you have lain in her embrace," Guy Chapman wrote, "you can admit no other mistress."[16]

The question as to whether the war was justified produced very mixed answers in the works of most British soldier memoirists. Most believed that it had started out meaning something, and yet wound up meaning nothing. It was a game with rules, and then someone tore up the rule book. The game never came to an end; it began to devour or dominate everything around it, and even years or decades after the Armistice the soldiers of the Great War were still trapped, in their minds, still going over the ground again, still at the front.

The Importance of Being Earnest About the War: French Responses

Much of this sense of war as a setting never to fade away is also evident in French intellectuals' responses to the Great War. But there are powerful distinctions to be drawn between such writings and those of British intellectuals. These contrasts arise from different subject positions of the writers. Some of these stances are straightforwardly political, in representing a point of view associated with a party or parties. Others are less obvious, in their voicing a kind of antipolitical stance based on the moral authority of the trench soldier. Both are missing by and large in Britain.

Henri Barbusse's *Le feu*, published in 1916 and quickly translated into a dozen languages, set a standard for soldiers' memoirs, a standard which was recognized by many who did not share his political outlook. Céline for once was in the mainstream when he wrote that Barbusse's book was valuable for puncturing the bloated prose of *les embusqués*, the shirkers who dreamed of war without risking their necks. Barbusse's style of rustic populism fitted in well with the political position he came to adopt as a leading communist intellectual. But that very fact indicates a politicized context about how to represent the war in which irony didn't fit easily. Satire and sarcasm are another matter entirely, as any viewer of the work of Brecht and Weil can attest.

The same unironic stance about politics marked those writers in the political centre like Genevoix, whose voice reverberated throughout the veterans' movement of the interwar years.[17] These were men, as Antoine Prost has shown magisterially, who saw it as their moral mission to make a future war unthinkable.[18] The central motif of their discursive practice was based upon a juxtaposition of a world of human values, which the *génération du feu* knew in their bones, to the world of "politics," understood as the arena of those who literally wallow in shit. To read their letters or their journals is to appreciate the depths of this hatred of the politicians. The wrath of these men extended to fantastic rhetorical gymnastics. What they did was to concoct a whole vocabulary of insults surrounding the notion that politicians were beneath contempt. One set of terms is derived from *politique* by adding a suffix: *politicards, politiqueux,* associated with *bistrot* and *boor,* and *politicaille, politicailler, politicaillerie, politicaillon,* all referring to the world of hangers-on, pigs around the trough, old stagers, windbags.

The ferocity of this indictment of politics is stunning. It also accounts for the political weakness of the veterans' movement itself. Drawing its strength from small market towns, and from small businessmen, petty tradesmen, and farmers remote from the capital, this was the politics of *la France profonde,* trying to go above the heads of the partisan crowd in Paris, to speak to the people of France.

The failure of this crusade was built into its mode of operation, its deliberate bypassing of Paris and the centers of power. Their aim was a kind of moral disarmament, a message to children and to the world at large that war was an abomination. But even antipolitics is a kind of politics, whose contours developed in an entirely unanticipated direction. Some even followed their general, Pétain, into collaboration in 1940.[19]

If the political road taken by Barbusse described one form of response to the war, then that of the mainstream of the veterans' movement, and many intellectuals among them, described another. What they all shared was a set of moral convictions which ruled out irony and displaced it with righteous anger. If space permitted, it would be important to nuance this brief *tour d'horizon* by adding qualifications with respect to many other voices which do not fit into this too neat framework. A mere glance at the writing of Barrès, Cendrars, Drieu de la Rochelle, Giono, and Céline disturbs any effort to unify French intellectual responses under a single rubric. Let me just say that the cadences and forms of French war literature are strikingly and consistently different from its British counterpart. Recourse to irony is certainly not absent, but it is less dominant, one would even say less ubiquitous, than it is in the imaginative landscape of British war writers.

Giraudoux and the Theatre of Ambivalence

Now for the exception, and what an exception he was. One way of highlighting the divide which separates the majority of British and French commentators on the Great War is to draw attention to one figure who, in terms of sensibility and style, managed to bridge the gap. Jean Giraudoux was that rare intellectual equally at home in entirely different cultural milieus, a cosmopolite without any trace of the Jewishness which in many eyes converted the word cosmopolite into a light insult. His internationalism in outlook and manner was more than a diplomatic facade; Giraudoux created a space where a kind of worldly, pan-European irony framed one of the enduring French masterpieces of the twentieth-century theatre of war.

I refer to *La guerre de Troie n'aura pas lieu,* first performed in Paris in 1935.[20] The title itself announces the game, which emerges in the very first exchange of the play. Andromache, Hector's wife, tells Cassandra that there will be no Trojan War. Cassandra bets her that she is wrong. We know that Cassandra will win the bet; so does the author, but Andromache is in the dark: thus we see the different communities of understanding which irony describes, all in a wager about destiny.

But right from the start, Giraudoux offers us an even greater irony. The opening lines spoken by Andromache are impossible. At the moment she speaks, Andromache could not have heard of the Trojan War, since it was called that only after the fact. Hence for her to say before its outbreak that it won't take place is to evidence knowledge—there will be a Trojan War—which undermines the content of her flat claim that it won't take place. What wicked game is Giraudoux playing here?

The subject of the play, and the choices it describes, are no laughing matter. Indeed, Giraudoux employs irony as a powerful defensive strategy in a world where war threatens. In the play irony is the last shield which Andromache and Hector wear to protect them and all of Troy from the scourge of war, and from those among them who turn bloodshed into poetry and carnage into heroism. Irony is the way they try to disarm the dangerous fools among them from triggering war. After the patriotic poet Demokos, the quintessential bellicose civilian, announces that killing a man gives a warrior the right to a woman, Andromache begs to differ. She tells him and her father-in-law Priam that women really love cowards, who are men who stay alive. Priam cautions her by saying she should be careful not to prove "the very opposite of what you want to prove." Priam doesn't see that she is speaking the direct truth: what is more honorable than dishonorable conduct in the pursuit of peace? "But which is the worse cowardice," she asks; "to appear cowardly to others, and make sure of peace? Or to be cowardly in your own eyes, and let loose a war?"

Her husband repeats this antiheroic principle time and again. In this respect Giraudoux's Hector is not Homer's. In this play, Hector believes that honor is a word which describes an inner state. To cast it off in public as the price of averting war is to lose only the outer trappings of true honor, which remains within. Here is the central strategy of the game he plays in this prewar period: the game of persuading the Greeks that there is no cause for war in the presence in Troy of Helen, snatched by Paris from her royal Greek husband. Ajax comes to take her home and finds that Hector invites him to have her. Ajax taunts Hector; what if I call you a coward, Ajax asks. "That is a name I accept," is Hector's reply. What if I spit, says Ajax; go ahead, says Hector. What if I slap? Go ahead, says Hector, and Ajax does. The slap leaves its mark, but Hector claims that the swelling shows he is healthier on that side of his face. Then the poet Demokos challenges Ajax, and to prevent them from conjuring up the casus belli they both are itching to find, Hector slaps Demokos himself, and then denies that anything had happened. War is averted, but in light of the general insouciance around him about the prospects of bloodshed, Hector has a sense that all these minor victories still do not add up to much: "I win every round. But still with each victory, the prize [peace] eludes me."

The next round is even more deliciously ironic. In negotiations with Ulysses, Hector declares that "Paris has not touched Helen." He is clearly lying, as the sailors aboard Paris's ship attest willingly. But Helen, whose heart is made of stone, is quite literally untouchable; Hector is speaking the truth, but not the one his companions think he is. Ulysses goes along with this conceit, and sees peace accomplished for a very paltry price: he will tell Menelaus that nothing had happened to Helen in Troy. "I have more than enough eloquence to convince a husband of his wife's virtue."

The soldier/diplomats withdraw and peace seems assured, until the very last moment, when the heroic fool Demokos shouts, "Treachery, and to arms" when he realizes that Helen is returning to Greece. Significantly enough, Hector kills Demokos, who in his last breath lies, and says that Ajax had killed him; this lie provokes the Trojans to kill Ajax, setting the war in motion. Hector is defeated, and the doom of his people is assured. The Trojan poet Demokos is dead, says Cassandra, "and now the Grecian poet will have his word." Homer's Trojan War, sung five centuries after the events in the play, is about to begin.

What a game Giraudoux has described. But its playfulness only masks the deadly seriousness of the drama. In a way, irony is the vehicle for a battle of representations, in which heroic notions of war collide with heroes stripped of those very beliefs. *La guerre de Troie n'aura pas lieu* is a duel between pacifism, represented by Hector, and heroism, expressed by Demokos. The poet is one of the old men who praise war without knowing it. He is a pale imitation of Barrès and others whose heroic aggression somehow had survived the carnage of Verdun and the Somme and had come to threaten the world again.

What the play describes is an ironic ambiguity familiar to anyone who—like Giraudoux—surveyed the French veterans' movement in the interwar years. As Prost has shown, they were men whose heroism could not be challenged; now, in the aftermath of war, they were determined to make war on facile notions of heroism. If they did not speak out, it would return. Like Hector, they had a sense of a mission constantly eluding them. The corrupt politicians and poets and propagandists were still there. To ex-soldiers like Giraudoux, who knew what combat was, another war was both unthinkable and just around the corner. That is what the interwar phrase *entre-deux-guerres* is all about.

It would be an injustice to an ironist of the stature of Giraudoux to limit his play to this single frame of reference. Yes, he had fought both on the Western Front and at Gallipoli; yes, he had been wounded twice and decorated with the Legion of Honor.[21] Yes, he was a diplomat who knew from many of his superiors and his adversaries what cheap, overblown language looked like. But his art is hardly autobiography; to assume so is to fall into a trap much cruder than his prose. I suggest that it is the tone of his voice which sets him aside from most French writers of the war generation as well as from the didactic cadences of the veterans' movement in interwar France. Irony sets him apart. And drew him sympathetically, temperamentally, to those other ironists across the Channel who meditated on the war. His ironic detachment, mixed with moral purpose, made his reactions to the 1914–18 war closer to those of Owen and Sassoon than to those of Barbusse and Genevoix.

It would be pointless to try to explain completely the complexity of Giraudoux's voice through his biography. The elegance of his prose would shrivel under such heavy-handedness. We know that his reach was European, and indeed extra-European. At the *École Normale Supérieure*, he wrote his thesis on "Quel but poursuit l'Allemagne en dévellopant sa marine de guerre?" ("What Is Germany's Aim in Developing Its Navy?"). Not much irony there. Nor was there anything unusual in a French intellectual's deep acquaintance with and admiration for German language and literature. What was somewhat more unusual was that Giraudoux's sympathies extended to the Anglo-Saxon world as well.

Here he benefited from a current of Francophilia deeply entrenched at Harvard. In part funded by James Hazen Hyde, son of an insurance tycoon, Harvard launched an exchange program which brought Giraudoux to Cambridge, Massachusetts, in 1907. When the professor of French was struck down with typhoid fever, Giraudoux delivered his lectures on eighteenth-century French literature. He was active in theatrical productions there, too. After a tour around America, he was introduced to President Theodore Roosevelt. It was at this time that Giraudoux decided to bypass the *Agrégation* in German and a future academic career and to concentrate on diplomacy.

That career would take him to the highest levels of the French diplomatic service. In the 1920s and 1930s, he traveled extensively, as inspector of French diplomatic missions. Naturally, the Franco-German dialogue was of major concern to him, as it was to all diplomats, but his gaze was not fixed on this one issue. His interests, as well as the sources of his vision, were multiple. The ironic voice he found was truly European, and through it he expressed without sentimentality the Sisyphean struggle toward a European peace always just out of reach.

All his adult life Giraudoux struggled with the duality of war and peace, and found in irony a way of expressing the tragedy of his generation, scarred by one war and seemingly unable to avoid another. That ironic voice was both distinctive and echoed others like it outside of France. In this sense he was a poet of the sentiments at the heart of the interwar French veterans' movement. But he was a poet with a voice of his own, one with ironic cadences with clear affinities to other literary responses to the war.[22]

Conclusion

If it is true that British and French intellectual responses to the Great War were different, and that irony is one facet of that difference, the question remains why should this be so. In brief it may be useful to draw on some conjectures which move intellectual history outside an older tradition which privileged the pure study of style and sensibility over cultural and political contexts.

My aim is to point to some disparities, some differences in emphasis and location which may be of interest in situating these materials. First, the notion of irony rests more easily with those further removed from the battlefields of the war. France was invaded; the bloodshed occurred on French soil, and the outcome of those battles determined the outcome of the war. There is not much room for irony on these points. But there are other, longer-term contrasts which may lay behind the different tone and emphases in these two countries' intellectual responses to the war. Some of these arose from the very different role played by ex-soldiers in postwar society. There was nothing in Britain remotely like the French veterans' movement. The proportion of ex-soldiers who joined veterans' groups in France was four times greater than in Britain. The absence of conscription before the war, added to the controversy over conscription during it, provided few supports for making veterans' experience a centerpiece of postwar political discourse. There wasn't even a minister for veterans' affairs in Britain, that business being handled by the Ministry of Pensions, set up initially in 1908 to help the elderly. Individual veterans became prominent in interwar politics, but when they tried, like Oswald Mosley, to introduce military forms into British political life, they failed miserably, consigned to an obscurity from which they never escaped.

It was not only that veterans' politics differed in the two countries. It was that the distance between intellectual groups and the political world in France and Britain was very different. Years ago, in doing some work on the French war economy, I was astonished to learn that the Minister of Commerce, Étienne Clémentel, would excuse himself from ministerial meetings so that he could walk over to the rue de Varenne where he was conducting experiments in optics in Rodin's house. Could that have happened in London? Perhaps, but I don't believe it did. And Clémentel was not exceptional; others like Clemenceau crossed the line between the arts and public affairs time and again. I might point to the well-known fact that British and French intellectuals live in a different proximity to the institutions of the state, and that this positioning might reinforce what Raymond Williams referred to as different structures of feeling, different styles of expression. One aspect of that difference is what I have called the ironic temperament, and especially its utility as a distancing device.

A word or two should be added about the structuring effects of irony on political protest. Irony both enabled and contained it. The British recourse to an imagery of games and gamesmanship, to fair play and decency, built into that irony a kind of limiting force. Games suspend time. When they come to an end, nothing in the real world has changed. Could not the same be said for irony as a sport, a game played for its own sake? The ironist could have his say, and then just fade away. In this sense, irony is both the fate of an intellectual class without a direct political function and a means of ensuring that this remains the case. Distance has its price alongside its privileges.

Above all, irony destabilizes. It rules out certain kinds of certainty. It is a mirror in which the gaze confronts something which is not quite what it seems to be. Confronting it means admitting that all interpretations, including this one, must remain up in the air.

CHAPTER 6

War Memorials
A Social Agency Interpretation

Historical remembrance is a process which occurs in space and time. So far we have had a look at photographs, war letters, plays, and novels. But the locus classicus of remembrance in the interwar years and beyond are war memorials. These sites, statues, and sculptures have been subject to a vast literature. To add a different perspective, I would like to offer a modest proposal that we not *de-construct*, but rather *shrink* the framework of discussions of commemorative forms in the twentieth century. I want to argue that shifting the scale of vision from the national and grandiose to the particular and mundane may help transform our understanding of war monuments, and of the forms of remembrance which occur surrounding them. In villages and towns throughout Europe, small groups of people have always stood between topoi and experience, between sites of memory and collective remembrance. It is their activity and their achievements which form the core of this chapter.

Why shift the focus from high to low politics, from capital cities to obscure towns, from first-order to second- or third-order actors in social life? One reason is that the great national sites of remembrance are exceptional, and their histories provide a misleading impression of thousands of others. Another is that in contemporary cultural history, multivocality is the order of the day. The thrust of much recent work in social and cultural studies has been away from an earlier top-down approach, which emphasized the capacity of dominant groups to act in effect as puppeteers, pulling the strings of cultural activity. That elites have tried to do so is self-evident, as we have noted in our discussion of cultural memory; less convincing is the claim that they effectively controlled the space within which all forms of cultural expression in general and commemoration in particular have developed. Cultural history is a chorus of voices; some are louder than others, but they never sound alone.

To adopt a pluralistic approach to cultural history has many advantages. It enables us both to respect national notations and forms and to avoid being blinded by them. Memories are both personal and social, and sites of memory are created not just by nations but primarily by small groups of men and women who do the work of remembrance. *They* are the "social agents" of remembrance; without their work, collective memory would not exist.

I want to argue that these "memory activists," in Carol Gluck's phrase,[1] frequently constitute powerfully unified groups, bonded not by blood ties but by experience. They share the imprint of history on their lives, and act as kin do in other contexts. They endure together, they support each other, they quarrel, and they act together. At times, their bonds are sufficiently strong to enable us to call them "fictive kin." It is the trace of these groups we find in the work of remembrance, and in many war memorials themselves.

"Fictive kinship groups" are the key agents of remembrance. What do we know about them? A great deal: they are goal-directed people, with an agenda, a project, whose traces may be found in local and national archives. The modest size of these cohorts is both their strength and their weakness. They can act in efficient and coordinated ways. Frequently such associations lose their power—and perhaps even their identity—once they grow beyond a certain scale. No one can say precisely what the threshold is that separates small groups of fictive kin, who share what Avishai Margalit terms "thick relations," from large groups, whose relations are "thin,"[2] and whose identity is much more diffuse and evanescent; but I have no doubt that such a threshold exists.

Wherever it is, the threshold falls well short of the nation. To be sure, nations have been termed families for centuries; the small stands for the whole in a metonymical manner. The czar was the "little father" of the Russians; the royal family in England was the model for the British nation, at least until recently. Political movements have used familial rhetoric too. Maurice Barrès liked to conjure up the political landscape in terms of "les grandes familles politiques de la France." But when we deal with mass movements or nations, we move from tangible realities to abstract, or imagined, ones. Once beyond a certain threshold, families are not agents but metaphors, and metaphors do not make monuments. Groups of people do. The question as to how and why they have done so in the twentieth century, and how we may do so today, are at the center of any discussion of collective remembrance.

After offering some thoughts on the concept of collective remembrance, I want to address the issue of social agency, and to relate the construction of commemorative forms to a prior and parallel process of the gathering together of groups of survivors who, through what I call "fictive kinship," do the work of remembrance.[3] Finally, I want to address the question of the continuity and the breaks between such activity in the first and second half of the twentieth century.

Collective Remembrance

A word or two is necessary about what I mean by the terms *memory, collective memory,* and *cultural memory.* Let me once again borrow from the work of Jan and Aleida Assmann to introduce the terminology of cultural memory into this inquiry. The Assmanns use the term to describe the re-usable and available texts, images and rites of each society, with the preservation of which it stabilizes and spreads its self-image; a collective shared knowledge, preferably (but not necessarily) of the past, on which a group's sense of unity and individuality is based. The topoi and narratives which appear in monuments need an institutionalized communication, without which their re-use cannot be organized. Therefore, we do not only inquire into the history, form and meaning of the monuments as artefacts, but also into the history of their use and their re-use.

I have serious doubts about the concept of "stabilization" as one of the functions of monuments, especially when some central issues surrounding the Holocaust can never be "stabilized." But in some respects this definition is a useful starting point. My remarks should be understood as attempts to refine and apply these concepts to the work of the small groups of people who create and re-create these sites of memory. The thrust of my argument is toward the presentation of a matrix of activity, in which the small scale is recognized alongside the aggregate, in which particular agendas are privileged alongside societal imperatives of legitimation.

To describe a set of social processes happening on several levels at once requires constant attention to *who* is *doing* the work of remembrance. I like to use the term *remembrance* to describe a *social* process; memory, both individual and collective, is its product. Remembrance has an active, transitory quality; it has a beginning and an end, an existence in space and time. Its very delimitation is its strength as a heuristic device.

The Collective Remembrance of War: A Social Agency Approach

The term *cultural memory* denotes more than the property of individual people, but it works best as a category of analysis when it is applied to the activity and products of groups and not to that of states as a whole. War memorials are a case in point; by any definition they are salient elements in the cultural memory of twentieth-century Europe. Some of these monuments are grandiose, self-serving tributes, to be sure; but many go beyond state-sponsored triumphalism to approach the regional, the local, the particular, and the familial realities of loss of life in wartime. I would like to draw attention to this latter category.

Here the dialectic between remembering and forgetting is visible, and is especially salient in nonofficial forms of collective remembrance. Such efforts are always the outcome of agency, the product of individuals and groups who come together not initially or exclusively at the behest of the state or any of its subsidiary organizations, but because *they* have to speak out.

Why? Here we are at the intersection of private memories, family memories, and collective remembrance. The men and women whose activity underlay the creation of war memorials lived through war as trauma, understood as an overwhelming, sustained, and mass experience. Many were in mourning; most were torn by war from one set of daily rhythms and were in search of another. Their decisions to act in public—by creating associations, by writing memoirs, by producing films, by speaking out in a host of ways—were profoundly personal. But they were not private matters only, since they existed in a social framework, the framework of collective *action*.

My argument, therefore, stands at a midpoint between two extreme and unacceptable positions in this field: between those (following Bergson) who argue that private memories are ineffable and individual, and those (following Durkheim) who see them as entirely socially determined and therefore present whether anyone acts on them. With Blondel, I urge that such approaches are best located in "the gallery" of useless "abstractions."[4] In between is the palpable, messy activity which produces collective remembrance.

In this as in other areas, agency is arduous. Its opportunity costs— time, money, effort—are substantial. *And* it rarely lasts. Other tasks take precedence; other issues crowd out the ones leading to public work. And aging takes its toll: people fade away, either personally or physically. The collective remembrance of old soldiers and the victims of wars is, therefore, a quixotic act. It is an effort to think publicly about painful issues in the past, an effort which is bound to fade over time.

This fading away is inevitable: all war memorials have a "shelf-life," a bounded period of time in which their meaning relates to the concerns of a particular group of people who created them or who use or appropriate them as ceremonial or reflective sites of memory. That set of meanings is never permanent; but it is also rarely determined by fiat. A social agency approach to the subject of "cultural memory" suggests that it is time to consider monuments not solely as reflections of current political authority or a general consensus— although some clearly are one or the other—but rather as a set of profound and yet impermanent expressions of the force of civil society, that space which exists in the shadow of and in dialogue, with families on the one side and the state on the other.

Fictive Kinship and Commemorative Activity

Those who initiated war memorials were almost always personally linked to the events themselves. In this sense they were witnesses. They had, of course, a variety of motives. Many were deeply personal. They acted in order to struggle with grief, to fill in the silence, to offer something symbolically to the dead, for political reasons. In most of their immediate concerns, they tended to fail. The dead *were* forgotten; peace did *not* last; memorials faded into the landscape. It is a moot question, at the very least, as to whether healing at the personal level followed.

To show what a social agency approach can yield, I would like to describe three kinds of social activity in different national contexts. The first is British—quintessentially British. It is the practice of observing a two-minute silence on 11 November at 11 a.m., a practice which operated at the local level in the midst of life between 1919 and 1946, and which may be coming back again today.[5] The second is that of the social bonding effected between disabled men with particularly horrific injuries—the French *gueules cassées*—disfigured men, men with broken faces.[6] The third is the work of fictive kinship surrounding the creation of war memorials, and one in particular, sketched in Berlin between 1914 and 1932.

I want to move along a continuum of memory work: from individual and internal memory during the two-minute silence; to isolated memory work among men whose disfigurement placed them outside of everyday life and who were forced therefore to look at themselves and to each other for support and human recognition; and finally to collective remembrance among those whose losses provided them with the unity of experience out of which commemorative activity emerged.

THE TWO-MINUTE SILENCE

The British practice of arresting the movement of ordinary life for two minutes on whatever day in the week happened to fall on 11 November emerged at the end of the 1914–18 war. It was sanctified by an extraordinary moment, when a temporary war memorial—the catafalque erected in London for the victory parade of 19 July 1919— became the permanent and imperial symbol of the wrenching losses of the Great War. The two-minute silence was first observed six months later, on 11 November, as an echo of the astonishing ingathering of more than one million men and women in London around the Cenotaph in Whitehall. The Cabinet never anticipated that the Cenotaph would be so magnetic; they imagined it would be a temporary form, and instructed Sir Edwin Lutyens accordingly to construct it out of light materials, easily assembled and disassembled. But after the people had voted with their feet to adopt this site as a permanent site of memory for the Lost Generation of the Great War, the Cabinet told Lutyens to reconstruct it, this time out of stone. There in Whitehall, in the heart of official London, it has remained to this day. Its simplicity and ecumenical character gave it its appeal. By saying so little, it said much about the moment of exhaustion and mourning which coincided with victory. By moving to pre-Christian notation, it announced that the imperial nation was honoring men who had died on active service, men who were not only Protestant or Catholic, but Muslim, Hindu, or Jewish—or who had no religion at all. Whatever Anglican clerics had to say—and their discomfort was palpable—ordinary people looked beyond the churches for a site which was sacred. And in the Cenotaph they found it.[7]

This was an astonishing, entirely exceptional moment. At that ceremony, the local and the national became one. It was never repeated, but instead, it was de-centered, reworked, reiterated at thousands of local war memorials built in the 1920s, and scattered throughout the country. That is where the two-minute silence was (and is) observed, in front of monuments dominated by names—the long lists of ordinary men from particular places who perished in a war in which sacrifice turned democratic.

The two-minute silence was a meditation about absence, about the million men of the British Empire whose deaths it so movingly symbolized. Each year between 1919 and 1939, the two-minute silence was observed on 11 November, when the King placed a wreath on the Cenotaph. What kind of moment was it? We know something about these individual, hidden memories through the evidence of the pioneering social survey group Mass Observation. In the late 1930s, this body sent out investigators to ask ordinary people throughout the country what they thought about during the two-minute silence. For our purposes, the answers most widely given are especially revealing. Mass Observation found that individuals did not think of the Empire, or nations, or armies, but of individual people who were no longer there. "It's for the people who lost theirs, it should be kept for them to think of the ones they lost," said one sixty-year-old woman.[8] The memory work was segmented: the loss of individuals in wartime was inscribed in *individual* memory, or rather in the meditation of *individual* people about the family members—fathers, sons, husbands, brothers, friends—who had died in the war.

The social notation of silence was secularized prayer. It forced people to remember, by suspending all other activities for a brief moment. Telephonists pulled the plugs on all conversations. Traffic stopped. Life was arrested. During the Second World War, the practice was suspended and, after 1945, removed to Remembrance Sunday. Taken out of daily life, the ceremony atrophied. But in the interwar years, it carried with it a powerful injunction to remember. I believe that that injunction had to fade over time, as other tasks and other memories crowded out the earlier images and gestures. Once the bereaved faded away, or moved away, or died, the original charge of the event was lost. The silence became just that—a void.

THE MEN WITH BROKEN FACES

What is most striking about the two minute silence is the *isolated* nature of this commemorative form. Here we *are* on the border of private and public recollection. Others lived their lives in this borderland, but in different ways. One such group of people was isolated by their wounds. These disfigured men, hideously scarred in many cases, had the war engraved on their faces. Their road back to a normal life was so obstructed by obstacles that many gave up entirely the struggle to demobilize, to go back home again. Instead they turned to each other, in an isolated brotherhood. In doing so, they formed organizations which pressed for their rights and created places where they could go without frightening little children in the street or on the beach. They constructed a social reality through which they could remember the simple dignities of everyday life that they had lost and would never recover on their own. Kinship here meant survival in very straightforward and mundane ways.[9]

Such groups existed in every combatant country. But their lives were very often isolated and private. They acted socially, to be sure, but in a way which confirmed their pariah status, while at the same time enabling them to construct an environment in which they could face each other and face themselves. They were themselves sites of memory, but of a kind so extraordinary that ordinary people had trouble even looking at them.

At this point we confront a paradox. These men bore the traces of war in so direct and unvarnished a way that it—and they—could not be faced. *They* had to be hidden, but that exile, that exclusion, was not the end of their story. Through marginalization, they created their own organizations, their own ceremonies, their own monuments, their own social lives. Theirs was a world apart.

THE ELDERS

A third category of remembrance is more general. It encompasses the emergence of groups of people bound together publicly by their experience of bereavement. They acted not in silence and not in the shadows. Private activity was the beginning, but not the end of the story. Unlike the people observing the two-minute silence in Britain, and unlike the work of the *gueules cassées,* most efforts to erect commemorative forms entered the public domain and stayed there. Inevitably, private memories accompanied public action, but here on this third level, the level of public, collective remembrance, a number of enduring messages were inscribed in a host of monuments by small groups of people. Such sites of memory rested on the work of small groups of men and women, on fictive kin, whose presence antedated these monuments and whose bonds frequently endured long after they were unveiled.

The gathering together of such fictive kinship groups took place in many forms. For those adhering to conventional kinds of religious belief, the churches were significant foci of activity. Others tried to bring the dead back to their homes through séances, frowned on by the churches, but popular nonetheless. Groups of spiritualists, either family members or fictive kin, met in a domestic setting where a medium "reunited" families with the spirits of the dead. Here the deceased hinted at the story of their lives after death, and offered the living consolation. Their message was frequently very simple: It's all right, the dead reassured the living; I'm safe and well. You can go on living.[10] And that is what they did, not in national units, or large collectives, but, through local affiliations and in the rhythms of their daily lives.

There is an evident contrast here. The *gueules cassées* had to cope with the need of many to hide the living face of war. In séances, bereaved people tried to bring back to visibility—if only for a moment—the hidden face of the dead. In both cases the gaze was a troubled one.

Troubling in a similar way is the gaze of another group of people engaged in "memory work" of this kind. This is a story on which I have written elsewhere,[11] but it is one which is part of a wider landscape of small-scale local commemorative activity which went on in homes and in private throughout the interwar years. Here we enter the prehistory of public commemoration, or (in other words) the secluded, intimate, hidden face of remembrance after the Great War.

The story of Peter Kollwitz and his mother, Käthe Kollwitz, is a familiar one. Peter, aged eighteen, volunteered for military service on 4 August 1914. He was one of approximately one hundred forty thousand out of four million German men mobilized who joined up voluntarily early in the war. These idealistic youths—overwhelmingly students or in middle-class occupations—have been taken to be representatives of *Kriegsbegeisterung*, of "war enthusiasm," in the nation as a whole. In fact, that "enthusiasm" was strictly limited to a few days and a narrow part of the population.[12] But among Peter's circle, it was real enough.

The sight of troops marching off to the war convinced Peter that he had to join up before the reserves were mobilized. "My fatherland does not need my year yet," he told his skeptical father, "but it needs *me*." Peter enlisted his mother's aid in getting his father to agree. He did, and Peter joined up, alongside his closest friends and classmates.

This acceptance of the principle of sacrifice by the youth of Berlin initially made some sense to Käthe Kollwitz. Throughout her life, her belief in a "calling" infused both her notion of what she must do as an artist and how to serve her people. Peter's decision to volunteer for the army fit into that framework. But as soon as the first news of battle and casualties reached Berlin, she began to see that it was "vile," "idiotic," and "harebrained" that these young men, at the beginning of their lives, were going off to war.

Peter Kollwitz left home on 5 October 1914. He said farewell to his mother on 12 October. Ten days later he was dead. He was killed in Belgium in a field about twenty kilometers northeast of Ypres. One of the friends with whom Peter had enlisted brought the news of his death to the family.

For the next thirty years Käthe Kollwitz grieved for her son.[13] For our purposes, I want to concentrate on one related theme. In an entirely different context, the historian Emmanuel Sivan has shown how, after 1948, Israeli families created kinship bonds among the friends of their fallen sons, friends with whom they had served and who were lucky enough to come back alive. At a different time, but in parallel ways, Käthe Kollwitz and her family did the same. Ritual attended this kind of bonding. The Kollwitzes left Peter's room intact. They put flowers on the chair next to his bed, and tried to conjure up his spirit in the room. Friends came by and read letters and texts there with the bereaved parents. They put a Christmas tree behind the bed, with eighteen candles for each of Peter's years. On subsequent Christmases and New Years, additional candles were added, to mark the age he would have reached had he been alive. Birthdays were marked there. This was a sacred space both for the family and for those who had joined in these acts of remembrance.[14]

Such gestures were not just extensions of traditional forms of family gatherings. They were there because the process of healing was so difficult, so slow. Käthe Kollwitz used to sit in her son's room and try to commune with him. At times she drew strength from this effort; at times she believed that "I walk in twilight, only rarely stars, the sun *has long since set completely.*"[15] The black sun, the aura of depression, was a constant companion.[16] And some comfort came from Peter's friends, with whom she found some solace, and whose visits she welcomed. To them she was "Mother Käthe" or "Mother Kollwitz." "I must retain my feeling of connection to the boys," is the way she put it on 9 October 1916;[17] they were part of her household, part of her life.

This informal "adoption" of those familiar young men who had shared Peter's fate, both the living and the dead, marked Kollwitz's life. It also became the centerpiece of her commemorative art. Before the First World War, her art encompassed many subjects. Prominent among them were historical and epic themes—peasant uprisings, great sweeps of protest and its suppression. After 1914, images of historical tragedy receded; images of family tragedy loomed larger. Her art became more maternal, more familial. In effect, the collective dimension of suffering portrayed in her drawings, etchings, and sculptures had shrunk to the nuclear family itself.

From early on in the war Käthe Kollwitz was determined to create a war memorial for her son and for his generation of friends. Initially her idea was to form a single family circle in stone. Her early sketches show two parents holding their dead son; over time, the son became detached from the parents and ultimately disappeared. Part of the meaning of this shift in iconography, from a nuclear family to an extended family, is located in the process of mourning, in the slow and terrible effort to let her son go. But part of the meaning is to be found in Kollwitz's commitment to gather to her family all those young men who had had to endure the war at its worst.

On 25 June 1919 she wrote hopefully, "If I live to see Peter's work [the memorial sculpture] completed and good, commemorating him and his friends on a beautiful site, then perhaps Germany is past the worst."[18] On 13 October 1925, she described the project as one in which "the mother should kneel and gaze out over the many graves. She spreads out her arms over all her sons."[19] Seven years later the memorial was inaugurated in the German military cemetery at Roggevelde near Langemarck and Ypres in Belgium. The sculpture is of Käthe and Hans Kollwitz, on their knees, in front of a field of graves, including that of their son. The mother's arms are not extended, but wrapped around her own body, as are her husband's around his. The representation of grief here is gendered. The parents strike different poses as they mourn for this "flock of children," this ill-starred generation, whose elders could not prevent the disaster which had enveloped them.

In the 1950s, German war cemeteries were consolidated in the Belgian countryside, and the remains of fallen soldiers in several cemeteries, including Roggevelde, were removed and reinterred a few miles away at Vladslo. Peter Kollwitz and his mother's two statues have found their final resting place there. It is only with difficulty that the visitor to Vladslo can find the plaque on which the name of Peter Kollwitz is written. He has become one among many, a child mourned by the two old people unable even to support each other in their separate grief. All they can do is beg on their knees for forgiveness, and offer their love and their grief, fixed in stone. (On a visit to the site a few years ago, I found not the two statues of "the elders," but green boxes covering them. The stone had been damaged by the elements and by time. Even granite has a half-life.)

In considering this monument, we are on the border between metaphor and lived experience. To say that at Roggevelde these were Käthe Kollwitz's lost sons is, on one level, poetic license. But on another level, her gathering of her son's generation into her family was an essential element in her effort to express the "meaning" of the war for her whole generation. Like many others, hers was a family which was defined by those who weren't there, and joined in an essential sense by other survivors.

By telling the story of her work of remembrance, we can begin to hear the dissonance between the tone and register of her activity, and the kinship, real and fictive, it describes, and the tone and register of national commemorative designs. In this sense, the smaller the canvas, the more continuous is the thread connecting topoi and experience, connecting sites of memory and the agents of remembrance. Once we leap to the national level, such organic links are almost always stretched to the breaking point and beyond. There are exceptions; the initial two-minute silence is one of them; Maya Lin's Vietnam Veterans Memorial, is another. But by and large only local activity, and small-scale activity at that, can preserve the original charge, the emotion, the conviction which went into war memorial work. Once we arrive at the level of the nation, we encounter politics of a different kind. Monumentality is never the language of the small social solidarities described here.

My argument should not be construed as a set of comments on the truism that "small is beautiful." Local politics can be as divisive and disturbing as national politics. I simply want to urge that when we speak of collective remembrance, we return to the original notion of Halbwachs, and recognize that different collectives, within the same state, socially frame their memories in very different ways. The nation is not the place where collective remembrance begins, though the local, the particular, and the national frequently intersect.

Conclusion

In this chapter, I have tried to illustrate the need to approach the history of collective remembrance from the angle of small-scale, locally rooted social action. Many of these phenomena were family-based, but others occurred among people whose ties were based on experience rather than marriage or filiation. I have used the term *fictive kinship* to characterize these associations. All these groups were agents of remembrance. Their activity antedated public commemoration and continued long after the ceremonies were over. Yes, on 11 November, these groups joined the nation, the wider collective. But that was not their origin, nor their center of gravity.

I have insisted that remembrance is an activity of agents who congregate on the borderline between the private and the public, between families, civil society, and the state.[20] This form of small-scale collective memory—the thought-process of kinship, both fictive and filial—was both powerful and brittle. At the time, it gave men and women a way to live on after the horrors of war. But as those agents of remembrance grew tired or old, developed other lives, moved away, or died, then the activity—the glue—which held together these cells of remembrance, atrophied and lost its hold on them. What has remained to this day are the traces of their work and the envelope in which they operated: the national framework which was but a thin cover over a host of associative forms arduously constructed over years by thousands of people, mostly obscure. Today we see the collective memory in national ceremonies; but in the decades after the Armistice of 1918, there were other, locally based collectives engaged in remembrance. They have vanished, but it would be foolish to merge these activities in some state-bounded space of hegemony or domination. What these people did was much smaller and much greater than that.

A final word about the relevance of these instances of commemoration, bounded by the tragedy of the First World War, for our consideration of monuments in the later twentieth century. After the Second World War, the same flaring up of older languages appropriate to a period of mass mourning did not take place. In general, commemoration was muted, a hardly surprising development in France or in Germany. In Britain, the names of those who died in the war of 1939–45 were simply added to those of the Great War. In part, this was a reflection of failure. The warning inscribed in war memorials—never again—was not heeded. In addition, there was a clear preference on the local level for utilitarian war memorials, useful donations or projects, fitting at a time when national reconstruction was the order of the day. The same body of opinion reflected in the Labour Party electoral victory of 1945 is to be found in the widespread discussion of commemoration in hospitals, schools, scholarships, and in the Land Fund. Statues, as one survey of 1944 disclosed, were not wanted.

There was a change too in artistic opinion as to forms of public statuary. Henry Moore stuck to the human figure, but many other artists turned to abstraction. Their work was thus both more liberated from specific cultural and political reference and less accessible to a mass audience. Whether or not these abstract images have the same power to heal as did older symbolic forms is a difficult question; my answer is probably not.[21]

The forms of commemoration may have changed, but in many places the impulse to create them has endured. And so have the controversies surrounding such projects. One of Käthe Kollwitz's sculptures, a pietà, was placed, amid much argument, in the Neue Wache in Berlin. It asks us to remember "the victims of war and dictatorship," thereby conflating those who perished during the two wars, the Holocaust, and under the East German dictatorship. Then there is the long, drawn-out saga of the effort to create a National Holocaust Memorial in the German capital. Perhaps the case of Berlin is exceptional, but it does reinforce my claim that, on the whole, the smaller the scale and the more modest the monumental project, the more likely it is that it will express the cares and sentiments of those who need to remember.

All I want to suggest in conclusion is that the same multivocality in the commemorative project persists now as was so evident a century ago. Here too we can see that however much we dwell on the Second World War and the Holocaust, the patterns which emerged during the Great War simply do not fade away. The history of commemorative projects launched in the period of the 1914–18 conflict and after show that remembrance is a process with multiple voices. They are rarely harmonious and never identical; they do not simply add up to a vague or ill-defined entity known as collective memory or national memory. Remembrance is always defined by its specificity—who, why, and where. The answers to these questions remain critical, and many of them can be answered only on the local level, by investigating the work of "memory activists."

Further difficulties have arisen when art is mobilized in the search for symbols appropriate for national monuments. Who can miss the underlying message of such projects? In Berlin, the message is hard to avoid: out of the ashes, the city and the nation have risen. Can such uses of the notion of aesthetic redemption be defended? I wonder. To reflect on these matters is still important, for the search for meaning in this the most violent of centuries, goes on. It persists, despite the urging of some postmodernists, like Jacques Derrida, that we give up the effort entirely.[22] I suspect that the activity of remembrance, and the creation of the topoi of collective experience which it entails, are irrepressible. They express some fundamental truths about the tendency of ordinary people, of many faiths and of none, to face the emptiness, the nothingness of loss in war, together.

CHAPTER 7

War, Migration, and Remembrance
Britain and Her Dominions

One of the central premises of the work of Maurice Halbwachs is that social groups frame the memories they share. That is, when collectives come together to recall significant events, events which tell them who they are as a group, then they create something he termed "collective memory." And when they no longer form a group, or when other life events intervene, and people age or move away or simply find other things to do, then the collective changes or disintegrates, and with it goes "collective memory." This sense of the socially constructed nature of "collective memory" is vital to historical study, since it precludes talking about memory as if it exists independently of the people who share it.[1]

One case which illustrates the way in which acts of remembrance bind together far-flung collectives is the way in which both British and Dominion populations came to mourn the "Lost Generation" of the Great War. At the same time as Australia, New Zealand, and Canada found during and after the war new meaning in a political and cultural life largely independent of Britain, the ties which bound these different populations together were reinforced by the social practices of remembering the dead of the 1914–18 conflict. It was an *Imperial* (now Commonwealth) War Graves Commission which gathered together the remains of those who had died and who built cemeteries to honor them.

After the Second World War, this sense of shared experience changed, not in any way to diminish the significance of the immense loss of life during the two wars, but to separate national practices and symbols into discrete parts. In 2006 Australians still make the pilgrimage to Gallipoli. The death of the last veterans of the Great War in Canada is front-page news, and poppy sales in Britain each November are robust. What changed was not the subject of remembrance, but in each country the composition of the population doing the remembering. After 1945, migration between Britain and the "Old Dominions" diminished just as migration from the "New Dominions" increased sharply. These black and brown Britons did not share the same "collective memories," in Halbwachs's sense of the term, and neither did new immigrants to Australia or Canada from Asia. It was inevitable that as cultural life became more pluralistic and less Anglocentric, even in England, acts of remembrance would reflect this new demographic profile. And so it has, not by diminishing the significance of the 1914–18 war, but perhaps surprisingly, by increasing it.

The key point here is that migration matters in the formation of collective remembrance, since migratory waves create diasporas with strong ties to the mother country. When migration patterns shift, so does the social base of "collective memory." The result is not necessarily forgetting, but more frequently the recasting of acts of remembrance into more discrete, distinctive national forms. It is no accident, therefore, that in 1993 the Australian government decided to bury in Canberra its own unknown warrior. They were no longer satisfied with the "collective memory" attached to the British unknown soldier buried in Westminster Abbey, who might well have been Australian; no one knows.

In this chapter, I first describe the ties which bound together the British Empire and Dominions in the twentieth century demographically. Then, by placing imperial demography and imperial commemorations together, we can see ways in which "collective memories" emerge and mutate over time. My fundamental claim is that demography created the British Empire, and now, by the twenty-first century, demography has laid it to rest. The project of peopling, in the euphemism of the time, "areas of white settlement" with British people was a remarkable one, with clear and visible outlines in the architecture and ambiance of Toronto, Melbourne, and Capetown. But deeper than the thoroughfares, the public schools, or the botanical gardens, what made the empire, the Dominions, and the Commonwealth a reality were the family ties which bound core and periphery together.

The demography of the British diaspora created the late-nineteenth-century British Empire and Dominions. But since the Second World War, the demography of migratory patterns has changed, and with it the ethnic and racial composition both of Britain and of her former dependencies have been transformed. In 1994, the city of Sydney won the right to host the summer Olympic games in the year 2000. The head of the Sydney committee, in a jubilant mood, announced, "We beat the Chinese," the other major contender as host for the games. His broad Australian accent did not hide the fact that he, himself, was of Chinese extraction; his family had come to Sydney thirty years earlier. He spoke for a new Australia, one with an Asian and Pacific character and consciousness very different from that dominant a century before. Migration matters.

This point leads me to my second argument: against the backdrop of this demographic history, distinctive cultural forms braided the Empire together. These forms have had a life history; some have withered away, others have endured. There is still today a common language, a shared sporting heritage, some facets of bureaucratic forms in general and educational systems in particular, all legacies of imperial administration. But other remnants of the imperial past have more specific referents, and have shown a surprising vitality despite shifts in ethnic and racial composition in both Britain and the former empire.

Some of these lasting cultural forms relate to the two world wars. In a way, remembering the terrible carnage of 1914–18 and 1939–45 has created a space in which imperial history could be written and rewritten every 11 November. Here is a moment during which the bonds which tied together communities at the ends of the earth could be (and still are) made manifest, respected, and honored. This is why the imperial monuments to the dead of the Great War still draw pilgrims by the tens of thousands today.

Many of them come to the flatlands of the River Somme, where the British army launched a massive and futile campaign on 1 July 1916. On those fields today are thousands of war cemeteries. Adjacent to them are national monuments. At Longueval, there is a South African monument; at Beaumont Hamel, the Newfoundland monument; at Villers-Bretonneux, the Australian monument; and at Thiepval, the monument to the 73,000 missing soldiers of the British Empire who died on the Somme but whose bodies were never interred. Their graves, the monument's central plaque affirms, are known but to God. These are all sites where remembering empire has been fixed in stone.

Even more powerful in its evocative and semisacred character is Gallipoli. Both there and in Australia, a dawn service is held commemorating the landing on the shores of Turkey on 25 April 1915. The public that attends these ceremonies is large and growing. And young. The date 25 April is at one and the same time Australia's day of mourning and her independence day. It is a moment when history matters.

The commemoration of the two world wars, and of the sacrifices made in them, is the most visceral and living form in which the "collective memory," in Halbwachs's sense of the term, the sense of a common history, is expressed. But it is important to register the mixed message of these occasions. The men who died in the two world wars stood on the middle ground between their countries and the British Empire. They died in an imperial effort; but they contributed not only to the survival of the Empire, but also to its supersession. The day Australians landed at Gallipoli is the day they mark the emergence of their separate and distinctive national identity. The Canadians whose deaths are commemorated at Vimy, near Arras, helped create a different kind of Canada, one with a more tenuous tie to the mother country. To remember the wars is to remember at one and the same time the apogee of imperial solidarity and the inexorable features of its demise.

Migration and Empire

The history of empire is an integral part of the history of population movements from and to the British Isles. This dual feature of demographic history is often underestimated. The demographic history of empire is marked by powerful centrifugal and centripetal forces. Only by measuring this two-way traffic can we appreciate fully the way British and imperial history have overlapped.

Out-migration in the seventeenth and eighteenth centuries was relatively modest: in those two hundred years, perhaps one million people left Britain for a new life abroad. That very rough average of five thousand departures a year was dwarfed by later surges of out-migration. Between 1815 and 1850, perhaps seven hundred fifty thousand people left the British Isles permanently. This outflow of roughly twenty thousand a year is almost certainly an underestimate. Migration statistics are a resultant of inflows and outflows. Many people chose to leave Britain for a better life, but first tried out nearby towns and then more distant cities. Internal migration prepared the way for more distant travel. Millions of people moved in a stepwise manner from country to town to city to an overseas destination. But then, sometimes years after arrival abroad, when things got hard, they came home again, only to restart the cycle. That is, by 1900 international passenger traffic was directed both ways and was repeated. Given the sharp decline in the later nineteenth century in the costs of transportation, overseas voyages became a normal part of the life cycle of a surprisingly large part of the population. How large a part it is difficult to say, but one passenger manifest from the turn of the twentieth century had it that a majority of the people on board had made the Atlantic journey at least twice in the preceding decade.

Thus the major period of out-migration from Britain in the nineteenth century, which helped people the Empire and Dominions, was also a period of return traffic from those who could not stand living abroad. That is why all migration statistics must be understood as registering multiple movements; double-counting in unavoidable. That is another reason why we should attend to trends rather than to absolute totals of immigrants whenever we address the subject of movement to and from the Empire.

One additional problem makes all British migration statistics nebulous. To this day, the movement of Irishmen and women into and out of Britain is both substantial and impossible to estimate with any precision. Migration to the United States or the Empire from Ireland took place both directly and through British ports. Those who embarked on return journeys to the British Isles landed in Ireland and in England, whatever their final destination. This is hardly surprising before the Irish Free State came into being in 1922, but it is still true today. British migration bound Britain and Ireland together even when people were trying to escape from one or the other or both.

Another major headache in handling these data is that they consist of information on people who went to imperial or Dominion territories, and those moving to the United States as well. Given the porous character of borders and the absence, prior to the First World War, of mandatory passports, we must treat overseas passenger traffic as capable of reaching a number of different destinations. In the 1880s, perhaps one-third of those who left Britain with the intention of residing abroad aimed to set up a new life in the Empire. The majority headed for America. After the turn of the century, a greater proportion of emigrants chose the Dominions over the United States.[2]

Whichever way they headed, emigrants followed well-trodden pathways. They had pretty good information on where to go and how to get there, provided by relatives, kinsmen, workmates, and friends who had come and gone, and, frequently, come again. They were making rational choices, determined as much (if not more) by the chance of a prosperous life in the receiver destinations as by disquiet or despair over their future in Britain. What demographers call the "pull" factor outweighed the "push" factor in most calculations.

With these caveats in mind, we can still provide a rough sketch of the peopling of the British Empire and Dominions over the last century or so. Figure 16 represents a summary measure of these demographic movements. It describes the pace and level of out-migration from Britain to extra-European destinations and the movement back of in-migrants to Britain from these same non-European sources. The difference between the two is the balance of population transfers out of Britain or into Britain. The net balance of migration was negative in all decades except the 1930s and 1980s. I shall return to this point in a moment.

Some significant trends began before the turn of the century and therefore prior to the time frame shown in Figure 16. There were two major surges of out-migration from Britain in 1879–93 and 1903–14. To give some idea of the magnitude of this movement of populations, we can use complete data for the years 1911–14, years for which accurate passenger surveys are available. In those four years alone,

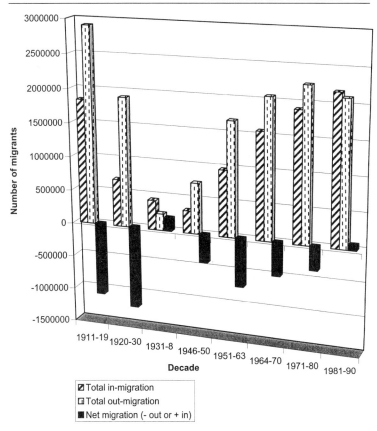

Fig. 16. Net migration in and out of Britain, 1911–1990.

more than 2.4 million people left Britain for extra-European destinations. But at the same time, more than 1 million people came
home from these very same foreign ports. That left the balance of
out-migration as exceeding 1.2 million. If two-thirds of these depart-
ing Britons reached imperial and Dominion ports,[3] and stayed
there, we can estimate the British population trying out the Empire
and Dominions before the Great War at about 1.5 million. Of these
people, half made their homes abroad.

These were exceptional years. The volume of this traffic was unparalleled and has not been matched since. Given the eighteenth-century average of about five thousand out-migrants a year, and the mid-nineteenth-century average of about twenty thousand out-migrants a year, we have reason to be impressed with the pre–First World War *annual* average of roughly three hundred thousand out-migrants.

The Great War ended this extraordinary chapter in the history of British migration. Indeed, the toll of human life in the war, as catastrophic as it was, was less than the total loss of population from Britain due to out-migration in the years 1911–14.[4] There was a net inflow of population into Britain from extra-European ports during the war, reflecting a return of British-born men to join the army as much as the shortage of shipping to deliver out-migrants to distant destinations.

Figure 16 illustrates the peak of British out-migration to extra-European destinations between 1911 and 1919. The post–1919 data are strikingly different. Out-migration in the 1920s diminished substantially, but in-migration fell even more sharply. Thus the net balance outward in the 1920s was higher than in the decade of the war. In the 1930s, migratory movements shrank substantially, and net migration turned positive, that is, toward increasing the home population. After the Second World War, out-migration picked up again, but in-migration grew faster still until the 1980s, when, once again, the British population was augmented by in-migrants. The break in the trend which peopled the Empire and Dominions is located in the decade of the 1914–18 war.

What made the war so decisive in the history of international migration was its effects on the political and economic context in which it took place. First, the gates came down on American immigration. Through three changes in immigration law in 1920, 1924, and 1929, the era of essentially free entry to the United States came to an end. Secondly, the economic troubles of postwar adjustment, and of the interwar depression as a whole, touched agricultural regions with particular force. These contractions made it difficult for receiver countries to absorb new immigrants, and for the prospective immigrants to calculate that they would do better in Auckland than in Accrington. Thirdly, the link between capital formation and migration in Britain and the United States, classically analyzed by Brinley Thomas thirty years ago,[5] began to unravel. The ties connecting the two sides of the Atlantic economy were transformed by the reversal of the creditor-debtor relationship as between Britain and the United States.

There were attempts after 1918 to restore immigrant pathways. An Overseas Settlement Committee (later Overseas Settlement Board) was established at the British Colonial Office in 1919. It oversaw emigration schemes, conducted publicity campaigns to advertise the virtues of settlement in the Dominions, and brought together interested parties such as philanthropic agencies, shipping companies, and veterans' organizations. These last were particularly important in the immediate postwar years, when the British government launched a Free Passage Scheme to assist ex-soldiers who wanted to start a new life in the Dominions. The Empire Settlement Act of 1922 provided £3 million a year to encourage British emigration. The Act was renewed in 1937 for a further fifteen years and dispensed a smaller budget, as did successor bodies empowered by post–1945 legislation to facilitate British migration to the Dominions.

These measures had some effect, and eased the passage of a steady but diminishing migratory stream in the postwar decades. But on balance, the effort to revive earlier demographic trends was unsuccessful for complex reasons located in the domestic history of the receiver countries as much as in the history of Britain itself. Many of the post–1918 schemes suffered from a surfeit of ideological conservatism. Some political leaders believed that people move across continents primarily for ideological reasons. Migrants had to follow the flag, so as to ensure the defense of the mother country. Others voiced, in so many words, older notions about the merits of getting rid of as many working-class men and women as could be siphoned out of an overstocked domestic labor market.

There were political echoes on the receiving end too. British migrants were of the right ethnic stock. To some of those in power in the Dominions, these British emigrants, unwanted in Lancashire, were at least better than eastern and southern European immigrants (or, later, African and Asian immigrants), who threatened to transform the ethnic character of Canada or Australia. Such notions were not unknown in Commonwealth Labor movements as well.

But what many proponents of British immigration to the Dominions ignored was the fact that the interests of Britain and of the Dominions were not identical, their labor markets were not symmetrical, and political slogans would do little to ease the absorption of newcomers to environments which were remote from Britain. The harsh realities of life on the Canadian prairies or on Australian farms were no secret; immigrants wrote home and came home. That is why, even during the worst years of the Depression, the period 1929–32, emigration from Britain never approached even a fraction of its pre–1914 levels. Indeed, as Figure 16 shows, British out-migration in the period 1931–38 turned negative. That is, more people were returning from extra-European destinations than were embarking on journeys toward them.

The Second World War was a second trough in the pattern of twentieth-century migration from or to Britain. But after 1945, the pace of migratory movement picked up. This is disclosed in Figure 16. But what we cannot see in the graph is that migration changed color.[6] The ethnic composition of in-migrants after 1945 was strikingly different from that of earlier cohorts.

In the immediate postwar years, 1946–50, both out-migration

and in-migration were constricted by the shortage of shipping, the stickiness of the labor market in Britain, and variations in demands for labor in receiver states. After 1950, migratory flows increased in both directions, while the net balance of out-migration fell in a stepwise manner, so that by the 1980s in-migration was greater than out-migration. In sum, Figure 16 discloses two trends: the first is the closure of the pre-1914 immigrant wave; the second is the transformation of Britain from being a net supplier to a net receiver of extra-European populations.

After 1945, American developments lay behind British trends. The McCarran-Walter Act of 1952 further restricted the right of entry of groups not already well-represented in the American population. Among them were West Indians, who increasingly saw Britain as their primary destination. In 1948, roughly five hundred West Indians immigrated to Britain. In 1954, the number rose to nine thousand. Between 1952 and 1961, about three hundred thousand West Indians came to Britain to stay.

By that time, they had been joined by a substantial inflow of immigrants from the Indian subcontinent. In the early 1960s, between seventy thousand and one hundred thousand people arrived in Britain from India and Pakistan. Then came one hundred eleven thousand Asian immigrants from Kenya and Uganda, fleeing from political disorder and persecution between 1968 and 1975. Successive Commonwealth Immigration Acts in 1962, 1968, and 1971 established controls for this inflow. Alongside these queues of newcomers were Europeans, many from eastern and southern Europe, and the perennial Irishmen. Their right to settle in Britain became entangled in the politics of European integration. By the late 1980s, the share in overall immigration of people from the old Dominions had been reduced substantially, to about 36 percent of all newcomers. As in all other domains, British history had entered European history, and by doing so, a chapter had closed both in the story of population movements from and to Britain, and in the story of the overlapping history of Britain, the Empire, and the Dominions.

The data in Figure 16 summarize these trends. There is a linear decline of out-migration in the three decades between 1911 and 1938. After the Second World War, out-migration to extra-European destinations rose again, but so did in-migration. Indeed the gap between the two continued to close, so that by the 1980s there was a net balance inward. Given the strength of in-migration from Conti nental Europe over the same period, it is fair to say that by the end of the twentieth century, Britain had become a receiver state for a wide array of people born elsewhere who chose to make it their home. The political economy of out-migration, so evident on the left side of Figure 16, was over.

The Audit of War

So far, I have surveyed the history of the peopling of the Empire and the Dominions in terms of the life decisions millions of men and women took (and took again) about where to live and where to stake a claim to a better future. I have shown that the peak of the imperial moment, registered in terms of high out-migration to the Empire and the Dominions, came before 1914. The Great War, therefore, inaugurated a period of diminishing demographic linkages between Britain and the old Empire, reconstituted first as Dominions and then as the Commonwealth.

This is an essential part of the story, but not the only one. There is a countervailing and, to a degree, contradictory story which works the other way. The Great War and, to a lesser though similar degree, the Second World War were periods when the linkages between the mother country and the diaspora grew stronger. That strength is reflected in Table I, enumerating the contribution of the Empire and the Dominions to the two wars in the stark category of loss of life.

Table I. Aspects of War Losses in the Two World Wars, in British and Some Dominion and Imperial Armies and Populations

	Population—1914 (millions, estimated)	First World War Population Killed (estimated) Total (thousands)	(per thousand)
Australia	4.9	60 (1.22%)	12
Canada	8.1	61 (0.75%)	8
India	321.8	54 (0.00%)	0
New Zealand	1.1	16 (1.45%)	15
South Africa	6.3	7 (0.11%)	11
United Kingdom	45.2	723 (1.60)	16
Total	387.4	921	

	Population—1939 (millions, estimated)	Second World War Population Killed (estimated) Total (thousands)	(per thousand)	As percentage of 1914—18 losses
Australia	7.7	21 (0.27%)	3	35%
Canada	11.5	41 (0.36%)	4	67%
India	380	36 (0.00%)	0	67%
New Zealand	1.7	13 (0.76%)	8	82%
South Africa	11.4	3.9 (0.03%)	3	55%
United Kingdom	46	254 (0.55%)	6	35%
Total	458.3	368.9		40%

Sources: J. M. Winter, The Great War and the British People, p. 75; Winter, "The Demography of the War," in M. R. D. Foot and R. Dear (eds), The Oxford Companion to the Second World War, p. 290.

The table provides information on prewar population totals, totals of military losses, as well as a rough comparison of these losses as a percentage of the total population.

As Table I shows, nearly 1.3 million men died in military service from these six countries in the two world wars. Over 900,000 died in the 1914–18 war. Whereas the total population of the six allies rose from about 387 million in 1914 to 458 million in 1939, an increase of 18 percent, the loss of life in the Second World War was less than half as great as in the Great War.

For our purposes, it is perhaps most important to underscore the total losses of Australia, Canada, New Zealand, India, and South Africa in the two wars. Over 300,000 men from what might be termed the "British diaspora" died during active service, and I want to chart that heavy, perhaps decisive, contribution to victory in the two world wars, and then turn to its commemoration as a subject which discloses the work of collective memory in creating another, still living, history of the Empire. After 1918, when the political, demographic and economic ties holding Britain and her dependencies together were beginning to coming apart, tens of thousands of families recovered those bonds through commemorative practices. Those sites of memory are well known, but perhaps less acknowledged is their power in turning the history of the Empire into family history, and family history of a tragic kind.

What commemoration succeeded in doing is to transform the history of nations into the narrative of thousands of family units. In the field of commemorative practice, small-scale activities usually last longer than large-scale ones, though there are exceptions to this rule.[7] Memorial services, pilgrimages, and other signifying practices on the local as much as the national level annually re-create families small and large; they even "re-create" the British Empire, understood in the fullest sense as a family of nations with a common history, if not a common future. That family remembers its dead anew each year on 11 November, and in Australia and New Zealand on 25 April. In recent years, more and more young people have flocked to the ceremonies, though any recollection of the Empire's *mission civilatrice* is not for them, nor is any Churchillian rhetoric on the empire as bulwark against communism. Their memory of empire is rooted in the experience of war and dominated by the shadow of bereavement.

Military Participation and Military Losses

The demography of Empire accounts for the mobilization of imperial armies in 1914. Formally, Dominions reserved the right to consider matters as weighty as a declaration of war; but in the event, Britain's declaration of war in 1914 spilled over through a kind of imperial osmosis to her Dominions. And hardly anyone objected.

The rush to the colors in Britain in 1914 was matched by a surge of voluntary enlistment in Australia, Canada, New Zealand, and South Africa. And this was hardly surprising. Half of the men who joined up in Australia had been born in Britain. That comma in the 1904 pledge of allegiance described the link between the two sides of their double identity—British and Australian. And an unstable identity it was. Return migration was a well-traveled path in the prewar period. Joining up in 1914 was a reflection of demographic realities. It described who the newcomers to the Dominions were: the bulk were young, British-born men of military age.

Enlistment statistics tell us who these men were in 1914, but not who they were to become in the subsequent four years of combat and beyond. And that is the great irony of the war. Military service began as a natural outcome of the geographical dispersion of the British population. But by 1918, the armies of the Dominions had, as it were, left behind the comma—and the imperial past it embodied. In Australia, New Zealand, and Canada a separate national identity emerged out of imperial military service and sacrifice. The men who returned from the field were less British than those who had gone off to fight. The tie to Britain was still there, though palpably and permanently transformed.

The statistics in Table I describe aspects of the heavy contribution the Empire and Dominions made to the war. The figures are incomplete, since they do not incorporate data on other dependencies, for instance Newfoundland or the West Indies, which also put men in uniform during the war. In addition, thousands of men from the Dominions served in British forces. Fuller statistics would only reinforce the impression left here. In Australia, Canada, New Zealand, and South Africa, over 1.3 million men enlisted. Of this total, 144,000 were killed. This proportion of one man killed for every nine who served is about the same as the British figure. Another 1 million men served in the Indian army, and of these 54,000 were killed.

These soldiers, and the war economies behind them, made a difference—some would say a decisive difference—in the outcome of the war. They provided the backup which the German army never had.[8] The shadow of empire mattered. And not only in terms of numbers. About one-third of those who served as pilots in British forces came from Canada. Australian engineers got the knack of the artillery war—and the crucial element of counter-battery operations— at least as rapidly as (and some would say much faster than) their British brethren. The Dominions and Empire not only sent men, they provided the cash to equip them, the wheat to feed them, and the loans which the mother country needed to finance the exponential growth in transport, communication, and services. The Empire helped in crucial ways to put these armies in the field and keep them there.

These Dominion troops are known by their role in particular military operations. The Anzacs, I have already noted, landed on

Gallipoli in the early hours of 25 April 1915. The expedition failed, and the landing force was ultimately withdrawn eight months later. But to most Australians, their landing was a victory. The defeat was a British, not an Australian, affair. Canadians, South Africans, New Zealanders, and Australians also separate the dignity of their men who fought and died on the Somme in 1916 or at the Third Battle of Ypres in 1917—both defeats—from the indignity of British military thinking and the incompetence of British military leadership.

That is one reason why those who believed in Empire or in a modified form of British hegemony through her Dominions could look back with pride on this moment of solidarity. But if there ever was a Pyrrhic victory, this was it. For the very defense of Empire helped ensure its demise. The toll in lives was too great ever to repeat; the costs were too high in every other sense to enable a weakened British economy even to contemplate a military effort on the scale of that of the Great War. What price victory? One answer was the unraveling of the British alliance of motherland, Dominions, and Empire.

A reflection of that change may be found in the statistics we have already surveyed of diminishing emigration from Britain to the Dominions in the interwar years. But another element in the story of what was lost in 1914–18 may be discerned in the nature and dimensions of the war effort the second time around, in 1939–45. The initial difference is that when Britain went to war on 3 September 1939, the Dominions took the news in, reflected on it, and then made their own decisions. Canada deliberated for a week, and then went to war. So did Australia and New Zealand. And so (with a bit more difficulty) did South Africa, then led by the veteran imperial statesman Jan Christiaan Smuts, who ordered the arrest of some Afrikaners who preferred the Nazis to the British. (It is to Smuts, by the way, that we owe the phrase "the Commonwealth of Nations," which he used in 1917 to describe the British alliance in the First World War.

The term "the Commonwealth" was officially sanctioned in the Statute of Westminster in 1931.)

The war the Commonwealth fought in 1939–45 was strikingly different from that of 1914–18. Statistics of military participation reflect this contrast. The population mobilized was greater, and the death toll was lower. This lesser degree of lethality in warfare had three sources. The first was the conviction in 1939, shared by leaders and public opinion alike, that the kind of bloodshed which arose from the stalemate of the Western Front could not be permitted again. When the Soviet Union entered the war in 1941, that carnage was repeated throughout eastern Europe, but not in those theaters of military operations in which British and allied forces operated. British and German soldiers did not use gas weapons against each other in 1939–45 as they had done in 1914–18. Secondly, military medicine had advanced so substantially that the chances of surviving a battlefield wound in the Second World War were much greater than in the First. And thirdly, the 1939–45 conflict was much more a naval war than the 1914–18 one. Supplying armies in both the European and the Asian theaters required an even greater emphasis on naval and shipping power than had been evident twenty-five years earlier. And naval war is less lethal than land war.

Again, a caveat is in order when surveying the data in Table I. These data are incomplete and illustrate only very rough estimates of casualty levels. They make no mention of the approximately sixty-thousand British civilians who died in the Blitz. The absolute values registered here matter less than what they tell us about the comparative toll in human lives taken by the two world wars. Approximately eighty thousand Australian, New Zealand, Canadian, and South African men lost their lives in the Second World War; this was approximately half the total of the First World War. There were variations: the total killed among New Zealanders who served in 1939–45 was roughly 82 percent of the total killed in 1914–18. But both British and Australian losses were roughly a third of those suffered in the Great War.

In general, British and Dominion forces fought together and saw their efforts as unified in the Second World War. But some military operations opened a yawning gap between and among allies. When Singapore was taken on 15 February 1942, 122,000 men surrendered. Some of the Australian men captured blamed the British for the disaster, and for the hardships of the next three years of incarceration at Changi prison camp or further north in Burma. The Canadian Second Division led the probe on German defenses at Dieppe in France in August 1942. This commando raid turned into a disaster: British losses totaled 132, Canadian losses 2,853. Canadian bitterness about the Dieppe raid has still not abated.

As in the Great War, the economic element in the allied victory was decisive. Here too the Dominions (alongside the United States) shored up a British economy unable to bear the costs of war alone. If the Great War substantially weakened the British economy, the Second World War impoverished it. Once the Atlantic Alliance was cemented—prior to the Japanese attack on Pearl Harbor—the time when Britain could claim to be a "superpower" was at an end.

And so was the dependent status of former Dominions and imperial possessions. Once more, the immigration statistics after 1945 prove the point. The ties between Britain and the Dominions were maintained, but the human flow which had created them diminished and changed in both character and color. From the mid–1950s, immigration to Britain from the West Indies and the Indian subcontinent outpaced emigration from Britain to the old Dominions.

The Second World War was a critical moment in this transition. India became independent in 1947, and after the fiasco of Suez in 1956, when the overwhelming weight of American power forced Britain to retreat from an imperialist venture to "protect" the Suez Canal, the notion that British power was reflected in her power to act anywhere in the world had to be abandoned. The use of military force against the Argentine army in the Falkland Islands in 1982 was like a nova—a brief glimpse of a world which had exploded long ago.

Commemoration

How has that imperial moment been remembered? What lingering traces exist in our own times? Here we confront a classic instance of nostalgic commemoration. When a phenomenon passes away, its shadow becomes fixed through commemorative practice. What the French historian Pierre Nora calls *milieux de mémoire* are replaced by *lieux de mémoire*.[9] At times, this act is manipulative. Elites create traditions to justify their own hold on power. But at other times, and imperial commemorations are a case in point, they also reflect broader cultural forces.

There is an abundant literature surrounding the theme of imperialism in British popular culture. My own view of the subject is that its significance has been greatly exaggerated. The Empire did matter in the vernacular of working-class life. It was there in music hall songs and vaudeville acts. But it did not have the hold on either the imagination or the political beliefs which some historians have supposed.

Empire Day is a case in point. It was established in 1896 on 24 May, Queen Victoria's birthday, to celebrate her realm and the imperial vision it embodied. The work of elites in broadcasting this message is evident. Empire Day became a national holiday in Canada in 1897, in Australia in 1905, in New Zealand and South Africa in 1910, and in India in 1923. There were Empire Shopping Weeks, proclaiming the virtues of goods from the Dominions, and an active Empire Marketing Board, with exports also in mind in the interwar years. The right-wing newspaper *Daily Express,* owned by the Canadian magnate Lord Beaverbrook, organized Pageants of Empire and sponsored song fests in Hyde Park to celebrate the Empire and Dominions. In 1924 there was a massive Empire Exhibition at Wembley in London. The King spoke at its opening, and the BBC broadcast the address. Its director general, Sir John Reith, was a fervent sponsor of this campaign. These broadcasts went on until the late 1950s, at which time Empire Day became Commonwealth Day.[10]

Now it is just a memory. When asked a few years ago, none of my students at Cambridge knew when Commonwealth Day was. To them the Commonwealth is a grant-giving body which subsidizes students coming to Britain—nothing less and nothing more. Imperial propaganda from on high has not left lasting traces, and (though it would be difficult to prove) it is my view that it had little effect even during its heyday. The reason is that when the demographic links that were tying together families scattered throughout the Dominions began to fade, when the apogee of emigration had passed, the Empire was only a marginal part of family history. Of much greater and lasting significance was (and is) war and the remembrance of the fallen.

This is why war memorials matter still. They convert world history into the history of the household. Ceremonies surrounding them bring the past into the rhythms of the present. They represent what the Australian historian Ken Inglis has called a semisacred space, a place where people remote from the churches can meditate on sacred themes.[11]

In the nineteenth century, core and periphery retained elements of a loosely defined Christian culture.[12] By the mid to late twentieth century, those forms had atrophied. It is not that a sense of the sacred is absent from British or Dominions' cultural life; rather, it is no longer sought within the churches. Instead, commemorative forms redefine sacred space in a way more palatable to a non-churchgoing, more heterogeneous, multiethnic population.

Many war memorials adopt an allegorical style, fashioning

figures or symbols of heroism, solidarity, and sacrifice, in a wide array of images and structures. Figurative art is much more prominent in First World War monuments than in those commemorating later conflicts. Styles change and so do commemorative forms. Christian notation is common in many war memorials located in churches and schools. But in civic space, more ecumenical messages were cast in stone. The most prominent of them all is Sir Edwin Lutyens's Cenotaph in London. It is a Greek form, an empty tomb. It bears a medieval sword in the shape of a cross, but the design was so clearly non-Christian that the Dean of Westminster nearly went apoplectic at its unveiling in 1919. Dean Inge's objection was not felt by millions of pilgrims who came to that spot and paid their respects to the dead in subsequent years. Lutyens's sculpture, to everyone's surprise, became both the British and the imperial war memorial. It announced that remembering the dead went beyond Christianity, since the Empire had lost sons who were of many faiths and of none. When the time came to recall those who had died in the 1939–45 war, it was obvious that the Cenotaph was the place to do so.

Cenotaphs are to be found throughout the Dominions. Other monumental forms repeat Lutyens's message. Sir Herbert Baker's Indian motifs in his facades surrounding the Indian Memorial at Neuve Chapelle created spaces for Hindu and Muslim alike. The cemeteries of the Imperial (now Commonwealth) War Graves Commission all bear an altar of sacrifice with words chosen by Rudyard Kipling from the apocryphal book of Ecclesiasticus, "There names liveth for evermore." But the cemeteries are hardly Christian in character, resembling a scattering of small- to medium-sized English country gardens in the countryside of Picardy and Flanders. Indeed, the war cemeteries of Republican France are more Christian, with row upon row of crosses, than are those of the Commonwealth, where each grave is marked by a headstone, not a cross.

Instead of providing a framework for a specifically Christian message, war memorials provided another kind of reference. Here the local took the place of the imperial, as if to remind visitors that those who died did so in the belief that they were defending very local landscapes. That is why the garden setting and floral displays matter so much; they are so evidently British in a stylized, bucolic way. Other local symbols reinforce the point in different ways. There is a caribou atop a rock on the Newfoundland memorial at Beaumont-Hamel. There is an Ulster tower near Thiepval, and a complete South African blockhouse at Longueval.

When we leave the battlefields and visit the tens of thousands of war memorials in towns and villages throughout the Dominions, this sense of place is stronger still. In the Australian city of Perth there is an avenue of oak and plane trees, planted in 1920 by relatives of the men of Western Australia who died in the war. It is a surrogate cemetery; the men who left this port city to go off to war and who died abroad lie eight thousand miles away. The names of the dead soldier and of the relative who planted each sapling are listed together on each tree in the Avenue of Honour, as though their bonds would be preserved by the spread of these ample trees, which form a majestic promenade today. "I do not know where the body of my boy lies," said a Perth woman in mourning for her son, "but his soul is here."[13]

In the vast majority of cases, Second World War memorials on the local level were affixed to those built to commemorate the dead of the Great War. The names were fewer, and the sense of the overlap between the two conflicts justified their elision in stone. More prominent regimental and national monuments to the dead of the Second World War were built, but it is to the local sites of memory that most commemorative practices are attached. That is where the names are.

Kipling was right. The names are what matter most. In the Antipodes, Canada, South Africa, or India, where distance makes pilgrimage very arduous, the names are indeed all which remain. Every one of them is inscribed on the walls of the Australian War Memorial in Canberra. But names matter just as much in Britain: two-thirds of all men who died during active service in British forces in the Great War have no known grave. The practice of naming on local war memorials is therefore profoundly significant.[14] It enabled ordinary people to locate this monumental moment in the history of the Empire within their own family narratives. The names help them to return to the family units which created the Empire and Dominions. In a sense, touching the names, or just visiting the war memorials and placing on them a poppy, is a vital element in the preservation of the memory of empire. Collective memory never exists in a vacuum; it is created by action, in this case by over eighty years of commemorative activity.

What did people understand by the term *Empire,* when located in this context? My belief is that when people spoke of the Empire at war memorials, they meant less a political or racial project than a collection of towns and villages scattered throughout the world but which still had something in common. There is an element of distortion in this view, to be sure. But in analyzing the way terms were used in the past when exploring the vernacular, we all too frequently miss the particular in the general. One soldier of the London regiment was asked by a journalist in 1915 if he was fighting for the Empire; he answered with a robust yes. He later explained to a buddy that what he meant was that he was fighting for the Empire Music Hall in Hackney.[15]

Now that the Empire is virtually a memory, what remains of it are the shadows of its history, shadows which are cast on many parts of the world. And yet this shared history is surprisingly alive today. For elites from the Commonwealth, a couple of years at a British university is still part of the breeding which up and coming men and women should enjoy. But there is a more popular, more diffuse bond between Britain and her former dependencies arising out of a common history. Fiction returns to it. In Australia it is to be found in the novels of David Malouf, *Fly Away Peter*, which is about the 1914–18 war, or *The Big World*, which is about the Changi prisoner-of-war camp in the Second World War. In Britain, it is located in the novels of Sebastian Faulks: *Birdsong* (about the Great War) and *Charlotte Grey* (about the Second World War, with a glance back to the trauma of the First).

In recent years, too, young people in Australia and Britain have taken up older commemorative forms and have breathed new life into them. As I have already noted, Australia's unknown soldier was buried in Canberra with full military honors in 1993. Here was a symbol of independence: no longer would the unknown soldier buried in Westminster Abbey stand for Australians who had died. Yet the tenor of the event was not anti-British; it reinforced the ties which led these men to fight alongside Britain. Those in attendance were of all age groups, though they were disproportionately young. The dawn service at Gallipoli draws increasing numbers of people. The campaign in Britain to restore the commemoration of Armistice day to 11 November and not leave it to the Sunday nearest to that date is surprisingly strong and, according to some, likely to succeed. Why does it matter still? Because collective memory is still firmly ensconced in family history. Acts of shared remembrance require a time and place at which they can be expressed. Without a place, or a substitute for a lost home, collective memory vanishes. War memorials create such a focus of attention, a site where a past can be evoked, re-created, perhaps misinterpreted, but in any event kept alive. If you want to find remains of the history of the Empire today, you should look beyond Hackney. They are present in thousands of villages and towns, in the countries of the Commonwealth, where the names of the fallen still face passers-by in market squares and before town halls. The family of nations which was the Empire is there, expressed not in grandiose rhetoric but in the local, the small scale, the ordinary: just names. Those names disclose a moment when family history collided with world history, leaving traces, indelible traces we can see to this day.

Those traces are now part of the landscape of towns peopled by men and women from other places and with other histories. The collective memories they bring with them when they immigrate are not the same. Their rich contribution to the cultural life of Britain, Canada, Australia, New Zealand, and elsewhere is overwhelmingly clear. My argument is that their presence in these countries has changed the character of the collective; and thereby, they have helped shift the pattern of remembrance in their new communities. Remembrance has become more decentralized, more linked to smaller groups, towns, villages, families.

In future what forms these cultural patterns will take is anyone's guess. But it is evident that students of collective memory must study the shifting demographic profiles of the populations doing the remembering. Demography matters in our understanding of the cultural history of remembrance, and scholars who ignore the links between them do so at their own peril.

Part Three

Theaters of Memory

CHAPTER 8

Grand Illusions
War, Film, and Collective Memory

One of the unfortunate features of the memory boom is the tendency of commentators to term any and every narrative of past events as constituents of national memory or collective memory, understood as the shared property of the citizenry of a state. Nowhere is this more evident than in the case of film. Time and again the claim is made that the way cinema presents the past somehow passes in an unmediated manner into something termed memory. A straight line is drawn linking imagery and memory on the national scale.[1]

To be sure, cinema and other visual images have been crucial lenses through which we have peered while sifting through the ground in our ruminations about the past. Cinema provides icons and frameworks in which we locate the stories we tell about the past, but to call the products of the cinema industry of a nation its national memory is to confuse choreography with content, and to ignore the complex interaction of the two.

I shall make reference later in this book to Walter Benjamin's aperçu that "memory is not an instrument for exploring the past but its theatre."[2] This statement finds no truer expression than in the cinema, that theater of memories which defies categorization in something as crudely constructed as the concept of national memory.

In this field mediations multiply so rapidly that the link between imagery and memory, however defined, immediately becomes tenuous. Consider but one level of mediation—the difference in the meaning of the term *memory* among different age groups, some who were alive when the filmic event in question took place and those who were not yet born. Films, documentary or fictional, may indeed evoke memories of events for people who lived through those depicted on the screen. What they take away from the cinema is a mixture of earlier memories and the filmic images they have just seen. However, if these people attend the very same film with their grandchildren, who were not born when the screen events took place, then it is impossible to conclude that the film evokes memories in their grandchildren in any way comparable to those the grandparents have. And yet many discussions of film and collective memory make this elementary mistake.

Memory is not additive. Different cohorts cannot simply and easily be conflated into something called collective memory, especially if it is packaged in national terms. Take but one example—Steven Spielberg's film *Saving Private Ryan,* to which we will refer in a moment. Second World War veterans who see the film may have memories triggered about their combat experience. Vietnam veterans may have their different combat experiences brought to mind by the film, and those too young to have fought in either war will respond to the film through the stories they have heard from their elders and from many other sources, including other films. Add up just these three groups' memories and you wind up not with collective memory but with collected memories stratified by age and experience. Different cohorts have different memories and draw on different representations which are not identical. They are exposed to various narratives of the past, and film is a very powerful source of such narratives, but to call these narratives collective memory is to turn a very complex phenomenon into something so vague as to mean virtually nothing.

In this context, Benjamin's reflections provide a better point of departure for a discussion of these issues. In a sense, there is no better instance of Benjamin's notion of theaters of memory than the cinematic. I use the plural advisedly, since it is evident that the theater of memory constructed by those who have lived through events is not at all the same reflective space inhabited by the rest of us. How much harder it is, therefore, to accept the claim that film is a source of one national "theater of memory" which we all, or rather all inhabitants of a particular nation, inhabit.

A more constructive approach sees film as one of the mediators of the memories of particular groups. Collective remembrance, as I have tried to employ the term, is the set of memories expressed in public by different collectives. The memories of these groups are mediated by collective cultural practices, one of the most significant of which is film, but the fact that we share and acknowledge common mediators does not prove that we share common memories.

One of the greatest problems with the contemporary memory boom is precisely this error. People refer to collective memory or national memory without reflecting on what these terms actually mean. The pathway many commentators sketch is clear: film produces memories among national filmgoers, who thereby imbibe particular narratives about the past. Whether political leaders or Hollywood producers pull the strings of this bit of puppeteering is irrelevant; the effect is what matters. This functionalist bias in our understanding of how memory—individual, social, collective—is manufactured is simply too crude to accept, and yet it is a point of view to be found in even the most sophisticated analyses of cultural constructions of the past in film, art, and literature.

As a counterpoint, I want to suggest that while film mediates the construction of individual and group memories, and in particular memories of war, it does so in ways which are never mechanical and which, in their variety and subtle power, reach different collectives in different ways. Film disturbs as many narratives as it confirms. Cinema in general, or any film in particular, seen as an uncontested, coherent embodiment of national memory is, I hold, a grand illusion.

The Grand Illusion

In the preliminary stages of work on the construction of a museum of the history of the First World War at Péronne on the river Somme, I asked a number of French veterans of the war what kind of films they wanted to have shown in the museum. Three of them responded directly to the question, and all said the same thing. The film they wanted to see in the museum was Jean Renoir's *The Grand Illusion*.

The choice made by soldiers who had seen combat, "ceux de '14," of poetry to express a "truth" about the war, in this case filmic poetry in one of the great imaginative moments in cinema, raises central questions about our understanding of the status and character of films about war, and the way they frame personal and collective memories. Renoir's film does not show a single combat scene, and yet I am not alone in the view that it is an unmatched elegy, an illuminated poem throwing a flood of light on what war is. That is what these men were saying by choosing this one film to be shown in a museum about their war, the Great War. Their personal memories of war were touched by Renoir's masterpiece.

But it is very difficult to see how this film evokes something which may be termed collective memory, aside from the memories of the groups of people who lived through the war. Is the film central to our collective memory? That is the question I would like to pose, and to answer in the negative.

When it came out in 1937, Renoir's film puzzled everyone. Was it pacifist? Hardly, when the "Marseillaise" is sung in a rousing scene clearly stolen a few years later in *Casablanca*. Was it nationalist?

Hardly; it was kind to the Germans; it showed Erich von Stroheim in tragic light; his stereotypical national stiffness as a Prussian officer was explained by a steel brace and other metal "gifts" in his body from his war service. Was it formulated in terms of class consciousness? Yes and no. Renoir was a man of the left, but in his film, Pierre Fresnay, the French aristocrat and counterpart of von Stroheim, gives his life for two commoners; in fact, one was a Jew. The world, Fresnay tells his social equal and captor von Stroheim, has no further need of them. Here is the vision of the Popular Front. What did the title mean? That war would return; that after the war, the commoner hero, Jean Gabin, would return to the German widow he came to love, Dita Parlo? Seventy years later we are still perplexed by this work of genius.

The Grand Illusion is a unique work, in some respects unparalleled in the history of cinema. But its example does suggest the danger of treating any film directly and in an unmediated way as a text of collective memory, however that concept is defined. To be sure, this is especially the case in works of artistic originality and power.

Like poetry, film—film at the highest level—does not instruct or indicate or preach. It ministers; it challenges conventional categories of thought; it moves the viewer. Other films do so to a lesser degree, but no film is strictly didactic, since images have a power to convey messages of many kinds, some intentional, some not.

Even if we take account of the exceptional nature of *The Grand Illusion*, it is still evident that the linkage between film and collective memory presents real pitfalls. Understanding the power of film to serve as a mediator of prior and current memories helps us appreciate the dangers of analyzing film as if it were a transparent and unproblematic device for the construction of acceptable narratives about the past.

There is one further problem which emerges here. The film

industry was international virtually from the start, but one of the difficulties in much of the literature on the role of film in the construction of memories of war is that it treats collective memory as national memory. Three studies of filmic representations of war in Britain, the United States, and Russia are cases in point. In reviewing their arguments, we can appreciate more fully both the current fascination with memory and the consistent imprecision with which scholars attempt to bridge the gap between representations of war and collective memories of it, however that term is defined.

Grand Illusions: Film and Collective Memories of the Second World War

The three scholars in question are eminent practitioners of twentieth-century history. Geoff Eley is one of the foremost historians of modern Germany and has written authoritatively as well on the history of the European left in the twentieth century. John Bodnar is among the leading cultural historians of twentieth-century America. Denise Youngblood has done pioneering work on the social history of Soviet cinema. Their mastery of the sources is unquestioned. but when even scholars of this level of distinction enter into the field of memory, they seem to lose some of the rigor so patently evident in the rest of their work.[3]

The framework of analysis in all three cases is similar. Each author relates film to an inchoate yet dynamic category roughly termed *collective memory,* understood in national terms. Perhaps the term collective memory is intended to follow Maurice Halbwachs's original usage; perhaps not. The term is simply used without interrogation. Since we are never told precisely what this category is, it is difficult to see how it might relate to other adjacent notions used in these articles: "popular memory" (Eley, p. 31), "authentic memory" (Youngblood, p. 32), or "cultural memory" (Bodnar, pp. 4, 17).

Without precise categories of analysis, the structure of interpretation is bound to remain vague and to a degree unsatisfactory.

Thus we are invited in these essays to relate film to something called collective memory and to do so in the context of cinematic reflections on the Second World War in Britain, the Soviet Union, and the United States. What is it that we learn of these three countries' cultural history from the authors' analysis of film? In Bodnar's discussion, we learn that Spielberg's *Saving Private Ryan* encapsulates a shift from framing the war experience in terms of collective trajectories—democracy, freedom, welfare, the icons of politics in the 1940s—to individual trajectories. Indeed, Bodnar follows de Capra in seeing the turn to the past, in this case past of the Second World War, in terms of individual memory, as a renunciation of political commitments tout court. This is his reading of the last scene in *Saving Private Ryan*, in which the surviving hero visits the graves of the men who died in the mission which brought him back home. He asks his wife to confirm that he was a good man and had led a good life. The individual, Bodnar suggests, is the measure of the worthwhile character of the sacrifice of soldiers in war.

Consider an alternate reading of this scene. In pilgrimages to cemeteries and battlefields, the notion of symbolic exchange dominates the structure of feeling and behavior. Those who return to these places confront the names of people who gave everything. What can the visitor give in turn? A small bunch of flowers, a personal offering, perhaps? But of equal importance is the statement that the sacrifice palpably evident in the cemetery has produced something which transcends it. The search for some redemptive meaning is at the heart of social and collective languages of mourning. These are hardly matters of individual valuation or construction. *Saving Private Ryan* ends on a collective note: the gesture of redemption, here secularized, has many equivalents in both world wars. What makes it sustainable in this context is that it dealt with the Western Front of the Second World War. When applied to the east, and in particular to the Holocaust, then it is much harder to justify.

But Spielberg himself has tried to do so. The end of *Schindler's List* shows the descendants of the men and women Schindler rescued putting pebbles on his gravestone in Jerusalem. "The people of Israel live," is how a religious person might configure it. The collective survived, and Schindler was one of those who, by saving a single life, saved the world entire. Spielberg is clearly interested in individual stories, but his notation is hardly the denial of collectivities Bodnar imagines it to be.

Other facets of Bodnar's handling of the subject of memory and collective behavior make one pause, too. He claims that "contests over public remembering were certainly not pervasive in most nations after World War II" (p. 5). This statement flies in the face of an avalanche of recent scholarship on precisely such contestation. Pieter Lagrou has shown convincingly how narratives of Resistance in France, Belgium, and the Netherlands were strategies of restoration, needed to revive political cultures damaged or destroyed by occupation and collaboration.[4]

The struggle to displace communists from their rightful position within the Resistance community was intense all over western Europe; the same harsh contest over who resisted and who did not punished social democrats, liberals, and Catholics in eastern Europe. And this does not even begin to touch the question of the eclipse of Jewish accounts of the war. All this was contested terrain. It is true that by the 1960s, the process of political stabilization in both east and west had taken its course, and that then and only then other narratives of victimhood could emerge fully. The Eichmann trial was a catalyst in this respect. But it is not true that the representation of what Bodnar calls "homegrown victimization" was limited to Europe.

Precisely in the field of film, such victims were visible. As Pierre Sorlin has shown, from very early on cinematic narratives adopted the voice of the child as the core of cinematic tales about the war. Anyone who saw René Clément's *Les Jeux Interdits* of 1952 or Rossellini's *Roma città aperta* of 1945, or Hans Muller's *Und finden dereinst wir uns wieder* of 1947 would be puzzled by Bodnar's assertions. Children are the quintessential victims in war; they cannot be blamed for its viciousness or its stupidities; they just have to endure them.[5]

Such filmic presentations of children at war demonstrate the danger of any argument that, in narratives dealing with the Second World War, images of victimhood were a late-twentieth-century phenomenon, following and displacing a different and prior collective memory of collective aspirations toward a better world. The lonely, isolated, damaged, or suffering individual in film could and did point to the need for collective action. The filmic children of postwar Europe were hardly icons of the triumph of individualism over collective action.

There is another problem in this kind of analysis. Bodnar takes issue with work on traumatic memory, understood as an underground river of recollection, likely to erupt unbidden when triggered by some external stimulus. He argues that trauma may not be so much buried as displaced, and in part displaced onto film. The problem here is the direct transposition of a category of individual psychopathology into the arena of cultural production. The notion of "trauma" is in itself contested terrain.[6] It is understood, in psychiatric or neurophysiological terms, only in a very rudimentary way. How is it possible to take the term and apply it to a culture as a whole?

Here is one feature of the discussion of collective memory that is at the heart of the problem. The assumption is that individual memory and collective memory are related in a linear or aggregative way. I know of no study in neurology or cognitive psychology which justifies such a rash conclusion. The language of collective memory or cultural memory is simply too vague to bear the weight of such an argument.

Bodnar's claim is that film served as a field of traumatic displacement. Cinema "articulated" anxieties arising out of "popular nervousness over brute force in both wartime and peacetime America" (p. 6). What film showed is that "violence could be homegrown." This imagery therefore enabled a "substantial amount of the trauma and anxiety, at least in the United States" to be not so much "restrained . . . as displaced into the narratives of mass culture" (p. 8). In this context "trauma and anxiety" evidently become collective phenomena. It is hard to know what evidence would help us evaluate these massive claims. Did Western films before the Second World War or gangster films of the 1930s serve the same purpose? And African-Americans, victimized in a myriad of ways by segregation, hardly needed a demonstration of the proposition that "violence could be homegrown." The generalized form of this kind of claim about cultural memory makes it virtually impossible to evaluate its validity.

The same problem mars Eley's essay on British film and the Second World War. History, he posits reasonably, is both a "relation to something that really happened" and also "a container of meaning, a representational project" which was of use to certain elements in British politics. What Samuel Hynes calls "the war in the head," meaning the war imagined,[7] offered what Eley terms "an active archive of collective identification" (pp. 2–3). This set of images associated with the fiftieth anniversary of the end of the war contributed to "an insidious postmodern gesture" whereby the history of real events was "erased in the very act of its recuperation." His central argument is that through war remembrance, imagery occluded history.

Sometimes this occurred in very indirect ways. Kenneth Branagh's bold interpretation of *Henry V* clearly cut across Sir Laurence

Olivier's film version of the play, produced as stirring wartime drama in 1944. But to Eley "Branagh ventriloquized Thatcherist rhetoric in spite of himself." Here's the rub: how in the world do we validate such a statement? Representations perform functions independent of their authors, to be sure, but why adopt this one interpretation when others seem equally valid? The chaos of battle is much more evident in Branagh's film, when Brian Blessed walks right across his king's postbattle path. This device seems to remove some of the fictive order of battle and its aftermath, and thus works entirely against post-Falklands Thatcherite posturing. I do not want to argue that my interpretation is any more valid than Eley's; just that his method of analysis rests on a set of unexamined and doubtful assumptions about what memory is and how it is manipulated. Vagueness here opens the door to tendentious political interpretations of the effect of film, in the form of stating that Kenneth Branagh inadvertently spoke for Thatcher, interpretations which are at best difficult to evaluate.

Film does indeed have power in projecting national stereotypes and narratives. But the purposes of film are not at all the same as those of political argument, such as that over British national identity in the fourth quarter of the twentieth century. In this regard, the range of reference in Eley's essay is unnecessarily limited. He is right to state that "something like a renegotiation of national culture has been taking place" in Britain since the 1960s, but he defines this process too narrowly. Thatcher certainly tried, Canute like, to stem the tide, but so much was against her that her failure was inevitable. Europe sealed her fate. Surprisingly for a German historian, Eley spends little time on the revolutionary implications of British integration, albeit hesitant and incomplete, into the European community. For at least a century, what is British has been defined as against what is European. "Lesser countries" (in Dickensian rhetoric) had to follow a path which the more fortunate British had bypassed. Now that is no longer the case. How has film accommodated this sea change? Are European stereotypes less or more evident in British film now that integration is a troubled reality? Here is an issue arguably central to a "renegotiation of national culture," but one on which Eley offers no clues.

Another difficulty in Eley's unanchored approach to collective memory and cinema concerns his handling of specific filmic material. "It's impossible," he tells us, "not to read [the] boyhood memoir in [Boorman's] "Hope and glory" of a wartime society of women against the Thatcherized political language of the 1980s." Is that really so? Images of childhood, as Sorlin has demonstrated, have been salient features of Second World War films from the later 1940s. Their power is in confronting war from the standpoint of someone who could not possibly be implicated in causing or fighting the conflict, but whose life is shaped by it anyway. Thus I remain unpersuaded by Eley's claim that the film "does have a metanarrative about the Second World War after all, though one coded through the formally depoliticized reconstructions of everyday life" (p. 13). But whether or not I share Eley's views is less important than the fact that he offers no criteria through which to evaluate them. Take it or leave it seems to be his approach to the study of memory, politics, and film. On balance I'd prefer to leave it.

Elsewhere, Eley speaks of "the promiscuous use" of the trope of nostalgia in the last two decades tending to flatten "the specificities of particular periods and their place in collective and personal memory" (p. 16 n22). There is force in this claim, but it fades rapidly when it is used to reach a political conclusion, namely that being nostalgic about the war tends to shift attention away from the period 1945–51, when the Third Labour government created the basic institutions clustered under the heading of the "welfare state." This period of political achievement, Eley notes, was the one in reference to which "collective memory" had been "organized," and the postwar consensus had been "characterized." Remembering the war in nostalgic film is thus, from Eley's point of view, a way to avoid remembering the postwar years, years when the welfare state was born. To turn away from this period served the interests of Thatcherite conservatives who aimed to undo that postwar settlement. Filmic settings in wartime Britain accommodated many different thematic readings. For but one prominent example, it would be useful to consider the egalitarian message of Michael Powell and Emeric Pressburger's 1943 film *Life and Death of Colonel Blimp*. Here is the stuff of nostalgia, nostalgia in huge quantities, married to a message deeply offensive to traditional conservatism. Apparently Churchill wanted to ban it. And this film is far from the only filmic war narrative with a powerful populist flavor.

I understand that Eley is not making an argument about history as past events, but rather about their imaginary reconstruction. His argument would have been more persuasive, though, had he adopted a more pluralist stance, enabling him to engage in multiple filmic readings of the war—and multiple forms of public recollection in recent years which move in different directions. When John Major tried to turn the fiftieth anniversary of 1945 (literally) into a picnic, veterans made him think again. There was too much bitterness and too much suffering for their collective memory to be inscribed within the rhetoric of the Conservative Party.

These are issues which ought to be studied and debated at length. My point here is that the attempt to correlate the imagery of film with something called collective memory, and to relate both to political contestation about national identity, is a program fraught with difficulties.

In Youngblood's essay on Soviet film and the Second World War, some of these same problems recur. Once again, the absence of a clear working definition of memory causes problems. Youngblood's interpretation is based on a juxtaposition of official lies about the war with filmic "truths," "truths" which "succeeded in returning to the Soviet people an authentic memory of the conflict" (p. 27). And yet what makes one memory authentic and another false? Even if we set aside Stalinist shibboleths, how can we know where the "truth" about the war lay? And how can we know that a particular film or set of films came to embody something called "authentic memory"?[8]

The authenticity of narratives about war is a highly contested subject. Some veterans continue to claim a proprietary interest here. The same assertions emerged after the 1914–18 war, and they are just as unconvincing. Essentialism cannot get us very far in dealing with imaginings of war. The experience was too varied for anyone to claim a privileged viewpoint; furthermore, if rough casualty figures can be believed, more civilians than soldiers lost their lives as a result of the 1939–45 war. There can never be such a thing as an "authoritative" eyewitness to such a multifaceted catastrophe.

Multiple witnesses must yield multiple narratives, of which film forms but one element. To evaluate cinematic images of war, perhaps the best way forward is to interpret film lightly. Film surely cannot bear the weight of heavy interpretative agendas. This is not to reify film nor is it to suggest that film has no political echoes or origins; on the contrary, it is rather to urge a more complex and textured approach to works which are simultaneously artistic, thematic, formulaic, commercial, and political.

And, above all, visual. In all three essays, the visuality of film is given less attention than its textuality. But surely imagery can (and frequently does) escape the confines of written language. And here a final set of problems emerges, related to the impossibility of visualizing battle and other facets of war. There is a substantial literature on this problem, related to the chaos of combat and the absence of a vanishing point or a visual center around which the space of combat can be configured.[9] It is at least arguable that all war films construct a geography of engagement which is inauthentic. The best film can do is to approximate the human or physical environment of war—an environment it can in no sense replicate accurately; the scent or stench of combat will never be there. An authentic war film, pace Youngblood, may be a contradiction in terms.

Film is never the same as text, and the ways in which cinema presents past events is never direct or unmediated. The authors of these essays have had the courage to enter a field insufficiently theorized—the field of collective memory—and have tried to relate film to various ways of understanding it. Their presentation of the issues is of importance, and ought to lead to much more systematic work on the matrix of activities, including film, through which both individuals and collectives configure the past. Much interdisciplinary work is currently under way in precisely this spirit.[10]

In this effort, greater rigor in the use of the concept of collective memory is clearly essential. Alon Confino has made a similar point,[11] and his remarks are particularly relevant in the context of historical accounts of film and memory. The term *collective memory* must be handled with precision because it may be at the heart of a matrix indicated though not spelled out in these essays. Collective memory may be understood as a set of signifying practices linking authorial encoding with audience decoding of messages about the past inscribed in film, or indeed in other sources. All three authors offer acute comments on the ways scriptwriters and directors encode political and social messages in their films. Some of these hidden agendas are carefully and subtly inserted: living under Stalin required no less. Other messages arrive in what may have been a semiconscious or unintentional way: such is the nature of Eley's claims about the subliminal "Thatcherite" echoes of Branagh's *Henry V,* or Bodnar's argument concerning individual rather than collective configurations of the Second World War in American film. Let us for a moment grant the force of these arguments; the problem still remains as to how such messages, once imprinted on film and projected to a wide audience, are decoded by it. The answer is complex and related to areas of the history or reading and reception well known to literary scholars.[12] There are conventions at work here, and their character in the context of films about the Second World War is informed by various kinds of images and memories, some personal, some familial, some social, some ethnic, some gendered, some national. One way of understanding these conventions is to term them collective memory; that is, the memory of different collectives about the past.

Here we encounter one crucial analytical distinction which these three authors do not make. Collective memory is not the same as national memory. National collectives never created a unitary, undifferentiated, and enduring narrative called collective memory. Nations do not remember; groups of people do. Their work is never singular, and it is never fixed. The anthropologist Roger Bastide wrote thirty years ago of the chorus of voices which address the issue of memories about the past. Some members of the chorus are closer to the microphone, others have louder voices, but no one orchestrates them in a unified way. A cacophony is inevitable.[13] For this reason alone, any study of collective memory must approach the issue from a pluralist's point of view. In addition, the concept of collective memory as a continuous message floating somewhere in the air cannot be sustained. What Carol Gluck has called "memory activists" are people who do the work of remembrance in public. When they cease to act, their collective's collective memory fades away. Someone else or some other group speaks in their place. Maurice Halbwachs provided the rudimentary form of this story seventy years ago.[14] Its implications are still of fundamental importance to the study of memory and history. It is both a chastening and a challenging thought that the task he embarked on prior to the outbreak of the Second World War, a war in which he lost his life, is a task which still remains to be done.

Conclusion

Liberating film from the burden of carrying something called collective memory has many advantages. Among them is the space this move creates to explore the ways in which film serves as a mediator, a multitiered theater in Benjamin's sense, in which the overlaps and elisions between our understanding of history and memory are performed again and again. In other words, the individual viewer of a film brings to that film personal memories and historical narratives. We are touched by film, sometimes powerfully evoked, so that our responses to film help restructure and fortify our notions of history and our personal memories. What we build up is a set of scripts about the past. We engage thereby in a process I term "historical remembrance," a way of "seeing" past events through exposure to discursive fields like film.

Historical remembrance is not the same as family remembrance or ritual remembrance in a liturgical framework. In film, and especially in war films, there is a narrative of the past which matters, and which is taken into account by filmmakers; the Germans didn't win the Battle of Stalingrad; the Blitz failed, and so on. But that narrative is the framework within which epic or realistic or ironic themes are worked out. To be sure, film carries myth with great ease and power, but it also carries historical narratives which affect the way viewers think about the past. Going to the cinema is a way of bringing history and memory together. The outcome is never stable and rarely predictable. Film viewers do not always get the message the directors or producers want them to get. When the subject of the film is war, there are too many other influences at work to enable anyone to predict the precise effect of the images on the screen on the viewing public. What we can say is that the power of film is such as to bring historical narratives into the scripts moviegoers construct about the past. Those scripts are infused with their own memories, and with stories they have heard from survivors. The amalgam of reflections individuals take out of cinema is therefore complex and volatile. Never adding up to something as grandiose as national memory, processes of historical remembrance are nonetheless crucial elements in the way individuals and groups perceive the past, and place their own lives within it.

CHAPTER 9

Between History and Memory
Television, Public History, and Historical Scholarship

Over the past two decades, the field of historical work has expanded rapidly toward what is termed public history, history outside the academy, linking historians to the broad population interested—sometimes passionately—in historical inquiry.[1] I want to suggest that this development has created spaces in which the overlap and differences between history and memory are visualized. In this chapter, I want to discuss television history. In the following chapter, the focus shifts to the field of museum work.

In both chapters the question arises as to how to visualize war. And because the visual dimension is so powerful, and because the public drawn to these representations of war is so large, it is important to specify how public history mediates between history and memory. In the case of television history, there are particular problems we need to address about authorial independence, finance, and political pressures. But the key point is that television documentaries, based on historical research, have the power either to confirm or to challenge other, earlier narratives about war. Some of these narratives arise from the recollection of participants. Others emerge from different sources. But whatever their origin, there is a substantial body of people who, while watching television history, bring their own memories or their family histories with them. If the television history is accurate and compelling, it may have a bearing on how the stories people tell each other about the past—past wars among other events—are told. Historical remembrance is an activity which has among its aims bringing professional scholarship more centrally into contemporary discussions about our common past.

Most historians do not engage in this kind of dialogue with the broad public. Their audience is their colleagues and students. The engagement with public history is controversial within the historical profession itself. Doing public history has risks attached to it. But, as I will argue below, not doing it has risks as well. One is leaving the field open to those unaware of current scholarly developments. Another risk is in terms of the way we separate "history" (something done in and for the academy) from "memory" (something done by laymen) into rigidly separate compartments. What I have termed "historical remembrance" is the negotiation of the space between the two. This negotiation happens in many forms, but among them are television history and museums, the subject of the following two chapters. My argument is not only that public history of this kind can and should happen, but that doing it has benefits for the way professional history is written.

Individualism, Collective History, and Public History

The first element in the creation of public history is prior scholarship. There is no narrative without such historical work. But in the construction of television or film documentaries about the past, and in particular about war, the work to be done is intrinsically collective. And there's the rub. Public history matters, but its collective character stops many people from going into it. Why? Because the fundamental ethos of the historical profession is individualistic. Collective venture is daring, risky, and rarely yields the recognition which young scholars in particular need at a time of vanishing university posts and cutbacks in university funding.

And yet the field of collective historical writing is not only thriving, but also almost certain to expand rapidly over the next decades through television and video audiences, interactive systems easily plugged into a desktop or portable computer, and the growing world of museums and historical exhibitions. The field of historical remembrance has been revolutionized by the expansion of visual media, and sooner or later the historical profession will have to come to terms with the new environment in which we work.

The challenge is clear: at a time of stagnant or limited academic audiences, public audiences have never been larger. Part of the source of this interest is the memory boom itself, sketched in chapter 1 of this book. While the profession of history is under financial constraints in the universities, it has a clear avenue to expand. The audience is there; the public service is there. But the means to arrive at the destination challenges cherished assumptions of our profession: namely, that what we do is individual; and that the "authorial voice" is the core of our enterprise. But even if individualism is worshiped as the sine qua non of wisdom, there is still room to share our profession with another kind of colleague, the public historian, who speaks primarily to society at large, and does so as part of a group of scholars and other professionals working together.

I want to introduce some aspects of work in public history in both this chapter and the next, which deals with museums. Here I refer to a joint BBC/American Public Broadcasting television series on the First World War. I served as co-producer and writer of this series. Then I would like to suggest ways in which this kind of project, while likely to play an increasingly important part in historical study, has difficulties imbedded in it: difficulties better faced when exposed to the light of day.

First the bad news. In a nutshell, the problem is that public history is publicly funded history. No one else will pay the sums needed for public history projects—television series, museums, exhibitions.

And as soon as official or state organizations commit themselves to pick up the tab for collective projects, the autonomy of the individual scholar is curtailed. Our holy of holies—the right to speak out about the past without financial or institutional shackles—has been invaded. These brief remarks aim at opening a debate about the benefits and costs of public history with special reference to the place of television history in our profession.

First, is it worth it? My answer is a resounding yes. The first point about collective projects in public history is that they are unavoidable when confronting gigantic issues of wide public concern. With certain notable exceptions, no individual alone can produce a history of most of the major subjects in contemporary affairs. The documentation is too vast, the issues too complex, the necessary linguistic skills too daunting. Either we work together or we don't work at all on a host of issues. Some such subjects spring to mind easily: fundamentalist Islam, international migration, urbanization, the information revolution. No one scholar can even keep up with the mountains of documentation produced day by day, let alone add to it in a rigorous manner in academic publications or in other ways.

There is another, less parochial, reason for doing this kind of work. Collective history is the only way to break down the hold of national history in our discipline. There is nothing wrong with national history: it simply throttles comparison. The celebration of the "peculiarities of the English" or Welsh or Scots or French or Germans assumes the other, but the rigorous rather than the rhetorical pursuit of such comparisons is rare. Public history can cross boundaries, and does so in Europe at precisely the moment when the creation of transnational histories parallels the emergence of transnational institutions and (in time) transnational identities.

The concept of collective work is, therefore, not one we can do without. But since university jobs are decided on the basis of the individualist ethos, it is unlikely that young people will put their careers on the line by embarking on risky projects in which their personal contribution cannot easily be specified. This must mean that universities will continue to be bastions of individualism in scholarship. The people who can "risk" collective projects, such as those which reach a television audience, are those already established in the profession, that is, middle-aged and tenured. The logic of appointments (and inertia) is a conservative force. Public history is not, because it is intrinsically collective. Creating a museum, or an exhibition, or a television series, can never be a one-man show. Collective work is how it has to be done, and if the lead is to come from anyone, it will have to be from those of us sheltered from the job market with an already established reputation as "conventional" historians.

Television history is collective history. Now that the mode of creation, production, and editing is entirely digitized, and images, sounds, and words are all reduced to computer files in (for example) the AVID system, group production is upon us. Today sets of people design, meld, and display historical programming for mass audiences on television throughout the world. In all of them, the contribution of any one person is inextricable from the collective. What matters is the quality of the interpretation on the screen, and that interpretation is (and has to be) collective.

The case for this kind of public history is clear. Historical understanding is part of the equipment of citizenship. Those millions of people outside the academy who care about history are part of our audience whether we academics admit it or not. And their craving for some kind of history on the television screen creates jobs which our students may find compelling and even rewarding.

Prominent among the subjects which attract large television audiences is warfare. Its drama, its documentation, its monumental scale all make it suitable for television documentary presentation. To see a series about war is to negotiate the space between public remembrance and private memories. The linkage between family history and universal history is writ so large in narratives of war that their appeal is unlikely to wane in coming years. Here again is one of the links between the theme of armed conflict and the contemporary "memory boom." Television, and now the Internet, have broadcast these stories to unprecedentedly large audiences.

Resistance Among Professional Historians

Public historical representations of warfare on television and elsewhere are ubiquitous. But there the problems start. Some are internal to the trade. No one should underestimate the resistance inside the academy against such collective historical work. Partly this is simply old-fashioned elitism. Partly it reflects a style of life, in which subtlety and irony are valued to the point that at times nothing clear-cut can be said; or rather, it underpins the notion, more commonly voiced than you may suppose, that anyone who speaks clearly is presumed to think simply. Television history, from this point of view, is simple-minded history. Any academic who engages in it is, therefore, risking his professional reputation.

Then there is the old goddess of jealousy. Most academics I know are either politicians or actors manqué; they like performance, but only when *they* are on stage. Others who speak to them from a television screen are bound to touch nerves among a profession both craving public attention and at times suspicious—even contemptuous—of it.

Finally, there is the question of "objectivity." Any one approach to a major problem in history is bound to select evidence and material on the basis of what the French call a *problématique,* a set of questions a generation of historians chooses to address. What about the questions historians of the 1960s, 1970s, or 1980s addressed? Do they get a look in? In some cases, the answer is no, and that is one point where the fur flies.

When the field of study is the history of war, as it so frequently is, the quarrels intersect with more general fault lines separating military history from cultural history, as if either could live in majestic isolation each on its separate peak. No one who enters this field is likely to leave it unbruised, another reason why young scholars may be prone to stay out of it.

The Great War Project

So the risks for a professional historian venturing into this arena are real, but so are the fruits of such work. Let me try to illustrate both by reference to a television series on the First World War entitled "1914–18: The Great War and the Shaping of the Twentieth Century." Conceived by Blaine Baggett, a television producer then working in the Public Broadcasting System in Los Angeles, the series aimed at telling military history from a cultural historical point of view: that is, by showing how people caught up in war encoded their experience in languages and gestures of lasting significance.

Baggett saw the potential in this new area of historical research and recognized that it was a transatlantic achievement. It is no accident that Americans have been prominent in the study of the cultural history of the Great War, that icon of the futility and carnage of organized violence in the twentieth century. One of the most powerful stimuli to a new generation of historical thinking on the First World War has been the Vietnam War. In large part as an echo of that war, there appeared a rich historical literature on the 1914–18 conflict. The dimension specifically governing this literature is the sense of the war as a cultural phenomenon, for soldiers and statesmen as much as for artists and audiences. Scholars such as Paul Fussell in *The Great War and Modern Memory,* John Keegan in *The Face of Battle,* and Eric Leed in *No Man's Land,* produced seminal work in the mid–1970s just after the end of the Vietnam conflict.

These works altered our understanding of the 1914–18 war. Fussell's book was consciously written as the reaction of a veteran of World War II to (and against) the Vietnam War.[2]

These scholars (alongside others) redefined the Great War as an event which transformed language, shifted radically the boundaries between the public and private realms, obliterated the distinction between civilian and military targets, occasioned witch-hunts for internal enemies, challenged gender divisions, and opened a new phase in the history of race and empire. In more recent years, Modris Eksteins in *Rites of Spring* and Samuel Hynes in *A War Imagined* explored the shadow of the war in astonishing and seminal works of art, as well as in more mundane features of cultural life.[3]

In Europe there appeared a similarly rich literature of the cultural history of the war. Jean-Jacques Becker and Marc Ferro opened new avenues of research on popular opinion in France and Russia, and George Mosse and Stéphane Audoin-Rouzeau explored the war's brutalizing effects on social norms and at times on civilians and soldiers alike. Antoine Prost enriched our understanding of both veterans' movements and commemorative events.

The work of these people, among others, created "the new cultural history" of the war.[4] It is based on the assumption that to understand the Great War, and its enduring repercussions, we must jettison outworn distinctions between "high" and "popular" culture, and between them and the political, economic, and military history of the day. In the 1914–18 conflict, all were mobilized; all were transformed. This was the heart and soul of the series; this was its agenda, and making this scholarship available to a wide public was the challenge at hand.

That project was recognized in open competition by a substantial grant from the American National Endowment of the Humanities in 1994. Following that core funding, the BBC joined the consortium, put in a substantial sum of money, in part from its education division, in part from programming, which enabled the completion of an eight-hour series on the war. The cost of the enterprise as a whole was about five million dollars.

The production took the following form. First came a series of meetings among a dozen or so historians about how the eight hours should or could be divided. This led to the drafting of summaries or treatments of each episode, specifying the historical argument driving the narrative of any one period. The first episode was called "Explosion"; the second "Stalemate," and so on. The chronological narrative of the war was clear, but each episode was told from the viewpoint of cultural history.

That meant searching for obscure or well-known first-person accounts of the events described in each episode. Hence storytelling created both the narrative flow and the analytical force through the accumulation of insights from personal testimony. One case should stand for the rest. The third episode, covering developments in 1915, was entitled "total war." This was a critical episode, since it described the spread of the conflict geographically and socially, as well as its power to obliterate the distinction between civilian and military targets. It began at Gallipoli, shifted to Britain, moved to Africa, then to the war in the air and at sea, turned to propaganda and the cultivation of hatred, and ended with a German doctor's account of the Armenian genocide. Here the meaning of total war—never really total but totalizing, tending to suck into the cauldron everybody and everything around it—appeared not through historical argument, but through narrative. It was the accumulation of elements of historical explanation through storytelling which, I believe, enabled us to show—vividly and viscerally—that in the Great War the whole was much worse than the sum of its parts.

Once identified, the stories had to be visualized. That meant location photography—at Gallipoli, at Woolwich Arsenal, but not in Armenia (through the Turkish refusal of permission to enter this

"military zone"). It meant too the search worldwide for period photography. Among the richest finds were those in Germany and eastern Europe. These enabled us to depart from the well-known sil-
houettes used time and again from the Imperial War Museum's
splendid collection of images and film. It also enabled us to tell the
story of the war from the German point of view, when relevant,
rather than retain the tired dichotomy of us and them still prevalent
in much military history. Cultural history departs from this bifur-
cated sense of the past.

Then came the hardest part of all: writing the scripts enabling us
to get all this into one hour. It is a chastening experience to see how
few words fill up an hour, but the slimming down of scripts showed
clearly how silence (and music) conveys meaning in television at
times more powerfully than words. The effects of images of shell
shock in episode five, or of mutiny or disfigured men in episode
seven, on the legacy of the war needed no comment. They spoke
volumes on the meaning of war.

Once fixed, the scripts needed air breathed into them. That
brought in the real princes of this aristocratic meritocracy—the actors. Most of those we hired were so prominent they didn't need the
work. But all wanted to do it because of its linkage to their own
family history. This was true of Ralph Fiennes, Liam Neeson, and
Judi Dench, as well as of virtually all the others who joined in the
project, and in my view gave it its music, its lingering power.

Then came the editing, all done on computer, and the composition of a score for the series and its location in the episodes. There
followed scrutiny and peer review by historians, who reported back
to the NEH. Thus the "product" emerged from Hollywood and
wound up in White City. There re-versioning and rewriting took
place, alongside an extended quarrel over credits. Why? Because the
Writers Guild of America believe in multiple credits—producer,
writer, director, and so on—in each episode, whereas the BBC's prac-

tice is to give each contributor one credit, no matter how complex the contribution. This was just one indicator of the different cultural codes with which two parallel professional groups operated. Just in time, the final respective versions were completed and then premiered in November 1996 on PBS and BBC 2. The series was shown in twenty-seven countries over the subsequent decade.

Historical Integrity and the Public Purse

This in a nutshell is how it was done. And it was collective work par excellence. I owe this to the executive producer, Blaine Baggett, because he brought the historians right into the center of the project, and there we stayed. We were not historical plumbers, called in to fix a leak or tighten an argument, and then dismissed with a pat on the back. We were part of the production team and recognized as such. This generosity of spirit is rare in television work but is likely to become more prominent as the boundaries between academic and public history erode.

In this context, it may be useful to distort slightly what has been a gratifying and complex experience, by dwelling not on the achievements and the fun, which were abundant, or on showing the series, which would be more illuminating, but in addressing the problems, which were also abundant. The difficulties in doing this work raise fundamental questions about the nature of the relationship between television and history, and although they are far from unique, they may have a broader interest than merely the reflections of one historian who was lucky enough to dip his toe in the pool of the television industry.

The first problem is money. With public money comes public influence of historical interpretations. In the United States, this meant entangling the project in the collision between the then newly triumphant Republican leadership of the U.S. Congress and the

National Endowment of the Humanities. Republicans went after this body, and its sister organization, the National Endowment of the Arts, with all the fervor of American anti-intellectualism. The outcome of the collision is still unclear, but the shadow over public funding of historical work of this kind was in our minds from the beginning to the end of our work.

As it happened, the tide of conservative puritanism—and hostility to public television—turned just as we made the series in 1994–96. This diminished the pressure on our work from within the funding body, the NEH, which has a rigorous set of peer assessments of projects it funds. We had to satisfy fellow historians and filmmakers, rather than keep looking over our shoulders at the Congress.

Much more contentious was the atmosphere and much higher was the price we had to pay to "version" the series, or clean it up for audiences on this side of the ocean. Satisfying the BBC was a major headache. Here the issues were varied. The first is the time-honored British condescension toward the American media and the supposedly infantile tastes of American audiences. The British version, it was argued, has to assume a high level of knowledge. My experience teaching the subject of the First World War at Cambridge over two decades did not support this claim. Still, a complex re-versioning of the American product, created in Lost Angeles, took place.

Here entered two other issues, further complicating historical work. The first was the status of the BBC and BBC documentaries, underlying their relatively conservative outlook on what an historical series should do and be. There is a wonderful pool of talent in White City, but occasionally it appears to be frozen over. Why? Many reasons come to mind, relating to the fractious atmosphere of the Thatcher years, and the structural changes fragmenting the BBC into competing divisions, each deeply worried about its future under contracts which offer very limited security. While working on this series, I taught at a university encrusted by traditions, some vibrant, some entirely atrophied. But I have never encountered a more feudal institution than the BBC. There decisions were made entirely vertically. The comptroller of BBC 2 spoke up at Cannes, and the money appeared; the comptroller took the decision as to scheduling and even entitling the series. All depended on one man. And that does tend to put a crimp into a highly imaginative system. But there is also a matter of style, of ponderousness; of taking itself a bit too seriously. "Auntie," if you will, preens too much in front of the mirror. By staring fixedly in that mirror, she may miss what is interesting in other, non-British directions.

Documentary television has developed remarkably in the United States over the last decade. Indeed, one reason why the Great War series was funded was the profound success of an American television series on the American Civil War. This moving documentary relied heavily on contemporary letters and photographs, and showed that an American mass audience had an attention span of more than ten seconds. The attraction of the approach to audiences in many countries was clear: here was documentary history with feeling. And feeling is not the core of BBC documentary work. Thought is. The American version uses more silence and visuals; the British one taught. It is a matter of temperament, to be sure, but also a matter of the BBC as a channel of record, a repository of history as the "nation" sees it; or more properly, as the guardians of the BBC want the nation to see it.

Emotion is conveyed through music, location photography, stills, and voice-overs. And here too the BBC has trouble with the American way of doing things—with good reason, in some instances. There is a tendency in American documentary work to shift from emotion to emotionalism, to make too much of the moon, or leaves in water, or other pastoral forms easily trivialized. Here national conventions of television work do link with clichés about national temperament and sensibilities. These arguments are exaggerated;

there is nothing more soppy than the British treatment of animals, especially jumping ones, but the stationary ones at times get the same mawkish treatment. No nation has a monopoly on bad taste, or on probity, whatever the Eurosceptics or anti-Americans have to say. The argument about national styles of documentary television is about long-standing differences of style and idiom, but there is a second problem of working through public television in Britain which goes beyond stereotypes about national character. License-fee payers support the BBC. Viewers cannot be "offended" without a public row following it. Given the fact that the First World War is imbedded in the family history of virtually everyone in this country, the subject is bound to be more sensitive here than in the United States. This led to a series of questions about the need to present a "balanced" interpretation, to bring "all viewpoints" to the screen, and so on. In short, nothing very radical or contentious would do.

One example will suffice to show the problem. From the start of the project the episode on the great battles of 1916–17, the Somme, Verdun, Passchendaele, was entitled "Slaughter." Lots of documentary evidence does the same. The French use the word *boucherie* for Verdun, one of their greatest "victories." Wouldn't it be more sensible, thoughtful BBC voices suggested, to call that episode "Sacrifice"? The answer was absolutely not, and "Slaughter" it remained. The issue was not just historical judgment or political sensitivities. It was the need for a state-run institution to try to avoid broadcasting the claim that the loss of life of three quarters of a million men had no redemptive "meaning." Sacrifices redeem; a slaughter does not. This is not just semantics; it is the marketing of heritage in politically acceptable forms. It is a term almost always applied to the political left, but at least as powerfully relevant to criticisms from the political right, an injunction to be politically correct. We resisted it, but not without a struggle.

The effects of the re-versioning, though, were palpable. In comparison with the American version of these crucial events, the BBC version is more cautious, more elliptical. Whereas in the American version I wrote and said on screen that the Battle of the Somme in July 1916 was a tragedy, one that no one had ever seen before, but the Battle of Passchendaele, from July to November 1917, was a crime, this statement was eliminated in the BBC version. The stated reason was the need to cut down the American television hour of fifty-three minutes to the BBC hour of forty-seven minutes. The real reason was damage limitation.

The BBC version is more cautious in another sense too. The American series is eight hours in length; the BBC version is seven hours long. The reason for the shorter series here is the BBC view that we tried to do too much in the American series. We tried to link the genocide of Armenians with the Holocaust in the Second World War; we linked attacks on civilians in the First World War with strategic bombing in the Second; we showed much more about Woodrow Wilson (admittedly less interesting to British audiences) and much more about revolution, counterrevolution and Western intervention in Russia. These segments do not appear in the British series, and in my view rob it of both the emotional force and comprehensiveness of the American series. We tried to show that what was thinkable, what was imaginable, about human brutality changed in the course of the 1914–18 war, and that all of us have lived with the consequences. Here there are grounds for professional disagreement. The BBC had a point, but it was (characteristically) the conservative point. If the world be divided between risk takers and risk averters, I think I know in which category the BBC of the late 1990s should be placed.

Another pressure toward the "mainstream" and the familiar came from the Imperial War Museum, whose film archives of this period are unparalleled. This institution has helped and advised the BBC over decades. Surely, the same thoughtful BBC voices purred, it would not do to have the *Times* report on the day the series is aired:

"Imperial War Museum says BBC series is historically inaccurate." Of course it would not do, but that is because inaccuracy is anathema, whatever the IWM has to say about it.

So every episode went twice before the military historians of the Imperial War Museum: once for the American version, to get the professional opinions needed to get professional questions right, and once for the British version, to smooth ruffled feathers even before they were ruffled. Here there was an additional element of re-versioning. It was to ensure that other voices, more conservative, more conventional, more reassuring, were placed on the screen.

The message was clear: do not squeeze out the old guard, do not be too hard on Douglas Haig, whose son had many well-placed friends; if you have to be unkind to his father, don't forget to wheel out someone who can put in a good word for him. And so we did: not for purposes of currying favor, but to show the liveliness of historical debate in this field.

One such defender of Haig is John Terraine, the chief historian of the 1964 series which helped launch BBC 2 and which the PBS series was intended to update. He duly appeared in episode 4 to defend Haig's record. Peter Simkins of the Imperial War Museum duly announced that the British army went through a "learning curve" in the 1914–18 war; and it was right that he had his say. So did others who were not so sympathetic to Haig and spoke of a "bleed-ing curve" as the only real trajectory which mattered. All this dis-agreement is healthy, and the series reflected the robust nature of research in this field.

It also showed that historical scholarship has not stood still since 1964. That was the justification for the new series in the first place. In the earlier series, there was no room for an African soldier, no footage on shell shock, no Otto Dix or Ludwig Meidner, no Käthe Kollwitz, no Yashka and her Women's Battalion of Death, no Armenian genocide. And no female narrator. So at the BBC's suggestion, a "broader" range of commentators was added to give the series "weight" in this country, for which you may read conservative credibility.

Some people were neither satisfied or amused. This was not at all surprising, though the apoplectic nature of some criticism was. Dame Judi Dench is one of the great figures of the British theater. Her voice is remarkable. But it is a woman's voice, and to A. A. Gill in the *Sunday Times* and Corelli Barnett in the *Spectator,* women have little or nothing to say about war. Barnett did fume in print that if he met me on the street, he would feel like punching me in the nose. Rough and tumble stuff, perhaps, but it does indicate where the sensitivities lie.

The Corelli Barnetts of this world would never be satisfied by the series, because it melded cultural history and military history in a way which located battle in the framework of the notions ordinary people held about their lives and the upheaval through which they lived. It did so using the voices of many of the finest actors in Britain and abroad: Jeremy Irons as Siegfried Sassoon; Ralph Fiennes as Wilfred Owen; Ian Richardson as Sir Ian Hamilton; Liam Neeson as the Irishman John Lucy and the Ulsterman Kenneth McCardle; Helen Mirren as Lady Helen Rhondda; Michael York as Robert Graves; Yaphet Kotto as the African soldier Kande Kamara; and so on.

This extraordinary array of talent gave weight and force to the words of these individuals, and to those of others, prominent and obscure, whose language is really the heart and soul of the series. This is what cultural history is all about: it presents the codes, the phrases, the images through which people understood their own times. Their words are among the most powerful legacies of the war; they frame our own language, our own imaginative landscapes, our own sense of the world. These idioms have helped shape the rest of the twentieth century. They matter intrinsically, but they are not the stuff of conventional military history.

This innovative approach struck a chord in the United States, but apparently not in Britain. This may help account for an interesting transatlantic contrast in terms of reception. First, PBS—a minority channel competing with several hundred competitors for viewers—widely advertised the series in the United States. It was shown over four days in two-hour segments, from 9 to 11 pm, starting on 11 November, which is not a special day on the American calendar. But it was prime time, and as it happened, also the prime week for what is called "the sweeps," or the annual television ratings of all channels.

The initial reception was very gratifying: approximately five million households tuned in. The critical response was huge and overwhelmingly positive. Reviewed fairly and critically in most major newspapers and periodicals, the series has received the Producers Guild of America Award for the Best Series of the Year, the Peabody award for best series of the year, and an Emmy award for best documentary series.

Public responses have been voluminous. PBS put in a discussion page on the World Wide Web, and 250,000 messages about the series were registered over the six-month period following its airing. I have no firm idea as to their character or content. Some people who left messages were abusive, others annoyed, others moved. That is normal, but it is clear that the series did fulfill the hope and potential of public history—to bring educated people into the forum of historical debate and share with them the excitement of historical narrative.

In Britain, the response was much more muted. There is no similar tradition of prominent reviewing of these series in the press, and it is certainly the case that computer addicts are more numerous on the other side of the ocean. But it may be worth reflecting on some of the reasons why the same series, toned down for a British audience, produced much less interest, though relatively high viewership—perhaps three million homes tuned in.

The first reason is timing. The BBC scheduled the series for Mondays from October to Christmas, but did so late in the season. Here is feudalism in action: everyone held their breath to hear the master's voice. When he spoke, they moved, but not a second before. That meant that prebroadcast publicity was almost impossible. One former student of mine pointed out in the *Guardian* that a few days' notice is not enough for a major daily to give a television series the coverage in Britain which it had in the United States, where PBS scheduled the series six months in advance.

Timing mattered in another way. The series was shown in Britain at 7 pm. To the producers of "Timewatch," the BBC history series, this is prime time for documentaries. But not to everybody else. It is dinner time. And some of the footage we provided did not suit collective digestion. Shell-shocked men, the disfigured, the bereaved were there in abundance, all presented not after the 9 pm watershed, but two hours before it. Why? One possible reason is that the BBC wanted to cover itself against any political fallout a series of an unconventional kind would produce. A 7 pm slot would enable the network to show it without fuss or fanfare. Our mix of historical narrative, contemporary film footage, and dramatized voices, drawn from contemporary documents, is an unusual way of doing history. A 7 pm slot would enable it to fade more quickly from the scene.

And that it has done. But there is another aspect of the echo effect of the same series shown in the United States which has a bearing on our subject. The Public Broadcasting System sponsored the creation of a set of high school teaching materials enabling the series to be shown as part of history classes. To my surprise, this was remarkably successful, and the takers stretched all over the country, from final year high school courses (O-level equivalents in Britain) to final year university courses. Here is another facet of public history, which will expand the interest in history and in the innovative ways it can be presented in the coming years.

In effect, my brief and limited experiences indicate that the linkage between academic history, public history, and television audiences is managed in a much more conservative fashion in Britain than in the United States. Let me clarify the argument. I am not saying that the American way is the best. It can be superficial and predictable, but its failings in the field of documentary television are those of experimentation, not tradition. My claim is rather that vestiges of elitism survive in some British institutions in ways which limit the options and vitality of the field of public history. Elitism rests uncomfortably with this kind of history. Professional habits die hard, both in the academy and in the media. But surely it is essential for us all to recognize that public history is here to stay and the more of it the better. The wisest course is to face not only its attractions but also its risks and pitfalls. The danger of public history is the danger of a drift toward the center, a desire not to offend, a search for consensus, and a consequent loss of nerve. For those who have both a fascination for historical narrative and a relatively thick skin, this is an attractive path, a path less trodden on, full of possibilities. To apprentice historians, the message is simple: try it out; moving into public history from the confines of the academy can be invigorating and exciting work. After all, as Orwell might have put it, you have nothing to lose but your academic "aitches."

These remarks on public history have a bearing on our overall concern with the linkage and overlap between history and memory. A too rigid distinction between them is behind some professional historians' suspicion of the narratives presented in museums or television documentaries. A too promiscuous interpretation of the relationship between the two—that is, that individual memories aggregated together somehow constitute history—produces a kind of uncritical populism which is equally indefensible. History is about questions, hypotheses, speculations. The traces of memory help establish their validity, but in and of themselves memories do not create history. What makes more sense than to draw walls between them is to see them as overlapping. This shared space is what I have termed here historical remembrance. It is not at all the same as liturgical remembrance or familial remembrance, both of which have a different sense of evidence and of time. Historians do something different. They cannot rely on eyewitnesses alone. Their narratives must be based on archival materials, specified so that anyone can check for herself the provenance of any element in it. This is as important with respect to photographs and film as it is to letters and memoirs. Indeed, public historians have an even heavier responsibility to tell a completely documented story, since those who come into a museum or watch a television documentary are not trained to sift through archival evidence. They are likely to suspend disbelief, and can be fooled if that is what the public historian wants to do.

More insidious is the tendency for public history to reinforce national myths and heroic stories. But this danger exists on the other side of the academic fence as well. An exponential growth in the audience interested in history has not changed one iota the basic standards which we historians have always accepted. What the memory boom has done is to expand the audience interested in history, and to provide more sites than ever before to present historical interpretations to the public. And in that task, the distinction is where it always has been and always should be: not between public or academic history, but between good and bad history.

CHAPTER 10

War Museums
The Historial *and Historical Scholarship*

In recent years, museums dealing with contemporary history have succeeded in attracting very substantial populations. Why do they come? In part, because it is in these sites that family history and world history come together. Nowhere is this more evident than in museums of the two world wars. These pillars of public history have been essential vectors of the memory boom.

War museums mediate between history and memory in particular ways. I want to discuss how this happens in a particular instance, that of a museum I helped design, and in whose research center I have worked since 1989. The story of the construction of this museum tells us much about how professional history and popular narratives about the past intersect. On the one hand, such museums draw on historical scholarship in order to present the past with some degree of rigor and authority. But on the other hand, scholarship itself develops in positive ways through such encounters with the public and its multiple memories of war. While history and memory can never be conflated, the construction of a space between the two—the space of historical remembrance represented in a museum—can change the way academic history is written.

Scholarship and the Museum

First came scholarship and then came the museum. The Historial de la Grande Guerre, at Péronne, Somme, is the only international museum of the Great War, reflecting the military and cultural history of Britain, France, and Germany at the site of the Battle of the Somme, the place where, Ernst Jünger tells us, the twentieth century was born. This chapter addresses the gestation of this museum and its intersection with historical scholarship of the 1980s and 1990s.

The dual character of this project gave it its originality and distinctive style. It was at once the fruit of international scholarship on the Great War, and a collective meditation on how to represent that scholarship to a broad public in three countries whose history is inscribed in this place. We entered into the arts of representation, a concept which was in process of transformation at the very moment we set to work. In the mid–1980s, Jean-Jacques Becker, Wolfgang Mommsen and I were first invited to begin the conversations among professional historians which ultimately produced the historical narrative on display in this museum. At the very moment we set to work with many others to help construct a museum of some kind in the eastern corner of the Département de la Somme, there occurred one of those sea changes in historical thinking which are difficult to see at the time, but which shifted the landscape of our work. The way the museum looks, and the way its scholarly community has developed in the two decades which have followed, reflect that shift.

Prior to the 1980s, the basis of cultural history, particularly in France, was the study of *mentalités*, or the enduring mental furniture of past generations. By the 1990s, for a host of reasons, a paradigm shift occurred, producing a new formulation of cultural history as the domain of the study or representations. Without intending to do so, by creating this museum, and engaging in its daily life through a symbiotic relationship with the *centre de recherche*, we have joined in the current of opinion which defines cultural history primarily in this way, as the history of representations. In effect, what we did was to create a museum which offered visitors, scholars, and laymen alike a different kind of representation of war, remote from that of other historical museums which address the subject.

That new representation, or rather set of representations, emerged here by accident, as it were. In the first stages of the project, a romantic, sensitive, powerful, at times grandiloquent vision informed the design. This was the phase dominated by Gérard Rougeron, who chose the word "Historial" as a midpoint between history and memorial, between the academy and public commemoration, or (following Halbwachs) between cold, dispassionate, precise history and warm, evocative, messy memory. The term "Historial" has been used elsewhere, but Rougeron gave it his own distinctive character. There was absolutely nothing cold and dispassionate about Rougeron, and this emotive, explosive side of his character helped bring about his demise. He left the project in a huff midway through, but some sense of what he had in mind can be found in two places in the museum. The first is adjacent to the cafeteria, where there is a *maquette* designed by Rougeron of a French infantryman, a poilu. The initial idea was to have this life-size figure at the entrance to the museum. The soldier was to be placed in a transparent telephone booth, and through a simple water-circulating system he was to be made to endure eternally the rain of the Somme. The second trace of Rougeron's vision is in the museum's film theater. On permanent showing is a film of the life of one British soldier, Harry Fellowes, who volunteered for the Northumberland Fusiliers at the age of nineteen and who survived to tell the tale of most of his mates who did not. Fellowes died during the making of the film, further adding to its elegiac character. This life history, as it were begun and ended on the Somme, was powerfully inscribed by Rougeron's talent for romantic figuration, and for mixing the mundane and the sacred against the backdrop of the staggeringly powerful music of Benjamin Britten's *War Requiem.*

When Rougeron withdrew from the project, his place was taken by a creative team of museographers led by Adeline Rispal and her firm, Reperages. Stéphane Audoin-Rouzeau and I were in Amiens for the selection of this new team, who had less than two years to completely redesign the museum. And redesign it they did, with the help of a series of Friday meetings in Paris with the *comité directeur* of the *centre be recherche,* meetings which led me into the mysteries of the link between French confusion and French creativity. How the first led to the second is entirely beyond me, but nonetheless it did.

How we got into this act requires a brief digression. In one of the early meetings with Max Lejeune, *président* of the Conseil Général de la Département de la Somme, and M. Petitjean, a stalwart administrator and friend of the project, I convinced Lejeune that a museum without a research center would atrophy. Dust would settle on exhibits which reflected one moment of scholarship, bypassed by students and colleagues bringing new approaches and sources to bear on our understanding of the Great War. An example is the Musée des Arts et Traditions Populaire, in Neuilly-sur-Seine, with rows of farming tools fascinating not to us but to an earlier generation of anthropologists. Historians can offer a field of debate and creative disagreement which would, I argued, help keep the museum alive. I made my point, and after an inaugural conference in Amiens in 1989, at which forty scholars came from as far as Australia and California to help in this effort, the research center was born, three years before the museum officially opened.

In this way a group of us was able to engage with the *conservateur*, Hugues Hairy, and his team, and with Adeline Rispal and Reperages, in creating a site of memory of a kind which I believe, immodestly, to be strikingly original. Without intending to do so, the team which built the museum—the architect, the *conservateur*, the museographers, the historians—managed to create a space which is at once elegant, scrupulous in its historical scholarship, and challenging in its narrative. There is one particular point about the narrative offered in the museum which needs emphasis. The ideas about war, and the forms in which they are expressed here, somehow managed to synchronize with or even to capture other intellectual movements in our field about the nature of historical representation itself.

This museum challenges us with the question, how is it possible to represent battle? How is it possible to represent war? The representations which we have chosen do not answer these questions either fully or directly, but challenge the visitor to pose them. This sense of history as an unending interrogation is one of the strengths of this design. And of course to say that the question is still open is to reject other, older ways of approaching it. If you want to see what the Historial is not, go to the Imperial War Museum in London, or to the Memorial in Caen. Older representations of war are there in abundance.

Representing War

In what ways is the set of representations of war offered by the Historial different? Let me summarize them under four headings. The first is in the beauty of Henri Ciriani's architectural design. Its simplicity, its use of clear, straight lines and arcs, its purity were clearly distancing devices. No pseudo-realism here; no sounds, no voices, no mimetic recreation, no appeals to the familiar and the comforting. Instead we have a museum which enables people quietly to contemplate the past—a cruel and violent moment in the past— without being told that they can share the "experience." The beauty of the museum disturbs and disorients in a museum on war. Thus

Fig. 17. Historial de la Grande Guerre, Péronne, Somme, France. (Historial)

the pristine white of the walls, and the high polish of the floors, are distancing devices. They present a face which is radically other than that of the subject, and thereby force us to think about what the art of historical representation is all about.

The second feature of the Historial which gives it its striking character is its explicitly comparative framework. In the *vitrines,* or display cases, three horizontal lines offer the visitor items and images from Germany, France, Britain, and their dominions at war. Everything in the museum is arranged in a tripartite fashion. Since the Battle of the Somme was fought here by the British, French, and German armies, the least we could do was to reflect that fact, rather than maintain a national framework with some reference to the visitors who made their way to this part of Picardie. The staggering character and implications of the Battle of the Somme, so significant in the overall history of the twentieth century, cannot be understood if only national units or national cultural forms are addressed.

The third way in which the museum made a distinctive statement was through its use of space. The most striking features of the floor design are the *fosses,* or shallow dugouts which are arranged in rooms 2 and 3. Two features of this design help account for its power. The first is that to privilege horizontality is to exit from a certain heroic discourse of war. The vertical is the language of hope, and anyone who has seen the great painting *Christ in the Tomb,* by Hans Holbein, now in the Kunstmuseum in Basel, will know that to adopt the horizontal plane as a principle of the organization of space is a three-dimensional way of challenging conventional representations of war and beliefs about its redemptive features.[1] What made this form so appropriate is that to point downward is to recognize where most soldiers lived their lives when they came to the Somme. Like the museum itself, they went into the earth and emerged out of it to fight the battle and the war commemorated in it.

The use of these *fosses* fits in well with the overall design of the building. The sense of a vector which moves from below ground to the surface and beyond is strikingly visible if you take the time to view the museum from across the adjoining pond, where on a clear day you can see the white walls of the building emerging from the water and rising to the sky. The war is clearly engraved on this landscape; it is under our feet (fig. 17).

The fosses, which we designed as central features in the museum, were puzzling to some colleagues from the Imperial War Museum who shared in the preparation of the Historial. They felt the arrangement would fail. The fosses were filled with valuable objects—uniforms and the stuff of ordinary life in the trenches—and it was inevitable that children would fall in, or that objects would be damaged or stolen. The introduction of an alarm triggered by proximity to the fosses did not satisfy them. By and large, their fears have not been born out. And here it is, the power of horizontality, which may explain the power of the design. There is a kind of funereal quality to these rectangular spaces, in which the uniforms of soldiers are laid out in a pristine manner. The clean, pure, arranged quality of the exhibit undercuts the sense that the visitor is approaching a grave, but the unavoidable impulse to look down changes the angle of vision of visitors and arrests their attention. Perhaps the correct metaphor is to an archeological dig, though now, after the carnage of 11 September 2001, the two may be seen as more proximate than they were in 1992.

The horizontal has other meanings in the museum. In room 1, on the eve of war, three maps of the world are placed on the floor horizontally to represent points of conflict—armaments, empires, territories. On the left are showcases and displacements which deal with what Europeans had in common, vertically arranged. Standing between the showcases and the maps, we can see the choice of war on the right and peace on the left. This spatial narrative makes the critical point that war was not inevitable, and that the sources of rapprochement were just as visible as the sources of antagonism prior to the outbreak of war.

Secondly, in the adjacent room, the *Salle des Portraites,* the verticality of hope, represented by ten floor-to-ceiling columns on which are displayed faces from ordinary family photographs, stands before the horizontality of horror, in the fifty gravures which form Otto Dix's terrifying series *Der Krieg.* Before descending into the war, and into rooms 2, 3, and 4, the visitor is invited to shed what might be described as the "Star Wars" mentality, where combat is individual and noble and vertical. The Great War was by and large another kind of war entirely.

Fourthly, the museum challenges the viewer by developing different forms of representations of war in its displays. Once again, I want to emphasize the accidental and the coincidental, in order to highlight how what we did merged with independent developments in the field of cultural history outside of our own specialty. Through the creation and evolution of this museum, we have added our voices to those who study cultural history centrally as the history of representations.

A word or two is needed on what the term *representations* has come to mean. At the same time as we were at work, a substantial literature on the nature of representation in cultural history emerged. One of its prominent spokesmen is Roger Chartier,[2] who (following Louis Marin[3] and Michel de Certeau[4]) has specified three levels of representations at issue in historical narratives. Once again, without intending to, we built a museum using these distinctions, without any awareness that we were doing so. Perhaps Hegel was right; there are some currents that are just in the air, and we breathe them in whether we know it or not.

Consider these categories of representations explored by Chartier. The first is taxonomic. Representations of this order "embody within individuals the divisions of the social world and . . . organize schemes of perception by which individuals classify, judge, and act." Anyone gazing at the maps on the floor in room 1 is confronting this sort of representation, in which taxonomies of international power are visually charted.

The second defines representations "as signs and such symbolic 'performances' as images, rites, or gestures." Consider two items in room 2 which fulfill this definition. There is a widow's gown, placed in this, the first room to deal directly with the war. This is its proper place, since 1914 was the most murderous phase of the conflict for France, and mourning hit the civilian population with brutal force from the outset of hostilities. Then again, there is a wooden sign, originally left on the destroyed town hall of Péronne by withdrawing German troops in 1917, collected by Australian troops who entered the town, who then donated it to the Imperial War Museum, who returned it to us for display in the museum. The sign says "Nicht ärgern, nur wundern": don't be angry, just be amazed. Here is a sign as well as a symbolic performance of military power, following military conventions to level the ground of an abandoned strongpoint. No atrocities here, says the sign. Religious objects, paintings, sketches: all these representations associated with "images, rites, and gestures" are visible in room 2.

Then there is a third meaning of representation as metaphor, or, in other words, as "the embodiment within a representative (individual or collective, concrete or abstract) of an identity or a power" evidently and unmistakably beyond that of the specific object itself. Thus the Crown prosecutes in Britain; the Euro rises and falls in value, both of which stand for legal authority and economic power reduced to a phrase or a bill of exchange. Such representative forms compress narratives into a snapshot or a very reduced phrase pointing to something powerful and something which isn't there.

Consider the three fosses right at the entry to room 3. Here we have a set of representations forming a syllogism which says much about the nature of combat. On the left is a fosse dedicated to various kinds of weaponry used here. In the middle is a fosse containing items of defense, some cunning, some positively medieval. Who would have thought of chain mail as a protection against machine gun or artillery fire? Or of an upside-down wheelbarrow, behind which soldiers crawled on their knees, an image replicated in one of the films shown on the video monitor on the right-hand wall. But the representation is only complete when we turn to the end of the syllogism: we move from thesis—killing power—to antithesis—protection, and finally to synthesis, in the form of a fosse dedicated to surgery and medical care, graced by the surgical kit and flute belonging to Georges Duhamel. This is a three-part narrative in which, as Jünger put it, machines were arrayed against men, and the machines had the advantage.[5] The objects are organized in such a way as to tell a story about "combat," or, as Duhamel himself wrote ironically, about "civilization,"[6] or, if you will, about "catastrophe," the human results of which are shown in the filmic material of the broken bodies of soldiers in front of the surgical fosse.

This set of representations is about something which is not there, but which must be recalled to enter the world of battle: namely fear, suffering, blood, and carnage. In the same space of the museum, without even a notice, there is another metaphoric representation of something not there—the Battle of the Somme itself. In this museum dedicated to the history of the war in general, and to the war on the Western Front in particular, it may seem odd that there is no visual representation of this battle. Nor can there be. By leaving a blank wall on your right between rooms 2 and 3, and adjacent to the audiovisual room, we confront you with the radical impossibility of representing the Battle of the Somme. This absence, or silence, or void, if you will, is an anti-monument, a challenge to our comprehension of the anticipation, the terror and exhaustion, and pain, and anguish, and ugliness which constituted the battle perhaps one million soldiers knew on both sides of the line. What was it like to be here, on the Somme at 8 o'clock on 1 July 1916, or 1 August, or 1 September, or 1 October when the battle was still going on? We simply do not know in a way we can represent in this museum. We do not offer "the trench experience," as does the Imperial War Museum, or a mock recreation. We bring the visitor, through a set of spatial metaphors, to the limits of representation itself.

Let me hasten to add that this kind of approach to history is about real absences, irreplaceable losses, a void in the societies waging war which could never be filled. Behind the representations lie these losses, as any visitor to the cemeteries dotted throughout this countryside will know. What has been lost as well is a set of representations of war, common before 1914, about the nobility of arms, the cleansing effects of combat, the redemptive character of sacrifice. We are at a great distance from these values and the cultures which created and affirmed them. The design and museography of the Historial de la Grande Guerre expresses this distance, and asks the visitor to gaze over it to a time and a place very far from where we are today.

Challenges

The Historial points to a European future which is not only political in character, but one which will also take new turns in scholarship. In this latter context, I would like to offer a few remarks about ways in which the experience of creating a museum has affected my approach to scholarship, and then offer a word or two about some of the ways in which we have fallen short of our original goals.

So far I have referred to the effect of scholarship on the museum. What about the reverse effects? Being forced to represent history through objects and images has reduced the scale of my own historical writing. Watching Gérard Rougeron, Jean-Pierre Thierry and the staff of the museum, and other collectors such as Gerd Krumeich made me reduce my field of vision, to miniaturize it, as it were. Perhaps helping to create a museum is the way to discover that small is beautiful. I do not see anything accidental in the linkage between our collective work in the museum, so dominated by objects in the Historial—objects at once so fragile, so transitory, and so pregnant with meaning—and Stéphane Audoin-Rouzeau's work on micro-history,[7] or Annette Becker's work on one remarkable individual, Maurice Halbwachs.[8]

Secondly, the use of video screens to provide visitors to the museum with documentary film of remarkable quality stimulated me to work on the power of contemporary film to inform and at times to distort our understanding of the past. In particular, films made by army physicians to show other doctors what shell shock looked like—some of which are on display in room 3—have been central to my own work on traumatic memory.

Thirdly, working in French and in a French project introduced me to a highly unusual and little valorized part of our profession— namely collective scholarship. We in the *centre de recherche* enjoy passing through a museum we helped construct, not despite but perhaps because none of our names appears on its walls. Being at the center of this kind of public historical project was a once-in-a-lifetime opportunity. No one of us could possibly have done it alone, but our profession does not recognize or value such collective activity. Perhaps later generations will shed some of the fetishization of the authorial voice which afflicts our own, and accept that some essential projects are simply too big for any one individual to encompass.

In one other important respect, the work we have done on the museum has made me revise my scholarly views. As I have already noted, the Historial is an experiment in comparative history. I recall well a moment when we were editing the papers of our inaugural conference of 1992, and I suggested to our group that the better title for the papers was *"Cultures [pluriel] et guerre, 1914–1918."*[9] That suggestion was adopted, but I do not think we recognized the implications of the addition of a single "s" to our book.

That "s" made me wonder about how truly comparative is the historical scholarship which has emerged from the *centre de recherche.* In its spatial narrative, it is emphatically comparative. But in the way we do history, I wonder if this is so. This question led to others. Perhaps the robust survival of national historiographies is the outcome of a comparative approach. Why? Because in some respects national cultural histories may not be comparable. Instead of a collective memory of the Great War, perhaps what we have unearthed is an "uncollective memory" of the past, fragmented into national units. We started off here to produce comparative cultural history but have wound up creating comparative cultural histories. Why the plural? Because the way cultural history has developed over the last decade or so, in the Historial as elsewhere, suggests that the comparative approach abounds, but its purpose is to offer insights which enrich rather than displace national histories.

Perhaps too this return to the national unit as the destination of comparative cultural history is unavoidable. The agenda of comparative cultural history may be both futile and fertile. It is an ideal type which can never be realized but whose very existence as an ideal helps enrich national cultural histories in profoundly important ways.

What follows is not the end of comparison, but its reconfiguration. Perhaps the best way to move forward from this point is not to give up the effort, but to treat comparison in a different way, one in which it discloses the ineluctable, irreducible differences and particularities of national cultures. Comparative history may be the path to our understanding of precisely this uncollective memory, those bits which do not make it across borders and cultural frontiers.

Perhaps a better way of capturing both the spirit and the utility of the historical work we have done in the Historial is to describe it as *relational history*.[10] That is, the framework is comparative, but the outcome of the comparisons is national. In effect the salient features of the national case are brought into relief by juxtaposing them to other, distinctive national cases. At the center of the conceptual space is, for instance, the French soldiers' newspapers, their *journaux des tranchées;* deepening our understanding are studies to the right and left of it on British and German trench newspapers and flysheets.[11] You can repeat the exercise by highlighting female labor,[12] or French songs,[13] and the same geometry appears. The core case is illuminated by reference to comparisons from peripheral ones.

Another way of making the same point is mathematical. Comparison establishes a relationship between variables which may have different valences, but which are entities of roughly the same kind. What I term "relational history" is different, in that it does not treat two or three cases as equal, but rather chooses one as the focus, and heightens that focus by putting alongside it other instances of a similar kind.

I suspect that much work which falls under the rubric of comparative history is very similar to this asymmetrical geometry of relational history, in this context, a history of an individual country or culture at war, placed in spatial and temporal proximity to other nations at war. Perhaps it is time for comparative historians to come out of the closet and admit what is really in their hearts: that they are doing national history in imaginative, sometimes daring, ways.[14]

In a way, this is a very positive development, since the notion of a common European historical curriculum or educational system is still well over the horizon. Our students still study national history as part of their preparation for citizenship. And given the challenges of European integration, the defense of national histories is likely to intensify in coming years. In French scholarship, the Historial has helped erase the occlusion of the Battle of the Somme by Verdun. In German scholarship on the Great War, there is much emerging today that would have been impossible to foresee a decade ago.[15] And in Britain, the boom in Great War studies and films and novels and tourism continues, bringing together military historians and cultural historians in a perhaps still slightly uncomfortable proximity, but a proximity nonetheless.[16]

What has not emerged is a European history of the war. In Britain, the Anglo-German antagonism still dominates the literature of synthetic works, from Sir Michael Howard to Niall Ferguson.[17] Both in the general literature and in the Historial we still have precious little to say about the Eastern Front. Austria, Italy, Russia, Serbia, a whole world at war is there, but not here. And the role of colonies and dominions in the war is only barely touched on. Indeed in room 2 there is a *fosse* dedicated to imperial participation which shows how deeply French the discourse of the museum is. Alongside

North African uniforms and paraphernalia is the gear of an Australian soldier, as if these self-reliant, independent Antipodean men were no different from inhabitants of the French or British empires. I can assure you that in Canberra they were not amused. But from a French perspective, one can see what it means and how it happened.

The challenge for the future is to rectify these omissions, and to extend our gaze not only spatially but also temporally, to the way the shadow of the war has fallen on later conflicts and later generations. Displays must change because historical debates move on. The history of the museum has much to teach us about the way scholars learn from forays outside the academy.

Located behind and juxtaposed to a medieval castle, the Historial shows the hiddenness of the history of the war. The sequence of the two buildings, constructed precisely so that you can't see the Historial from the market square in front of the castle, heightens the sense that we are very remote from the nostalgia and romance of ruins. This museum speaks of ruins of another kind—the ruin of the hope of progress, the ruin of millions of lives, the ruin of the idea that war can be predicted, controlled, imagined. To be sure, we are the bearers of a narrative about loss, but it is a narrative constructed in such a way as to be revised and renewed by the next generation of historians who will tell it here in their own way.

CHAPTER 11

"Witness to a Time"
Authority, Experience, and the Two World Wars

In the aftermath of war, there is a tendency for those who create representations of the conflict to wear the mantle of consolation. Tolerable or sanitized images of combat and violence against civilians are seductive and politically useful, since they present observers with elements of hope. They make war thinkable, even in the aftermath of terrible carnage. At times these positive narratives become intolerable to some of those who lived through these events. Such men and women then decide to take a stand. They speak with what Joan Scott has termed "the authority of direct experience,"[1] and aim to strip away from our understanding of war and repression romantic or heroic readings of the past.

This rejection of anodyne or bowdlerized approaches to war and violence is evident in the testimony given by many people during and after the two world wars. Such individuals form a general category of observers, whose significance has grown over time. Witnesses have proliferated in part because war crimes trials have taken place all over the world. But not everyone who gives evidence in a courtroom shares the same outlook or perspective.

Some of these observers have been called "moral witnesses." Such people are witnesses, not in the religious sense, pointing out someone prepared to affirm her faith by dying for it, nor in the legal sense, indicating simply someone who testifies at the bar. They are rather storytellers of a special kind. They are individuals with a terrible tale to tell, people whose very lives are defined by that story. What sets aside the narrative moral witnesses have to tell is that it is based on the individual's direct and personal experience of what Kant called "radical evil."[2] Avishai Margalit has investigated the philosophical claims of "moral witnesses" and argues that such people are carriers of what he terms our collective memory of radical evil and of those destroyed or disfigured by it.[3] Witnesses have special standing as spokesmen for the injured and the dead, and in particular for those who suffer through war, political repression, and racial persecution.

Moral witnesses testify at trials, and, to be sure, trials are theaters of memory, places where memory is performed. But moral witnesses speak out in many other ways. They write memoirs; they give interviews; they present evidence to the reading or viewing public. Some become public figures. Rigobertu Menchu and Elie Wiesel, both Nobel-prize winners, come to mind in this context.

The moral witness carries a particular kind of memory and makes special claims to our attention. In a book on memory and remembrance, this group of people deserves special attention. In this chapter we examine the moral witness as an iconic figure in the memory boom, and address some of the difficulties imbedded in his or her testimony.

The basic argument is that moral witnesses have a story to tell, but it is frequently one which is constructed as against the grain of conventional wisdom. In the aftermath of the two world wars, narratives of heroism and romantic notions of armed struggle spread widely. Some survivors went along with these tales; others were revolted by them, and decided to expose the lies and distortions imbedded in the generally accepted story. In doing so, they stood up as moral witnesses.

Such people told their stories out of anger. They framed their words and thoughts in the context of discursive fields which troubled them and which they could not abide. When they reached this conclusion, they tried to set the record straight. At times this happened in a courtroom, but not always. Moral witnesses live among us long after the termination of the wars which disfigured their lives and long after judicial proceedings are closed. They claim the status of truth-tellers, with a story to tell and retell. But they are also determined to stop others from lying about the past or from sanitizing it.

In this chapter, I will first consider the nature of moral witnessing, as Avishai Margalit has constructed it. I will then consider two distinct instances of witnessing, each of which has the reactive, adversarial character of setting the record straight. I will conclude by trying to draw out some of the difficulties in the claims moral witnesses make and how witnesses of this kind have helped shape the memory boom.

Moral Witnessing

Avishai Margalit has provided a powerful sketch of what he calls the "moral witness." This is an alloy, a composite noun, in which the two parts cannot be separately analyzed. Let us consider his argument first. The category he explores includes those who know through their own experience "the combination of evil and the suffering it produces: witnessing only evil or only suffering is not enough." It is this double burden—what he terms "knowledge-by-acquaintance of suffering"—which separates the witness from the observer or the victim.[4]

It is not only the awfulness of the experience, but the nature of the risk taken by the witness which sets her apart. Risk here means not only having been targeted for persecution or injury, but also facing danger in the very act of telling the story itself. Those who accept that risk and speak out anyway are "moral witnesses," those "whose testimony has a moral purpose."[5] That purpose—ensuring that the story is told—gives the witness a standing utterly different from that of a reporter or an historian. These groups try to establish the facts, and their position in the story is outside of it. The witness, in contrast, is inside the story, and his very survival is essential in the storytelling he has to do. Thus, in Margalit's terms, "The moral witness has to live in order to serve."[6]

This storytelling is based upon a hope, and a slender one at that, "that in another place or another time there exists, or will exist, a moral community that will listen to their testimony."[7] What makes this hope so sober is that it flies in the face of the tendency for those subjected to radical evil to despair and to conclude that the notion of "a moral community" is an absurd and mocking illusion. The witness says no. Though no religious source is needed for this denial of despair, there are many religious statements which support it. Margalit refers to the language of the Mishna on this point, enjoining us to act in the following way: "Where there is no human being, be one."[8] The minimal moral community established by the act of witnessing is one, or rather one person now and the same person later—the first person is "the current self," close to the events being narrated; the second is "one's future self," who will somehow still retain a moral outlook. Beyond the teller of the story is an audience, perhaps of uncertain size and skepticism, but made up of people who may come listen and understand some day.

Witnesses are guides to an experience most of us never have to face. And as they write or speak about their lives, they establish not only a set of facts, but what it felt like to be marked indelibly by them. Margalit uses a meteorological metaphor to make his point here. "To be a truthful chronicler is to be a perfect historical seismograph, to record accurately the vibrations of history. But a seismograph does not tell us what it is like to be in an earthquake. For that we need a moral witness."[9]

Witnesses uncover evil, and without them the perpetrators can bury their crimes along with their victims. It is the very act of speaking which establishes the case against the deniers. But the witness, Margalit holds, has no political agenda. His voice stands whether or not something long-lasting—a treaty, a convention, restitution, compensation, or a guilty verdict—actually happens. The testimony is what matters, not its instrumental uses.[10]

The witness's tale is a first-person account, a "personal encounter";[11] the prosecutor or legislator or banker or diplomat creates third-person narratives, stories about what happened to others. The political witness may tell it "like it was," but the moral witness tells it "like it felt, that is, telling what it was like to be subjected to such evil."[12]

For Margalit, moral witnesses are, therefore, crucial carriers of memory. Through them we can learn about terrible events in the past, but more importantly, we can learn crucial moral lessons from them. They speak for a group whose ties are with others who passed through the fire; they have what Margalit terms a "thick identity" based upon "thick relations," personal bonds which only they shared. Thus they speak for a particular group, but in doing so they reach out to us all. Some manage to speak for humanity as a whole, since "a moral witness may well give voice to an ethical community that is endangered by an evil force."[13] Speaking out, as a first-person witness to evil, Margalit suggests, is a symbolic act of great significance, one which may affirm the power of language itself to reach into the darkest moments in history.

Witnessing and Setting the Record Straight

My claim is that looking at particular moral witnesses in time and place requires some revision in the argument Margalit has advanced. What we need to do in particular is to contextualize the figure of the witness, to locate him or her within a marketplace of narratives, some political, some not, and some of which are distorted or mendacious, even when they are constructed by those with direct experience. In other words, the witness never speaks in a vacuum. He or she can stop others from either lying about the past with impunity or mobilizing narratives in the service of a cause beyond the events they recount. I want to argue, using Scott's frame of reference,[14] that they assert the authority of direct experience, but they do not do so alone. Others were there, too, and tell stories which vary widely both in content and in context. Witnesses, I hold, frequently speak against the grain, as it were. They expose "untruth" or truth hijacked for a host of purposes of which they, the witnesses, do not approve.

And there is always a lot of "untruth" about. In this chapter, I shall discuss witnesses who wrote about their lives in the two world wars against the grain of other narratives. One was a survivor of the First World War; the other a survivor of the Second. Their lives were very different, but the anger underlying their moral purposes was similar. Witnessing to the Holocaust is by now a very well-known phenomenon. But a generation earlier, there was also a group of moral witnesses, truth-tellers, men who saw the slaughter firsthand, and who were determined to expose what they took to be "false" accounts of what had happened. Witnessing the horrors of war did not start with the Nazis. Here again, we see ways in which cultural forms developed in the First World War point to modes of expression and remembrance during and after the Second.

Veterans and Witnessing

Before turning to the "witnesses" of the carnage of the Great War, it is important to meet the objection that those who fought voluntarily or as conscripts in the 1914–18 conflict can never be compared to those who were deported and exterminated in the Nazi Holocaust of the Second World War. There is certainly no parallel in terms of volition or in terms of the capacity of one side to inflict injury on the other. Great War soldiers killed and maimed other Great War soldiers; Jews did so to Nazis only in the fantasies of the killers.

What is similar is the tendency of the survivor of both conflicts to form groups of what Margalit calls "thick relations," people bonded by their experience of violence and suffering and who construct narratives about their lives in similar ways. Here the experiences are not comparable, but the signifying practices which contemporaries fashioned to give meaning to them are comparable. Some moral witnesses had worn a soldier's uniform in the Great War; the uniform (and life) of a concentration camp inmate was very different. But many of the stories told about the horror of the trenches, and those told about the Holocaust, were written and spoken by people who shared one feature in common—that is, they were determined to tell the story they knew without sugarcoating it with moral uplift or romance.

Many veterans of the Great War were as much witnesses, in Margalit's sense, as were those who passed through the concentration camps and death camps of the Second World War. Many soldiers of the 1914–18 conflict were determined to tell their story as witnesses to the butchery which took the lives of nine million men. They certainly had "knowledge-by acquaintance of suffering." They knew what risk-taking was all about, and many took risks by standing up and speaking their minds after the war was over. Their testimony emphatically had a moral purpose; they ensured that what they took to be a truthful story about the war was told, whether people believed it or not.[15]

Many of these witnesses had some kind of religious education or outlook; others were entirely secular. And, in Margalit's terms, they tell us not only what happened, but what it felt like to be subjected to a kind of warfare no one had ever seen before, a war of machines against men. To them their testimony is what mattered, and the last thing they wanted was to make political capital out of it. Others saw politics as a continuation of war by other means.

Adolf Hitler wrote about his war in *Mein Kampf,* and he too had the "authority of direct experience." The purpose of his memoir was to unfold the political program he helped shape alongside other veterans in the 1920s. Politics was the destination of memory. The same was true of the French veteran Henri Barbusse, the author of a war memoir entitled *Le Feu,* published in 1917 and translated into English as *Under Fire.* Barbusse spoke out against war, and used the proceeds of his award-winning novel to help fund one of the first French veterans' organizations. He later became a leading communist intellectual and political figure.

There were others, though, who claimed to reject politics of any kind—right, left, or center. This strange configuration requires a bit of elaboration. As Antoine Prost has shown, for many French veterans between the wars, politics was not something natural, but rather something disgusting, something done by little pigs wearing elegant clothes who win elections only in order to get closer to the trough. To them the term "politician" was synonymous with self-serving, corrupt, stupid, and insensitive time-server. In their terms, to engage in politics is to debase oneself and become morally compromised by definition. Politics puts people off, it is "execrable," it is "vile," "shady," "repugnant."[16]

Why? Because it turns "truth"—what they took to be the "truth" known by the veterans—into lies, lies which are used by politicians in ways which make a mockery of the suffering of the men who went to war. What matters in this context is not the validity of the somewhat extreme argument French veterans advanced. It is the way their argument sketched out a role for them as "moral witnesses." As Prost put it, their lives are shaped by their link with the dead of the war. They speak out of a commitment to "witnessing, presence, and loyalty."[17]

And they speak out of anger. It is what gives them the energy and the determination to fight for their version of the truth. Moral statements are what witnesses offer; but they feel they are in danger of being shoved away from the microphone by political "vermin" who would not know what a moral argument was if it should hit them in the face. Such men are "refuse left over from before the war, shirkers, or failures," and the best advice a veteran can give is this: "Let these fucking guys leave us alone and get lost."[18]

In place of the politician, the veteran had to speak for those who were not there—the millions of dead men whose "thick relations" to the living veterans were made visible by processions in every town and village annually on Armistice Day. And this they did.

War Books and Witnessing

We have already alluded to the way memoirs and collections of letters constituted, in the interwar years and beyond, a vast and complex repository of the direct experience of war.[19] Some of those who produced war books took it upon themselves to speak and act as witnesses. Others did not, and pocketed the cash which came from a public eternally fascinated by the war. The distinction between the two kinds of writers of war books was a very delicate matter. Who spoke for the *poilus?* And who turned their suffering into profits? At times the moral character of moral witnessing is defined by immoral witnessing.

A clear instance of this witnessing by negative reference is the case of Jean Norton Cru. A Protestant Frenchman who spent his academic life in the United States, Norton Cru wrote two books which spoke of and for the witness. The titles themselves announce this mission: *Témoins* (Witnesses) in 1929[20] and *du Témoignage* (On Witnessing) in 1931.[21] The same nuances of the term *witnessing* in English color the French.[22]

Here is a case which poses the question of the divide between history and memory in no uncertain terms. Norton Cru argued that "true" history could only be written by those able to recount "true" memory. In the conclusion, I shall return to this unacceptable formulation of the nature of history and memory and narratives of both. But taking him on his own terms, it is important to see that from his position it is vital that history and memory be brought into line. When he wrote in the late 1920s, this, he believed, was not at all the case. The moral witness, in Norton Cru's project, aligns history with his or her memory, and thereby speaks for those who are not there—those who fought but did not survive.

Norton Cru was a veteran of the Great War. He had lived in the United States from 1908, but returned immediately to France on the outbreak of the war. From October 1914 to February 1917 he was an infantry sergeant serving in the trenches of the Western Front. In 1915 he served at Vauquois, which was a hill turned into what looked like a volcano—two armies perched on the lips of a giant crater. In 1916 he was on the Chemin des Dames. And then he joined three-quarters of the French infantry in the battle of Verdun, which lasted for ten unbroken months—probably the longest single battle in history. Then he was seconded to serve as an interpreter in the rear first for the British and then for the American armies. He was disgusted by the way the war was presented behind the lines; it was so near and yet so far from those—either soldiers or civilians—who did not see or did not say how terrible it was. Finally he was sent on a mission to the United States to rally support for the war; it was back in his adopted home where he learned the war was over.[23]

For Norton Cru, it would never be completely over. He made a pilgrimage to Verdun in 1922, and there he walked the ground of the battlefield to the sound of exploding shells, which were being detonated by those trying to clear the area of the deadly remains of the battle. He ate wild mulberries on the mutilated landscape, "And I did not think it would be a sacrilege: the dead excuse me, they know that I was once one of theirs."[24]

The sense of horror he retained about war was so deep that he came to dedicate his life to speaking out about it. He was also a man disturbed, shocked by the romantic stupidities and arid narratives which appeared by the bucketful in the decade after the war. When he read official histories, military histories, accounts of battles and military maneuvers, he experienced a kind of cognitive dissonance. In these pages were many things, but the war he knew as a front-line soldier was not one of them. He simply did not recognize there the reality through which he had passed. This moral shock is what turned him into a witness, or rather an arbiter of witnesses, a judge of those who bore witness to war.

His books are readings of war memoirs, based upon a view that the same "scientific" methods applied without much fuss to political history had to be applied in the same way to the history of war. That is why we have to evaluate the evidence of eyewitnesses, the writers of the memoir literature of war. It was crucial to strip it of its naturalness, which grows out of unexamined biases in many of these memoirs and about their tendency to configure the clash of arms as an utterly unfounded romantic episode in heroism. How can this be true, Norton Cru the veteran asked? In sum, he wanted to expose the ideology in many war memoirs in order to prevent people from lying about the war. Here is his prolegomenon:

> Has the question been raised whether the traditional conception of battle is in agreement with the objective and psychological facts observed by witnesses? Is there any evidence from witnesses? Where is it? Are the witnesses competent to testify? What are their credentials? I put these questions to myself, like many other soldiers no doubt, starting from that day in 1914 when the brutal shock of the first contact with the tremendous realities of war completely demolished my bookish conception of the actions and feelings of a soldier in battle.[25]

If this is a path to history, it is an unusual one, since it puts the historian in the story *and* in the evidence. Without pausing to consider the difficulties in this assertion, Cru affirmed that his subjectivity is his objectivity. Norton Cru's stated purpose is to examine the writings of his "brothers in arms." Their "thick relations" were consecrated in blood, and for them he speaks. He privileges war books written by fighting men in order to get to the first target—civilians and staff officers stationed far from the front who pretend to know what war is. The best of war books—arbitrarily defined—were written by soldiers who went through combat documents of moral witnessing totally out of reach of the civilian patriots such as Maurice Barrès, whose elevated prose spread lies about war.

What mattered most to Norton Cru was that witnesses could be separated from mere storytellers, false chroniclers who knew not of what they wrote. Moral witnesses are truth-tellers; false witnesses weave stories out of conventional cultural archives. We never see witnesses worthy of the name "fall into the vice of exaggeration or the fabrication of legend."[26] Their language is unadorned by the distortions of bias and the conventions of the past. Of three hundred writers surveyed by Norton Cru, twenty-nine pass the test. These are voices of very different men from very different walks of life who had very different wars. But they shared one thing which he believes was at the heart of the matter: the ability to record their sense experience "faithfully" in such a way as to make their accounts uncannily similar to those of other witnesses. Common sense, consistency, and an eye to details only those at the front could have seen inform their memoirs.

In contrast, the liars and distorters are legion. And to his chagrin, their words are taken by the reading public as having the same moral weight as those of true witnesses. Unless someone corrects the record, in the future ordinary people will believe the lies and delusions of those who pretend to speak of the war without knowing it at all.

The true witnesses will vanish in a kind of Gresham's law of war literature—the bad currency will drive the good currency out of circulation. Instead Cru aimed "to give a picture of war according to those who have seen it at close range; to reveal the feelings of the soldier, not those acquired by imitation or by suggestion but which are his direct reaction to contact with war; to uncover an entire literature, a whole body of testimony, an attitude of the mind, a faith, an ideal, the secret soul of this soldier community, all things not generally known or, rather, imperfectly realized and misunderstood, which is worse."

To correct the record is utterly critical, since in these true voices, there may be found "a confession at once courageous and soul-stirring, an energetic repudiation of age-old half-truths. What had to be faced is that war had pushed men beyond the limits of human endurance. "No, war is not a business for man"; it is inhumanity writ large. And any staff officer or military historian who was not there and who writes of battles through charts and maps and arrows is simply proclaiming his irresponsible ignorance. Only the "witnesses" can speak the truth.[27]

That is why it matters so much to Norton Cru to separate the wheat from the chaff. There are staff accounts, which are simple blueprints of battle; there are war memoirs infused with illusions, and then there are war memoirs, written from the bottom up, infused, Norton Cru argued, with "truth." These happy few are the moral witnesses to war and what it does to men. Out of their words, and only out of their words, can "true" history be written.[28]

And it is history with a message. From these witnesses we learn that "man comes to the point of making war only by a miracle of persuasion and deception practiced on the future combatants, in peace time, by false literature, false history and false war psychology." The profound sense of the frailty of the human body, the fear which seizes a man by the throat whatever his background or experience, that is what war is. This is what Norton Cru meant when he wrote, "If people knew what the soldier learns at his baptism of fire, nobody would consent to a solution by force of arms."[29] Only through such moral witnesses can we see the abomination of war separate from the forest of sanitized tales or lies which obscure it.

Len Smith has pointed out how Norton Cru's readings of war memoirs is profoundly engrained with a kind of Protestant literalism. The reading of texts which deal with life and death is not a neutral matter; like Holy Scripture itself, the word is the path to the sacred, though it usually is the road to the profane. In such terms, Norton Cru's emergence as a moral witness becomes clear. Here is how he put it: "There, in my trench, I took the solemn oath never to help those lies, and, if God should spare my life,—to bring back the sincere, unadorned relation of my experience. I swore never to allow my imagination or any desire for literary expression to make of my post-war self a traducer of my former fighting self. . . . I swore never to betray my comrades by painting their anguish in the bright colors of heroic, chivalrous sentiment."[30]

Interestingly, Norton Cru heaped opprobrium on the romantic antiwar memoir of the socialist (later communist) Henri Barbusse, *Le feu,* on the memoir of the right-wing novelist Dorgeles, *Le croix du bois,* as well as on what he took to be the romantic fallacies of Remarque's *All Quiet on the Western Front* and Ernst Jünger's *In Stahlgewittern.* All were guilty of resorting to conventional literary language about the romance of war, either for political reasons or to satisfy a commercial audience.

The validity of the argument that "truth" can be ascertained easily, and that there are those who can escape from the discursive field in which Norton Cru and the rest of us live, cannot bear critical scrutiny. We shall return to this point in the conclusion. Cru's position is less an analytically defensible one and more a cri de coeur. His project aimed to bear witness to the monstrous nature of war by exposing the shallow lies of most of those—in and out of uniform—who wrote about it. He owed it to those who did not come back to do so, for he was haunted in the postwar years by the sense that they would vanish without trace. Others would speak in their place and construct false accounts of the war. Norton Cru, the moral witness, did everything he could to set the record straight.

Witnessing the Holocaust: The Testimony of Leon Weliczker Wells

It is evident that the category of the moral witness antedated the Second World War. What moved the shape of this social formation onto another plane after 1941 was the Nazi attempt to conceal the crime of genocide. They intended that the victims would vanish like the ten lost tribes of Israel, and so would the manner of their extermination. The direct refutation of Holocaust denial is a familiar story. What is less well known is the way some survivors stood as moral witnesses against heroic narratives of resistance and revolt in the concentration camps and extermination camps of the Holocaust.

To be sure, simply to tell the story of what happened was an act of bravery. "I will bear witness," Victor Klemperer wrote in his diaries,[31] and he was certainly not alone.[32] Primo Levi's writing on his time in Auschwitz has become an indispensable text of moral witnessing.[33] But to bear witness against the Nazis is one thing. To bridle against heroic constructions of what the victims did under these harrowing circumstances is another.

One salient example of this kind of moral witness is that of Leon Weliczker Wells.[34] He was a very different kind of man from Klemperer, a mature scholar who had converted to Christianity at a young age, or from Levi, a young Turin chemist turned partisan fighter until captured and deported to Auschwitz. When the Nazis came to power Klemperer was head of romance languages at the Dresden

Technical University. Levi was born in 1919, raised in an assimilated Jewish family, and trained as a chemist. Leon Weliczker was younger; his education was still to come, and he was much closer to traditional Jewish culture and religious life than the other two men.

Leon Weliczker was born in 1925, in a small town, Stojanov, one hundred kilometers to the east of Lvov in Polish Galicia. His father came from a Hasidic family—part of the Belzer community—but moved away from this form of Judaism, though he was still an observant Jew. The senior Weliczker became a well-to-do timber merchant who had served in the Austrian army during the First World War. His grandfather on his mother's side was a Zionist. Leon was one of seven children, and the only member of his entire family to survive the Holocaust.[35]

At the outbreak of war they were in Lvov, but immediately fled the city, which was a major rail center, under aerial bombardment. Shortly after, the Russian army arrived, and by April 1940 the arrests of "enemies of the people" began. Leon and his father hid every night until they realized that their families would be arrested too. Life settled down and Leon and his older sister applied to study at the Technical Institute in Moscow. Their applications were accepted, but the invasion of the Soviet Union in June 1941 put an end to their plans, and to their entire world. Leon Weliczker was sixteen years old.

The German army entered Lvov on 30 June 1941, together with Ukrainian militia units. The Ukrainians took Leon, his older brother, and his father to the city jail. Along with five thousand other men they were assembled outdoors, and were both beaten unconscious, and then told they were about to be executed. They were not killed; it was a bit of theater to induce terror, and very effective theater at that. Most of the men were sent away by trucks to an uncertain fate. Leon and his father were arbitrarily released; his brother remained in jail.

In November 1941 the Jews of Lvov were concentrated in one quarter of the city. Once the ghetto was constructed, the critical step for survival was to find a work permit. This Leon and his father did in heavy construction. In March 1942 Leon was taken to a prison camp on the outskirts of Lvov. Later he was transferred to a bigger camp for two thousand inmates built off the Janowska road. In both places he did all kinds of manual labor and witnessed mindless cruelty and violence. He was a slave laborer, condemned to death but never knowing when the sentence would be carried out.

Typhoid fever was rampant in the camp, and Leon nearly succumbed to it. Feverish, he was marched to the sands near the camp and made to dig his own grave. Then he was ordered to drag another corpse to the mass grave. While doing so, he mustered the strength to run back into the camp and mingle with the prisoners. The guards assumed he had been shot, so with the cover of a dead man he evaded detection and could sneak out of the camp and rejoin his family. It was too dangerous for him to remain in Lvov, so with his younger brother he went back to the village of his birth, Stojanov, to stay with his grandfather. He worked on farms in the vicinity until one day— Yom Kippur 1942—he heard that his mother had vanished in one of the *Aktionen,* or roundups. He tried to commit suicide, but a doctor who lived nearby bound his wrists to prevent him from doing so.

Leon returned to Lvov and found work there as a glazier and a pipe fitter. At several moments he was convinced he was about to be shot, but he somehow escaped. Finally the SS took him and his two brothers to the Janowska camp. His youngest brother was shot, the other was led away to execution elsewhere.

That is when the darkest part of Leon Weliczker's imprisonment began. He was forced to join a *Sondercommando,* a Death Brigade, whose job it was to dispose of the corpses of the Nazi's victims. Astonishingly, it is this most harrowing phase of his ordeal that Weliczker was able to document in a diary. In the early parts of his autobiography, *The Death Brigade,* he reflects on his life before and during the German occupation in the past tense. When he was forced to work in the *Sondercommando,* everything is told in the present tense. The details of this horrifying ordeal described in his diary most probably were recorded shortly after they happened.

In this part of his memoirs he records aspects of the Holocaust which have become iconic. He refers to the orchestra of inmates which "serenaded" prisoners on the way to work or to execution. In his diary he noted that "we knew that for many, if not all, of us the music will someday play the "Death Tango."[36] This was the original title of the poem written by Paul Celan, whose parents died in nearby Czernowitz. Celan's poem, "Death Fugue," described the burning of the bodies of the victims. "We are digging a grave in the heavens," wrote Celan, and he repeats: "In the sky he gives us a grave." One of those who dug graves in the sky was Leon Weliczker.

What makes his story so unusual is that he is one of the few survivors of these Death Brigades. There were twenty-three such units, according to Weliczker. Twenty were composed of Russian prisoners of war, three of Jews. All but one *Sondercommando* were liquidated to cover up the crime they had covered up themselves. Weliczker was among the fifty or so survivors.[37]

What he witnessed in the ravine near the Janowska camp beggars description. His unit built a bunker there, and that is where they dealt with the dead. Some people were shot in the ravine and then burnt, whether they were still alive or not.[38] Many other corpses were brought to the site for burning. Then the remains were reduced to dust. Weliczker was among those who dragged gravestones from the Jewish cemetery to form the frame of the sifting area. The prisoners took the bones which remained after the fire and placed them so that they could be ground to dust by another group they called the "Ash Brigade." These people had to retrieve any "valuables"—jewelry, teeth, fillings, and so on—and give them to the guards. By day's end these men were covered in black ash, the remains of murdered Jews.[39] On occasion, the victims' clothes were given to the Death

Brigade to wear so they could look "clean and decent," in the words of their overseer.[40]

They opened other mass graves in the area; they disinterred and burned the bodies, and then covered up the crime by plowing and seeding the ground. Soon not a trace of the crime would remain.[41] Weliczker tried to avoid handling the bodies, but there were too many, and he too had to participate in unearthing them, flinging them into the fire, and sifting the remains of those he may have known.[42]

It is difficult to imagine a set of circumstances in which elemental notions of human dignity are so brutally called into question. Primo Levi wrote in his memoir of Auschwitz that what he saw was not the worst.[43] There may be no way of establishing where the "worst" was, but Leon Weliczker was certainly near it.

Throughout 1942 and 1943 there was talk among some prisoners of revolt, but the plans were shelved as long as their families just outside the camp were hostages. Everyone knew what would happen to their loved ones if they escaped.[44] But the deportation of the Jews of Lvov began in March 1942; a year later, in June 1943, the ghetto was liquidated, and, in November 1943, so was the Janowska camp. There was nothing more which could be done to the inmates or their families. They also knew that they would be killed as soon as the flow of bodies ceased.

To escape they formed two groups, one made up of "musicians" who would distract the guards, and another who would approach other guards with an offer of booty confiscated from the dead. This trade in contraband had become normal practice. Not everyone wanted to escape. One man who had lost his entire family and had no wish to live refused to go. On hearing of the escape plan, he took to bed and would not move. He wished the conspirators well and hoped that they would survive "and tell the world, as witnesses, how they murdered a people."[45]

To Weliczker's surprise, the plan worked. On 21 November 1943 the prisoners killed a few guards, and the others were sufficiently distracted to enable him and about fifty other men to get away. Two escapees were shot, but the rest made their way back to Lvov, along with another prisoner who joined up with them later. Together they found a barn where they could hide, together with twenty-two other Jews.[46] They were fed by a Polish farmer and his wife who took terrifying risks to do so.[47] In April 1944 the Russian army finally liberated Lvov, and all those hidden emerged safely from their cellar after nine months underground.[48] Their benefactor, the farmer who hid them, asked them not to return, since it would go badly for him with other Poles if they knew he had hidden Jews.[49] Weliczker, age nineteen, was one of several hundred surviving Jews out of a prewar population of one hundred fifty thousand in the Lvov area.

In the days after Liberation, at a gathering of survivors, he met historian Philip Friedman. Weliczker gave Friedman his diary. Weliczker later gave testimony to the Russian Justice Department about German crimes in the Lvov area, information used in the preparation for the Nuremberg trials,[50] and wrote an article about the killing of Polish intellectuals, the bodies of many of whom Weliczker had disposed of himself. He was indeed in a position to provide evidence about particular victims of the Nazis.

The danger to Weliczker was not at an end, though. Liberation was bewildering. He was alone, without ties of any kind. "Nobody wanted you. Everyone was scared of you for one reason or another. You were *witness to a time*."[51] He found work in a railway office in territory now under Soviet control, and was accused by the Soviet secret police of having been a German collaborator and a spy. The evidence was that he was still alive; the accusation was that those who had survived must have been compromised.[52] He was released, and got on the first train west.

There, in independent Poland, his life began again. He enrolled in the Polytechnic Institute in Gliwice intent on becoming an engineer. It is at this time that he got back in touch with Philip Friedman, then director of a Central Jewish Historical Commission in Lodz. This organization published Weliczker's memoir in Polish in 1946.[53] By then he had moved west to the American zone in Germany. In Munich he decided to continue his engineering studies, and he worked for the Jewish Historical Commission. After completing his doctoral studies, he emigrated to America, where he lives to this day (2003).

Witnessing the Holocaust: The Eichmann Trial

One way in which the case of Leon Weliczker Wells is so fascinating is that he encompassed multiple aspects of the work of the witness. He recorded the story while it was unfolding. He made sure that it would be heard. And he used it to bring justice to some of the killers.

In the last pages of his memoir, Weliczker described how his written testimony helped convict one of the Nazis in charge of the Death Brigade. In 1947 he confronted the man in custody, and confirmed his identity. Despite appeals by the man's family to Weliczker that he exercise compassion in his testimony—pleas described with scarcely veiled anger at the monumental refusal of these people to face what this man had done—Weliczker wrote to the Polish court in support of the prosecution, which indeed convicted the man of war crimes.[54]

Here Weliczker's witnessing entered another phase, which reached its apogee in Jerusalem. His testimony in the trial of Adolf Eichmann began on 1 May 1961.[55] He was present not because he had information on Eichmann. He could not link Eichmann to any of the German soldiers or SS men who had run the Janowska camp or the Death Brigade. He was there in part because he could document the conspiracy to exterminate the Jews in the Lvov region, and in part because he was practically the only survivor alive who could testify as to the steps the Nazis took to cover up their crimes. This point was crucial in establishing the legal principle that Eichmann was engaged in acts he and his colleagues knew to be illegal at the time they were committed. Such knowledge of illegality helped establish the credentials of a court which tried him for crimes committed long before the court, and indeed the State of Israel itself, had been established.[56]

The attorney general of the State of Israel, Gideon Hausner, introduced Weliczker Wells to the court as an engineer, a man of science, a researcher for a large American shipping firm, with patents and publications to his name. He was clearly a man of intelligence and one used to evaluating evidence in a systematic way. He told the court too that he was the only survivor of his extended family of seventy-six people.

He was also the author of a memoir of the Nazi occupation, introduced to the court as exhibit T 214. Here is the exchange between Hausner, asking the questions, and Wells, on the stand:

> Q. Before we continue, perhaps you can tell me, did you immediately after the War write the book in Polish by the name of *The Death Brigade, Sonderkommando 1005,* published in Lodz in 1946?
>
> A. I wrote it during the War. But it was handed over the second day after the War to the Polish Historical Commission, which published it a year later.
>
> Q. This contained the notes which you made continuously throughout the War?
>
> A. Yes. The original notes during the War were handed to Dr. Friedman, and he took it over, as the head of the Historical Commission to be published in Lodz. From these original papers, which I never rewrote then, only a part were published as *Death Brigade.* But these original papers contain the whole story of the whole time of the War.

It is this document which made Wells's testimony so valuable to the prosecution. He testified in 1961, eighteen years after his time as a member of the Death Brigade, and memories fade. The notes he had made in wartime confirmed his testimony.

Wells proceeded to recount graphically the multiple forms of brutality meted out to the Jews of Lvov from the earliest days of the German occupation. He told of his time in the Janowska concentration camp, and the tortures and murders committed there. He recounted the story of his escape from execution. He recounted seeing horrors of many kinds, including the death of his brother. Then Hausner asked him this question, which raised the issue of witnessing as a moral act:

> Q. Dr. Wells, before we go on, tell me—now you had seen all your family dead, you were now back in the Janowska camp—how could you stand it? How could you survive it? What gave you the will to go on?
>
> A. It was the will of responsibility, that somebody had to remain to tell the world that it was the idea of the Nazis to kill all the Jews—so we had a responsibility somehow to withstand this idea and to be alive. There was not one of us, as will be shown later, that had any interest whether it was he or the second man; it was always: who will be the best to survive and the others will go to death—so as to feel that one man or at least somebody would survive out of all of this.

Wells then came to the story of the Death Brigade. He detailed the ghoulish procedures followed, the disinterring of the bodies, their burning, the collection of gold items, rings, teeth, and so on, up to eight–ten kilograms a day, the grinding of the bones to dust, the meticulous enumeration of the number of people killed. He told how he and the other Jewish men were forced to eat their meals on the piles of corpses themselves, how some people were burned while still alive.

Wells told too of their constant thoughts about escape, and their continual fear of inflicting torture on their families if they did so.

Then came the liquidation of the ghetto and the Janowska camp, removing the last obstacles to an escape plan. But before telling the court about his escape, he was interrogated on a point which left a scar on him, one which helps us to understand why he continued to write about his experiences in the Holocaust in the years to come. It is a point making clear that as a moral witness, he had the duty to expose other, to him unacceptable, narratives of what had happened during the Holocaust. Hausner asked him the following question:

> Q. Now tell me—there weren't many guards for two thousand people: why did all these people go to be shot—why didn't they try at least, to injure their murderers before they were killed?
>
> A. First of all, the two thousand people were not together—they would bring them in groups of forty, thirty-five or fifty, shoot them, and then the next truck would come with another forty. . . . There were a lot of guards in proportion to each group, not against the two thousand. But secondly, in the beginning one always has somebody to lose, a family to worry about. . . . At this time, in 1943, nobody cared anymore—he was always one of the last, had lost everybody; and just to be tortured longer—the tortures were so more real to these people than their death, because life didn't mean any more to them . . .
>
> Q. You mean they wanted death without torture?
>
> A. To finish with it.

This exchange comes to the critical point: why did these people not resist more? Why did *you* not fight back? It is a question posed by many Israelis. And it was a question Wells considered "immoral."[57]

When Wells recounted his escape from the Death Brigade, he once more brought to the court's attention the terrible state of the prisoners, the desire of many for a speedy death, and the unwillingness of some of them to go back to a world in which all those they loved had been killed. All that remained was for someone to be a witness. This is how he put it: "On this night we decided that a certain group of people and also the musicians must stay till the last minute—[knowing that they would] be killed—because they will be cover for the other people. And they all accepted it very willingly because none of us had [any] interest [in] who [was] to survive. The only idea was that one of us survives and tells the world what happened here." Among the fifty or so people who survived the Death Brigade, Leon Weliczker Wells alone was able to tell the story.

Moral Witnesses and the Construction of Meaning

The testimony of Leon Weliczker Wells at the Eichmann trial was not the end of his time as a witness. He provided testimony at the trial in Stuttgart of the SS men who had been responsible for the Janowska camp. He published his memoir *The Janowska Road* (later entitled *The Death Brigade*) in 1963 and produced one further book of memoirs, as well as an historical account of the record of the American Jewish community during the Holocaust.[58] He also contributed a lengthy interview to the Fortunoff Video Archive at Yale University, which reviews many of his earlier statements.

In a host of ways, Wells is Margalit's prototypical moral witness. Wells had a mission, the mission he fulfilled first in Poland and then fourteen years later before the Eichmann tribunal in 1961. He was determined to ensure that at least one person told the story who had a firsthand encounter with suffering and radical evil. As Margalit put it, he told us not only what happened during a murderous earthquake, but what it felt like to be there. He spoke up in such a way as to restore some semblance of a belief in a moral order by describing in as clear and clinical a manner as he could manage the anatomy of genocide in one particular place.

And yet there are two other dimensions to the story of witnesses like Wells to which we must attend. The first considers the meaning of the story he told and the ways his own sense of it differed markedly from that of other contemporaries and other survivors. The second addresses the question as to how different generations respond to what the witness has to say. In both cases, witnesses find themselves in adversarial or isolated positions, facing those who take their story and turn it into something remote from their sense of it, or who come to it only after many years. Moral witnesses, I argue, are people who retain a sense of anger, of outrage, of frustration to the lies, distortions, reworkings, or sanitizations of their painful past.

Romantic Resistance

The testimony Wells gave to the Eichmann trial raised an issue which preoccupied him in later years. In his extended conversation about his time in the *Sondercommando,* preserved in the Fortunoff Video Archive, Wells returned time and again to the question put to him as to why he had not resisted earlier. True, he and his fellow prisoners had killed their guards and escaped in November 1943. But the questioning of Gideon Hausner in Jerusalem pointed out the fact that the guards were few and the prisoners, those about to be killed and those like Wells who would dispose of their bodies, were many. There were about one hundred twenty men in his *Sondercommando,* and when they did finally make their move, about fifty escaped. Why, then, did they not throw off their chains earlier?

Wells tried to account for his life in the Janowska camp and in the Death Brigade without flinching, and without embellishments. He said in his Yale interview that he had volunteered for the Death Brigade to escape torture and death.[59] He was forced to break every convention about respect for the dead; he desecrated graves, he ate on corpses, slept next to the pyres, and helped sift the bones for gold teeth and other valuables. How could anyone stand this descent into horror?

Hausner's question measured Wells's testimony against a standard of resistance central to the ideology of the Israeli state. Israeli commemoration of the Holocaust was from the start directed toward remembering the victims *and* the resisters, the people who died fighting or simply defiant, rather than descend to the state of men like Wells. His story did not fit into their narrative or that of others who have reflected on the Holocaust. To Wells, their arguments are offensive. To survive is not good enough from their point of view; to be a martyr is preferable. This "horrible idea,"[60] this notion that to cling to life is somehow ignoble or inhuman, is one which he rejected completely. Discussions of mass resistance among concentration camp prisoners were based not on any knowledge of the situation, but rather on a fantasy, a political myth, that of heroic revolt, a revolt which did not and could not have occurred. The question, why did you not fight back? was deeply offensive to Wells.

> It's immoral, and I have to blame some Zionist leaders of Israel, that they introduced . . . did you fight back. It is one of the lowest, and I resist always to speak about it. Today it is easy to ask a woman being raped, did you fight back? . . . I feel I have a right to live even if I don't fight back. No one has a right to kill me if I don't fight back.
>
> This idea of celebrating resistance, and so on. It is a horrible idea because I don't want to be a martyr, and nobody wants to be a martyr. Only other people try to make martyrs and fighters.[61]

Yes, he had killed his guards and escaped, but his story was not that of heroism. It was not the kind of narrative those wishing to find hope even in the Holocaust wanted to hear.

There is a substantial literature on the subject of "survivors' guilt."[62] Wells appears to have avoided this burden; the memories he carries are heavy enough. There is no one to whom he needs to answer for the fact that he is still alive. He did kill his guards and escape but refused to join in the narrative of heroism which others who were not there tried to construct. Not embellishing, not justifying, but describing what he went through was his task, and it has lasted a lifetime. "Since 1945," he states, "I have been a continuing witness, and repeat the same story which becomes newer and newer."[63] Someone had to survive to tell it; that it was he was pure accident, though his systematic mind has helped disseminate it, not only in his writings, but also in his idiosyncratic English.[64]

In a number of ways the story of Wells coincides with that of Norton Cru and his *Témoignage*. Both suggest that one defining feature of the moral witness is that he does not tailor his remarks to suit more romantic notions of what we would have done had we been there. The invitation to sweeten the story, or at least to dilute its bitterness, has been present throughout Wells's life; that he has resisted it is evident, and so is his anger and contempt for those who want to hear a different kind of witness.

Faith

If a romanticized version of resistance in the face of torture, degradation, and terror is one which Wells the moral witness cannot abide, there is a second comforting framework which he rejects as well. He has turned his back on the religious beliefs of his childhood and youth, and though he is still drawn to Jewish ritual and the poetry of the tradition, his faith—as he put it in the title of his last memoir—was shattered beyond repair.

His book *Shattered Faith* is told in the form of recalling a series of Days of Atonement, the holiest day of the year for his family and for the Belzer Hasidim among whom they lived. After lingering over the holiness of the day, as it was lived before the war, he comes to 1942. It was on this day that he learned from his grandfather that his four sisters and his mother had been murdered.[65] It was on this day that he seized a knife and tried to commit suicide. No more did he observe daily prayers. It was, he wrote, "the saddest day of my life."[66]

A year later, his Yom Kippur was spent burning bodies in the Death Brigade. That day, in 1943, he found papers and objects identifying the dead as Polish intellectuals who had refused to form a quisling government. This was no holy day; in fact, it was just another day lived in what he termed "Gehenna," the entrance to hell.[67]

Even after liberation, Wells went to synagogue on Yom Kippur simply to find survivors. Prayer was beyond him; his dreams were filled with the horrors he had seen. And so it remained when he started a new life in the United States. He could not "run away" from his childhood, but neither could he retrieve its certainties.

Wells is caustic about a story concerning the religious leader of the sect in which he was raised, the Belzer Hasid. Wells recounts that during the war this rebbi was spirited out of Belz, and later out of Poland, while his wife, his seven children, and all his followers perished. In later years the rebbi was silent when asked about the Holocaust.[68] And rightly so, Wells observed, because he had not been through the fire, but was deemed too holy to stand together with his family and the people who worshiped him as a mystical teacher. The Belzer Hasid was no witness to the Holocaust; his survival tells us nothing about God.

Wells's anger extends to those who take comfort from mystical tales emerging from the Holocaust. One described another rebbi, the Bulzhever rebbi, who was also a prisoner in the Janowska camp. The story has it that one of the SS decided to have some fun using a bomb crater which had been created in a recent air raid. The soldier brought a group of Jewish prisoners to the edge of the crater and ordered them to leap over it. Those who failed to reach the other side would be machine-gunned; those who succeeded would be allowed to live. One prisoner told the rebbi he would not perform for the Nazis. The rebbi demurred: life could not be given back to God; it could only be taken by him. "We must leap, and if we don't succeed, we will enter Paradise just a few seconds before all the rest," the rebbi said. The rebbi leapt and reached the other side. So did the reluctant man to whom he had spoken, and who now asked him: "Rebbi, how did you reach the other side?" The rebbi answered, "I clung to the coat-tails of my forefathers." The rebbi asked him the same question in return, and his follower responded, "I clung to yours." Here is "witnessing" in the original, theological sense of the term.

In contrast, Leon Weliczker clung no longer to Judaism or to a belief in God. He has clung instead to telling his story, even though, or rather especially because, it went against the grain of hope. That is what makes his witnessing moral. It does not fit into preordained narratives. It does not provide solace; it provides a story, his story, one which needs to be heard, one which no one can take from him and shape in an uplifting or comforting way.

Conclusion

These two moral witnesses help us see how important it is to locate what they do and what they say in a social context. Witnesses rarely speak in a vacuum. The collectives in which they live frequently use witnesses to fortify the stories they, the collective, disseminate about themselves. At times witnesses do not recognize themselves in these narratives. They express anger directed at those who construct what they take to be partial, self-serving, comforting, or blatantly false narratives about the world or events they knew firsthand. Since many witnesses speak out over time and do so more than once, they are constantly taking their distance from the words of others. Norton Cru could not stomach the bellicose banter of civilians, who had never seen a trench, or of veterans who should have known better but who retreated from what he saw as truth into romance. Wells had trouble with the implicit validation of heroic resistance in Israeli narratives of Holocaust resistance. To a degree, what makes their witnessing "moral," in Margalit's terms, is that they refused to conform to the conventions outsiders construct about the events through which they have lived.

Witnesses tell stories in different ways.[69] Cru wrote about other's narratives. He was a literary scholar who used his talents to dissect war memoirs and to detect distortions and romantic illusions within them. Wells wrote his memoirs, but he also wrote a history of the relative indifference of Zionists and American Jewish leaders to the plight of the victims of the Holocaust. By what moral right, he asked, do Israelis claim to act "for the slain Jews of Europe" when they did not do so in the 1940s when lives could have been saved? "As one whose parents, uncles and aunts, brothers, sisters and cousins were killed by the political madness that dominated Europe, I refuse to stand by now and allow their memory to be used to fuel the ideology of 'Kill or be killed!' that dominates Israel and Zionism today [1995]."[70] Over time, the moral witness is one who speaks out on moral and political issues of many kinds. Politics matters in the work of the witness.

Social context matters in another way as well. To a degree, such witnesses become a kind of fictive kinship group. They can talk to others who had been there, but perhaps not to the rest of us. This makes them hard people to live with, and gives to their style and demeanor a certain proprietary or intolerant tone. The story is their story; they are wary of others who come to it, and who may hijack it for unspecified purposes. Instead, many witnesses opt for family narratives, tales told for the edification of their children or their children's children.

Frequently a generation gap places witnesses in the company of much younger family members. We have already referred to the tendency of survivors to relate their stories not to their own children, who—in the hope of building an entirely new life—may wish to turn away from the history their parents endured, but to their grandchildren. This kind of transgenerational bonding may account for what Margalit calls the "thickening" of commemorative relations over time, the construction of groups with an increasingly deep commitment to acts of remembrance. The family memoir of Peter Balakian shows how this happened in one Armenian family.[71] David Grossman's novel *See Under Love* describes this trajectory of stories which can be told openly not to the second but to the third generation of survivors.[72] Generational ties also help account for increasing interest in the Great War seventy years after the Armistice, when virtually all the veterans have passed away.

This multifaceted, contextualized, and diachronic character of witnessing raises difficulties with Margalit's claim that "collective memory has agents and agencies entrusted with preserving and diffusing it" and that among such agents are "moral witnesses."[73] Witnesses like Cru and Wells work against collectives which construct consolatory narratives, those with reassurance. They stand against the grain of moral uplift, which can turn into a way of lessening or ignoring the enormity of these events. They offer affirmations not of collective identities but of the capacity of individual men and women to retain, against the odds, a belief that words matter, that they can reach other people, even over the desolate landscape of war and genocide.

Finally, it is necessary to examine the claims moral witnesses like Norton Cru and Wells make for the authority of direct experience and for the "truth" value of their memories. This claim, and the moral standing it confers, are at the heart of the memory boom.

We have already seen, in our discussion of soldiers' letters in chapter 4, that many of those who described war and the suffering it entails embrace an essentialist view of experience. They claim that experience is an entity, fixed, immutable, and identifiable by those who have had access to it. They internalize it and then, through storytelling, externalize it for those who weren't there.

This kind of positivist thinking is filled with difficulties. What makes it untenable is how it reifies events and places those who tell the story outside the narrative in which they themselves are imbedded. It is difficult to sustain the view that experience is a "thing," which has a material form verifiable by experimentation and confirmation, a form which follows physical laws. Instead, though they do not admit it, men like Norton Cru and Wells, narrators par excellence, use experience in an entirely different sense, one which contradicts their own claims to objectivity. Joan Scott has put the point well. Experience is not something which the witness has, but rather something out of which his sense of self emerges. To recapitulate, her argument is that experience is not "the authoritative (because seen or felt) evidence that grounds what is known," but rather the social construction of knowledge by people who define themselves in terms of what they know.[74] This is precisely what witnesses do. Experience from this point of view is constituted by subjects and thus highly volatile; it changes when identities change and has no inert, external, eternally true existence outside the person reporting it.

Both Norton Cru and Wells try to persuade us that their experience is positivist and not subjective. It is fixed, and they have access to it. That is why they know who is right and who is wrong about the past. That is why they can correct the record and stand up against the tendency to clean up or romanticize the story of war and persecution. And yet, their stories are just as much social constructions as are those they reject or rebuke. It is best to see their witnessing as an amalgam of both kinds of "experience." There is no need to deny the materiality of the events they describe, but they are not outside of the story; their witnessing is part of the event itself.

This set of difficulties does not diminish the significance of their words or their witnessing. It merely guards us against accepting their own claims at face value. For the monstrous nature of Norton Cru's time under fire or Wells's period as a slave laborer was bound to affect the way they tell the story. Some of those who went through similar times were unable to speak of what had happened to them.

We have discussed the way which these people carry "traumatic memory" as an underground river of recollection.[75] Witnesses, in contrast, are able to speak, and the way they retell the story is shaped by the lives they led thereafter. What moral witnesses offer is not unvarnished truth, but rather a very subjective construction of the extreme conditions under which they lived. That very subjectivity, the quirkiness of Wells's English or the angularity of Norton Cru's pedantry about every little detail of a soldier's narrative, tell us as much about who they were as about where they were.

And yet, whatever intellectual objections we make to the claim of the "authority of direct experience," it is clear that part of the current obsession with memory is fueled by it. Moral witnesses speak to us from the other side of a veil. They have seen radical evil and have returned to tell the tale. They embody memory of a certain kind, and remind us that remembering the cruelties of the past is not a choice but a necessity. They are part of the archive. They demand that we face them. Their plea for recognition, for active knowledge, or acknowledgment, is at the heart of the memory boom.

Part Four

The Memory Boom and

the Twentieth Century

CHAPTER 12

Controversies and Conclusions

"Language," wrote Walter Benjamin, "shows clearly that memory is not an instrument for exploring the past, but its theatre. It is the medium of past experience, as the ground is the medium in which dead cities lie interred."[1] In this book, I have followed Benjamin's lead and have explored multiple facets of memory as theater, memory as a medium of both personal and collective experience. In doing so, in exploring this overarching subject, this vast arcade of remembrance, I have focused on one particular historical setting. That setting is war and the effort of survivors to defer or to defy the slipping away of the faces, the names, the forms of those who suffer and die in war. This anamnesis,[2] or effort to remember, this work of re-cognition, of re-collection, of the victims of war and violence, is at the heart of what I have termed the memory boom. In the twentieth century, the two world wars have precipitated many commemorative forms. Though the subject of war and Holocaust has been at the heart of our recent meditations in this area, it is important to remember that there was a prior "generation of memory," one which was determined to find signifying practices appropriate to the scale of the catastrophe which they termed the Great War.

The Memory Boom and Historical Remembrance

The memory boom is overdetermined. It has many sources and many facets, indeed so many facets that the field seems to expand more rapidly than the conceptual tools we have to comprehend it. Here an archeological study has its merits. One key task has been to see how practices of remembrances have arisen, and against the backdrop of which events? When we pose this question, we are led inevitably to the subject of international war and violence, the traces of which are salient features of the memory boom in the twentieth century.

When we face this archeological effort, we confront a second task as well. It is the need to rethink the terminology we use to examine the subject of memory itself. The term denotes a process, not a product. It is a set of practices, not a fixed or static category or concept. It arises out of the activities of groups as much as, or even more than, those of individuals. In an earlier study, Emmanuel Sivan and I addressed this problem and offered a way out of the forest of linguistic imprecision we face today.[3] It is to see the term memory as a metaphor for practices of collective remembrance. That is, groups of people come together in public to do the work of remembrance. These groups may work in concert with the state, but they are never wholly subsumed by it. Remembrance is a facet of family life and of civil society, that space which reaches from the family to the state, and which includes the market. Collective memory—an equally abused phrase which can mean virtually anything or nothing—we redefine as the practices of remembrance of different collectives which come together in public to speak or write or interpret the past in a host of different ways. These collectives contest narratives about the past. They try to come as close to the microphone of public discourse as they can, and this *prise de la parole* is part

of what defines their collective character. Collective remembrance—
or, if you will, collective memory—is rarely what the state tells
us to remember. There are always too many people who construct
their own narratives which are either at a tangent to those constructed by politicians or their agents, or which are totally in-
consistent with what the state wants us to believe happened in the
past.[4]

Those who hold power always try to construct a narrative of the
past legitimizing their authority. But their voices are never the only
ones engaged in acts of remembrance. To recognize this multivocality in the field of memory work helps us avoid all kinds of dead
ends. It sidesteps the meaningless title of the Web site of the digitized
holdings of the American Library of Congress, misleadingly entitled
"American memory."[5] It deflects well-intentioned interpretations,
like those of the former American poet laureate Robert Pinsky, to
champion American poetry as a repository of "American memory."[6]
Whose memory? How can a nation remember? When did we nomi-
nate these people to construct or carry it? Do elites, the exceptional
people who write poetry, carry the memory of the masses? Reflecting on these conundrums does not disclose a particularly American
approach to this matter. The promiscuous use of the term memory
without any precise meaning at all is evident in many other national
cases. Once we recognize that it is extremely difficult to apply to
collectives the terminology developed by cognitive scientists and
others in their work on individuals, it is but a short step to seeing the
virtues of shifting our discussion from memory to remembrance,
from the passive to the active voice.

This conceptual premise is at the heart of this book. We all
recollect the past, but remembrance is generated by action. In considering the subject of remembrance, it is essential to distinguish
between and among its forms. Family practices are replete with

remembrance, and it is impossible to engage with the liturgical world of Islam, Judaism, or Christianity without entering the realm of religious remembrance. Alongside these practices, I consider a third set—those I incorporate under the portmanteau term "historical remembrance," acts and practices of groups of people who come together to remember particular historical incidents and upheavals. The focus here is on forms of remembrance triggered by what men and women consider to be major events which have touched their lives in significant ways. If they did not think so, they would not make the effort of remembrance. And we must not forget that it is always an effort.

In this process of historical remembrance, historians play a role. It is not a foundational role, or, at most times, a central role.[7] But it matters nonetheless. The script collectives express or develop in forms of historical remembrance can be challenged, and historians are among the arbiters of such challenges. So are lawyers and psychiatrists, who bring to bear their own professional training in sifting evidence and in dealing with contradictory findings or eyewitness testimony.

Historical remembrance entails not only first-person narratives, but scripts which later generations form and disseminate about significant events in the past. That is why any consideration of the contemporary memory boom much recognize the role of novelists, playwrights, poets, filmmakers, architects, museum designers and curators, television producers, and others in this varied set of cultural practices we term historical remembrance. Many of these people are in it for the money, and, viewed cynically, it is easy to see how some exploiters of the "heritage trade" turn a pretty penny out of the nostalgic clichés of "olde Englande" or Dracula theme parks. Most of those engaged in the business of remembrance, though, are not in it as a business.

War and Historical Remembrance

There is clearly a market for historical remembrance. What has triggered it? In the first chapter of this book I addressed some aspects of this question. There are many sources located in the thrust of what we now call "identity politics," in the structure of consumption patterns of educated sectors of the population, and in the spread of what might be termed broadly as psychoanalytic cultures in many parts of the world. This study recognizes the overdetermined nature of the memory boom and focuses on but one source of this powerful cultural current.

One answer to the question as to why so many people choose to do the work of remembrance lies in the subject of war and its aftermath. Among the most prominent sources of the flowering of public remembrance in the twentieth century has been the desire to recapture the profile and to keep alive the name of those who, because of war, are no longer there. Remembrance is an act of symbolic exchange between those who remain and those who suffered or died. They went through much; they lost or gave much; we give the little we can—starting with recognition and acknowledgment and then moving on, at times, to material expressions of both.

These terms show why the subject of memory has taken on such a powerful collective character. Acknowledgment—understood as active knowledge, expressed in public as the recognition, the rethinking, and the restating aloud of claims—moral, political, material—which other human beings have on us. Among those claimants are victims of war and violence. The least of their claims is that we not let them and their stories vanish without trace, that we face them, that we face what happened to them. That act starts alone, in our individual reflections on an injured or absent person, but acknowledgment, in the sense I am using the term, never ends alone. It is a public act, a kind of remembrance expressed by groups of people prepared to face their shared past together. When they come together, remembrance becomes performative. It is materialized in the gestures and statements of the actors, those whose actions constitute remembrance.

In the course of this book, I have explored modes of remembrance of many different kinds. Most are voluntary, but not all. Consider the discussion of shell shock in chapter 2. Psychiatric injury is a form of remembrance of a very special kind, one which has taken on many different meanings and associations throughout the twentieth century. To be sure, part of the memory boom is driven by our understanding that perfectly sane people become insane during and after war. Those ex-soldiers "whose minds the dead have ravaged," in Wilfred Owen's phrase, stand in a long line of victims of war and violence whose injuries are not physical but which are none the less crippling. These people are also the subject of the memory boom, and give it some of its tragic features.

And its political ramifications too. For acknowledging an injury in the service of the state is tantamount to accepting the right to material compensation. Pensions—and public expenditure—follow the recognition of the damage done to men and women in war. Since psychological disabilities were hard to diagnose and, even when diagnosed, hard to treat, such injuries were (and remain) the subject of much controversy. Some doctors and pensions officials saw malingering behind every claim of psychological disability. Others were more liberal in their labeling of frequently puzzling sets of symptoms. Over time, what we first termed shell shock and now call posttraumatic stress disorder received medical and administrative legitimation, justifying the acknowledgment of injury an the payment of pensions to those suffering psychological injuries related to war service.

In more recent times, there has been much discussion of the

claims for compensation for injuries inflicted by violent regimes against their own people or in the course of civil war. Here the problems are multiple. The same mix of psychological and physical injury presents complex problems of medical diagnosis and administrative responses. And now the claimants rarely wear uniforms; they were targets simply because they were there.

But whether we are dealing with the international warfare of the earlier twentieth century or the fragmentation of warfare since 1945, remembrance follows armed conflict, as night follows day. There is a vast literature on how this is done by the victors; most of it shows the choreography of state leaders, legitimating their power through contact with the suffering of those who put them there. This book addresses some—and only some—facets of the work of civil society in the unfolding of historical remembrance, a set of practices which brings together many different groups whose view of the past is rarely identical to that of the state.

In the twentieth century, warfare became everybody's business. Before 1900, commemorative statues mostly celebrated individual commanders; after 1900, and even more so after 1914, ordinary people became the focus of commemoration. That is why the preservation of names on war memorials is so important.

Later in the twentieth century, the democratization of suffering changed the face of remembrance. The soldier no longer stands at the center of the narrative of the historical remembrance of war and its victims. Precise figures cannot be established, but it is likely that more women than men died in the course of the Second World War. One million children were murdered in the Holocaust. Genocide since 1945 has targeted women and children, as the future of the population, to be exterminated. Other subject groups—Indians, suppressed minorities, ethnic groups, homosexuals—have asserted their own right to speak, and through their *prise de la parole* they have helped ensure that their stories and their lives were not erased by their persecutors. Their words appear in tribunals, in commissions of inquiry, in autobiographical memoirs, in archives of oral and video testimony. The archives of the memory boom are multiple and growing.

Beyond History and Memory: Critiques and Controversies

So far I have described an array of collective practices which constitute a major facet of the memory boom today. What Benjamin termed "theatres of memory" are indeed all around us. There is much which is significant and much which is moving in such forms of remembrance, but we need to acknowledge the dangers and pitfalls in these projects as well.

Memory As the Re-Sacralization of the Past

In the past decade a set of powerful critiques of the memory boom has emerged. These arguments are worth addressing. One such argument is that the memory boom is veiled politics, a subtle form of religious fundamentalism dressed up in the language of contemporary philosophy and critical theory. To Kerwin Klein, the memory boom is both ubiquitous and to be regretted. "Memory is replacing old favorites—nature, culture, language—as the word most commonly paired with history, and that shift is remaking historical imagination," creating a new "memorial consciousness" filled with "flaws and contradictions." Our new memory is both very new and very old, for it marries "hip new linguistic practices with some of the oldest senses of memory as a union of divine presence and material object." The memory boom, to Klein, is therefore a relapse into an earlier form of thinking, best summarized under the heading of the re-sacralization of the world. Thus we have the first indictment: the culprit is "memory as re-enchantment"; the offense—the betrayal of critical thought. "In academic and popular discourse alike, memory and its associated key words continue to invoke a range of theological concepts as well as vague connotations of spirituality and authenticity." Invoking memory provides emotional warmth, as against the coldness of historical analysis.

And what is worse, Klein notes, "Memory" with a capital *M* has come to take on a life of its own. The word assumes the capital letter when it becomes attached to material artifacts or to public property. "Ideally, the memory will be a dramatically imperfect piece of material culture, and such fragments are best if imbued with pathos. Such memorial tropes have emerged as one of the common features of our new cultural history where in monograph after monograph, readers confront the abject object: photographs are torn, mementos faded, toys broken." "Memory" thus emancipated from its sources and documentary or stated forms becomes reified. It turns into a freewheeling historical agent in its own right: "The new 'materialization' of memory thus grounds the elevation of memory to the status of a historical agent, and we enter a new age in which archives remember and statues forget."

This form of nonsense, Klein argues, has been embraced by premodernists, modernists, and postmodernists alike. Thus "the conservatism of the academy has asserted itself by assimilating a few empty slogans and offering up a "new" cultural history effectively purged of real intellectual radicalism." For the memory boom has led those who have fallen into its clutches "to re-enchant our relation with the world and pour presence back into the past." It is a fix for those who cannot stand the harshness of critical thinking or historical analysis. It is a "therapeutic alternative to historical discourse."[8]

Memory as History

The second danger some commentators see in the memory boom is parallel to the argument Klein has advanced. From very different perspectives, others have decried the dangers lurking in the total collapse of history into memory. On one level, most historians agree that the two categories cannot be separated completely, but neither can they be conflated. Not all memories can stand the test of history. The Nazis believed that the German army had been stabbed in the back by Jews and socialists in 1918, thereby turning a German victory into bitter defeat. This "memory" of catastrophe, inscribed in Hitler's *Mein Kampf*, as the source of his political career, is completely false. The German army lost the war in the field of battle, and many of its leaders used this self-serving narrative, turned into "memory" by German soldiers like Hitler, to lie about the past. Their memories constructed a history which had lethal consequences. There are many other similarly toxic memories which can be contained if not totally eliminated by documented historical analysis.

In less murderous environments, the collapse of history into memory, according to some interpretations, reflects the unraveling of state sovereignty since the 1960s. The memory boom, Pierre Nora tells us, both announces and hastens the death of the nation-state. In 1992—the year of European integration—he wrote that "the memorial model has triumphed over the historical model and ushered in a new, unpredictable, and capricious use of the past."[9] Instead of history, what we now have is patrimony, or group memories, defined in terms of the cultural capital of individuals or groups, rather than that of the nation. Commemoration of the "patrimonial type" is remote, Nora believes, from commemoration of the "national type," and the emergence of a host of local museums and celebrations of local culture in France and elsewhere are to him evidence of a nation in decline, one which has traveled "the distance between national history and what we may now call national memory."[10] His claim is that "the past without the organizing coherence of a history has become entirely patrimonial . . . the historical consciousness of the nation has been replaced by a form of social consciousness, so that history as action has been replaced by history as a completed tale."[11] A nation obsessed with memory is one which has exhausted its sense of a historical mission, *la mission civilatrice,* which—in the case he has made his own—spoke not only for France but for humanity as a whole.

The quest for memory is, Nora believes, a sign of profound political disorientation. As we have already pointed out in chapter 1, his project *Les lieux de mémoire* emerged in the late 1980s at a time when the pole stars of French political affiliation and history—Gaullism and communism—were fading rapidly. His enterprise, a huge success by any standard, was an effort to search for a new orientation, a new set of guiding lights. And when he looked around, he found not memory but an ersatz version of it. "Memory is constantly on our lips," he wrote, "because it no longer exists." Or rather it no longer exists in the midst of life.[12] Since "society has banished ritual," and thereby "renounced memory,"[13] everyone cries out for artificial or symbolic substitutes for what less rapidly changing societies have taken for granted. What we have is second-order memory: we collect, organize, exhibit, catalogue, but observe the form and not the substance of memory: "The trace negates the sacred but retains its aura."[14] Here the challenge is that the pursuit of memory is a sign of the decadence of older forms of collective identity, and their replacement by mere Potemkin villages, artificial sites of artificial memory.

Memory over Politics

There are similarities between Nora's position and that of another critic of the memory boom, the historian Charles Maier. In a number of characteristically incisive and wide-ranging articles Maier has advanced the view that we are suffering from "a surfeit of memory." The current fascination with memory, he believes, betrays "inauthentic and unhealthy" features, which add up to an addiction. From his point of view, the memory industry invites all of us into a narcissistic world, one in which the pleasures of loss or nostalgia are part and parcel of the bittersweet and profitable business of remembering. It is the self-reflexive character of remembering which gives what he terms "the experience of experiencing" its characteristic "bathetic" charge. History has causes; memory has moods; the inwardness of the memory boom has gone so far that "memory . . . has become the discourse that replaces history."

Such group narcissism loses track of a past and a future in the search for the fix of memory. This is why, in his view, that the current obsession with memory is the opposite of transformative politics. The memory boom unsettles the delicate balance between past and future and winds up undermining universalist projects, arising out of the Enlightenment and configured during what he terms the age of territoriality. Instead ethnic activists use memory to force others to acknowledge and recognize past injustices which define who they are; sites of memory become garrisons of identity politics, as well as bastions of exclusion and atrocity.[15]

When Maier's critique was first published in 1993, his pessimism made sense against the backdrop of Serbian atrocities in Bosnia and the patchwork of violence which followed the collapse of the Soviet Empire. But now, a decade later, I believe it is time to take a less jaded view of the memory boom and to see it less as a political dead end than as a political challenge.

The Challenge of the Memory Boom

There is force in many of these criticisms, which, taken constructively, constitute a powerful indictment of the trivialization or brutal exploitation of modes of remembrance for narcissistic or self-serving purposes. But each critique goes too far. To remember the dead of the world wars is not necessarily to re-sacralize their sacrifice. Pacifists used these moments for precisely the opposite purpose. And the notion, advanced by Nora, that memory has ceased to exist within our lives, but needs to be created in artificial forms, and that literature is dead, is curiously out of touch with cultural trends in many other parts of the world. Gabriel Garcia Marquez insists that his book *One Hundred Years of Solitude* is the inscription of stories he heard as a small boy at his grandmother's knee. *Milieux de mémoire* are alive and well, and so are oral traditions in many parts of the world.

As to his cri de coeur about the displacement of national history into patrimony, it is true that the construction of new European institutions has given regions and localities new space to breathe and new funding to celebrate their own cultural achievements. The de-centering of commemorative practices is no bad thing, but it is clearly premature to offer a eulogy to the nation-state. Much of this book addresses the issue of multivocality and shows the powerful multivalent character of remembrance in civil society. There is nothing in this effort which undermines the nation-state; the contrary is true.

Maier's view that the memory boom is an escape from politics is also both insightful and incomplete. In some cases, the quest for memory does offer a sense of the past in place of a plan for the future. But among Guatemalan Indians or Palestinians or Vietnamese villagers, the construction of narratives about a past recently disfigured by massive violence is no alternative to politics but its direct expression. The memory boom is so complex that there is room both for admitting some of the pitfalls these critics point out and for suggesting that it is not the act of remembrance which is problematic but rather the motives of some of those who engage in it.

On one point, though, the critical conversation about the memory boom has not gone far enough. All of the critics I have cited here base their arguments on a clear separation between history and memory. I have already noted that historical narrative can help examine the claims of memory. But it makes little sense to juxtapose history and memory as adversarial forms. They overlap in too many ways to be considered as pure categories, each living in majestic isolation on its separate peak. Historians engage in memory work and commemorative practices; their choices of subject matter are frequently subjective. And those very practices reflect, sometimes well and sometimes very imperfectly, the narratives historians have constructed.

Instead of drawing firm and unrealistic boundaries, I suggest we see the terms "history" and "memory" as describing a field of force in social thought and social action. In other words, I want to propose that what is most interesting about contemporary cultural forms is neither history nor memory per se but the overlaps and creative space between the two.

The category of historical remembrance acknowledges the significance of scholarship. Historians do help to prevent people in power from lying about the past. These professional "remembrancers," in Peter Burke's phrase,[16] do not always live up to their charge, but they do so frequently enough to matter in the work of historical remembrance. But scholarship alone is not enough. The active participation of men and women who are outside of the academy is both necessary and unavoidable in the practice of historical remembrance. What it promises is a dialogue between scholars and laymen, who have much to teach each other. This creative engagement in framing and expressing—in public—narratives about the past threatens the privileged position of some academics. Doing public history in this way, living with the neighbors, if you will, is not everyone's cup of tea. But its benefits are substantial.

Historical remembrance is a field which has helped bring affect back into historical study. That is one reason why so many students have been drawn to this field. It moves in the opposite direction from positivism; it makes us all consider our own subject positions, and the significance of commemorative issues in our own lives and communities. And yet the discipline of scholarship sets limits on our discussion of highly emotive issues. Yes, the spiritualization of the past can happen; so can the turn to memory when political programs fail. The crucial point is not that there is a lot of memory work about, but how sensitive we are to the ways in which it can be exploited or ruined. But that is hardly a danger restricted to this subject matter. Far more treacherous is a world in which "theaters of memory" are treated as if they are outside of scholarship, or somebody else's business. If we historians do not enter these theaters, someone else will.

Ending a book on a set of caveats is no bad thing. One of the aims of this study has been to promote critical vigilance in a field of central importance to cultural history. Caution in dealing with issues of this degree of sensitivity and explosiveness is healthy. And so is our engagement in the exploration of the arts of remembrance explored in this study. The field of international violence is not about to vanish; the list of its victims is likely to increase while you are reading this book. If this discussion makes you pause and consider them for a moment, then the dialogue of writer and reader will fold into the compelling and still ongoing conversation about history, war, and remembrance.

Notes

Introduction

1. Jay Winter and Emmanuel Sivan (eds). *War and remembrance in the twentieth century.* Cambridge: Cambridge University Press, 1999, esp. ch. 1.

2. One of the leaders in this field is James E. Young. For a guide to the literature, see his publications, in particular, *The texture of memory: Holocaust memorials and meaning.* New Haven: Yale University Press, 1993; Young (ed). *The art of memory: Holocaust memorials in history.* New York: Prestel, 1994; Young. *At memory's edge: after-images of the Holocaust in contemporary art and architecture.* New Haven: Yale University Press, 2000.

3. See Omer Bartov. *Mirrors of destruction: war, genocide, and modern identity.* Oxford: Oxford University Press, 2000.

4. Winter and Sivan (eds), *War and remembrance.*

5. Endel Tulving and Martin Lepage, "Where in the brain is the awareness of one's past." In *Memory, brain and belief,* edited by Daniel L. Schacter and Elaine Scarry. Cambridge, Mass.: Harvard University Press, 2000, pp. 209ff.

6. Daniel L. Schacter. *The seven sins of memory (How the mind forgets and remembers).* Boston: Houghton Mifflin, 2000, pp. 9ff.

7. On which see Annette Becker. *Maurice Halbwachs. Un intellectuel en guerres mondiales 1914–1945.* Paris: Agnès Viénot, 2003.

Chapter 1. The Setting

1. For four different discussions of this issue, see Charles S. Maier. *The unmasterable past: history, Holocaust, and German national identity.* Cambridge, Mass.: Harvard University Press, c1988; William James Bouwsma. *A usable past: essays in European cultural history.* Berkeley: University of California Press, c1990; Tad Tuleja (ed). *Usable pasts: traditions and group expressions in North America.* Logan, Utah: Utah State University Press, 1997; and Lois Parkinson

Zamora. *The usable past: the imagination of history in recent fiction of the Americas.* Cambridge: Cambridge University Press, 1997.

2. *Les Lieux de mémoire,* sous la direction de Pierre Nora. Paris: Gallimard, 7 vols, c1984–c1992.

3. James Joyce. *Portrait of the artist as a young man.* London: The Egoist Ltd., c1916, p. 253.

4. Avtar Brah and Annie E. Coombes (eds). *Hybridity and its discontents: politics, science, culture.* London: Routledge, 2000; Bernd Thum and Thomas Keller (eds). *Interkulturelle Lebenslaufe.* Tubingen: Stauffenburg, c1998; Rita De Grandis and Zila Bernd. *Unforeseeable Americas: questioning cultural hybridity in the Americas.* Amsterdam: Rodopi, 2000; Victoria E. Bonnell (ed). *Identities in transition: Eastern Europe and Russia after the collapse of communism.* Berkeley: Center for Slavic and East European Studies, University of California at Berkeley, c1996; and Homi K. Bhabha. *The location of culture.* London: Routledge, 1994.

5. Frances A. Yates. *The art of memory.* London: Routledge & K. Paul, 1966. See also Jonathan D. Spence. *The memory palace of Matteo Ricci.* New York: Viking, 1984.

6. I am grateful to Jan Assmann and Aleida Assmann for advice on this matter.

7. Charles S. Maier, "A surfeit of memory? Reflections on history, melancholy and denial," *History & memory* (1993), pp. 136–51.

8. This approach owes much to the Assmanns' seminar on cultural memory at Yale in 2002, and in particular to Aleida Assmann's comments on this issue.

9. On Bergson, see *Bergson: biographie,* begun by Philippe Soulez and completed by Frederic Worms. Paris: Flammarion, c1997.

10. On Warburg, see E. H. Gombrich. *Aby Warburg. An intellectual biography. With a memoir on the history of the library by F. Saxl.* Oxford: Phaidon, 1970.

11. On Rivers, see Richard Slobodin. *W. H. R. Rivers: pioneer anthropologist, psychiatrist of the ghost road.* Stroud: Sutton, 1997.

12. On Proust, the locus classicus is still: George D. Painter, *Marcel Proust: a biography.* London: Penguin, 1990.

13. See Annette Becker. *Maurice Halbwachs. Un intellectuel en guerres mondiales 1914–1945.* Paris: Agnès Viénot, 2003.

14. Maurice Halbwachs. *Les cadres sociaux de la memoire.* Paris: F. Alcan, 1925.

15. Maurice Halbwachs. *On collective memory.* Translated by Lewis A. Coser. Chicago: University of Chicago Press, 1992. For recent elaborations, see Iwona Irwin-Zarecki. *Frames of remembrance: the dynamics of collective memory.* New Brunswick: Transaction, 1994; and Peter Burke, "History as social memory." In *Memory: history, culture and the mind,* edited by Thomas Butler, 97–113. Oxford: Basil Blackwell, 1990.

16. Maurice Agulhon, "La statumanie au xixe siècle," *Le romantisme*, xxx (1981), pp. 20–30.

17. Eric Hobsbawm and Terence Ranger (eds). *The invention of tradition.* Cambridge: Cambridge University Press, 1983.

18. See David Cannadine, "The context, performance and meaning of ritual: the British monarchy and the 'invention of tradition,' c. 1820–1977." In Hobsbawm and Ranger, *The Invention of Tradition,* pp. 125ff.

19. *The National Trust, a record of fifty years' achievement,* edited by James Lees-Milne. London: B. T. Batsford, 1946.

20. Mark Girouard. *Life in the English country house: a social and architectural history.* New Haven: Yale University Press, 1978.

21. Raymond Williams. *The country and the city.* New York: Oxford University Press, 1973.

22. Ernest Renan. *Qu'est-ce qu'une nation?: conférence faite en Sorbonne, le 11 mars 1882.* Paris: Calmann Lévy, 1882, p. 28.

23. Jeanne Beausoleil, "La collection Albert Kahn." In *Autochromes 1901/ 1928.* Paris: Tresors de la photographie, 1978; and Jeanne Beausoleil and Pascal Ory (eds). *Albert Kahn 1860–1940. Realites d'une utopie.* Boulogne-Billancourt: Musée Albert Kahn—Département des Hauts-de-Seine, 1995.

24. For example, see Benito M. Vergara. *Displaying Filipinos: photography and colonialism in early 20th century Philippines.* Quezon City: University of the Philippines Press, 1995.

25. Madeleine Rébérioux, "La mur des Fédérées." In Nora, *Les Lieux de mémoire,* vol 2, pp. 220–62.

26. Maurice Agulhon. *Marianne au combat: l'imagerie et la symbolique républicaines de 1789 à 1880.* Paris: Flammarion, c1979.

27. Jay Winter. *Sites of memory, sites of mourning: The great war in European cultural history.* Cambridge: Cambridge University Press, 1995.

28. Pieter Lagrou. *The legacy of Nazi occupation: patriotic memory and national recovery in Western Europe, 1945–1965.* Cambridge: Cambridge University Press, 1999.

29. Frederic D. Homer. *Primo Levi and the politics of survival.* Columbia: University of Missouri Press, c2001; Pietro Frassica (ed). *Primo Levi as witness: proceedings of a symposium held at Princeton University, April 30–May 2, 1989.* Fiesole: Casalini, 1990; Myriam Anissimov. *Primo Levi: tragedy of an optimist.* Translated by Steve Cox. London: Aurum, 1998.

30. Annette Wieviorka. *L'Ère du témoin.* Paris: Plon, c1998; see also her essay "From survivor to witness: voices from the Shoah." In *War and remembrance in the twentieth century,* edited by Jay Winter and Emmanuel Sivan. Cambridge: Cambridge University Press, 1999, pp. 101–29.

31. Peter Burke, "The social history of memory." In Burke, *Facets of cultural history.* London: Penguin, 1990.

32. Primo Levi. *Le devoir de mémoire.* Paris: Éd. Mille et une nuits, 1994, p. 75.

33. *The sorrow and the pity; a film.* Filmscript translated by Mireille Johnston. New York: Outerbridge and Lazard, distributed by Dutton, 1972. See also Henry Rousso. *The Vichy syndrome: history and memory in France since 1944.* Translated by Arthur Goldhammer. Cambridge, Mass.: Harvard University Press, 1991.

34. Eric Conan and Henry Rousso. *Vichy: an ever-present past.* Translated and annotated by Nathan Bracher. Hanover: University Press of New England, c1998.

35. On Grossman, see Ilya Ehrenbourg and Vassili Grossman (eds). *Le livre noir: sur l'extermination scélérate des Juifs par les envahisseurs fascistes allemands dans les régions provisoirement occupées de l'URSS et dans les camps d'extermination en Pologne pendant la guerre de 1941–1945, textes et témoignages.* Translated from Russian by Yves Gauthier et al. Arles: Actes Sud, 1995.

36. On this debate see chapter 6.

37. Olga Clendinnen. *Reading the Holocaust.* Cambridge: Cambridge University Press, 1994.

38. Jean-François Lyotard. *La condition postmoderne: rapport sur le savoir.* Paris: Editions de Minuit, c1979.

39. Emmanuel Levinas. *God, death, and time.* Translated by Bettina Bergo. Stanford, Calif.: Stanford University Press, c2000.

40. John Felstiner. *Paul Celan: poet, survivor, Jew.* New Haven: Yale University Press, 2001.

41. Max Horkheimer and Theodor W. Adorno. *Dialectic of enlightenment.* Translated by John Cumming. New York: Continuum, 1972.

42. Charles Maier, " 'Lines of force': territoriality, technologies, and the production of world order in the modern era." Lecture, Yale University, 11 February 2000.

43. Communication from Nora, in an exchange and debate between us on "history and memory" at the Centre de l'histoire sociale du vingtième siècle, Paris, March 1999.

44. Gustavo Perez Firmat. *Life on the hyphen: the Cuban-American way.* Austin: University of Texas Press, 1994.

45. See Allen Megill, "History, memory, identity," *History of the human sciences,* xi, 3 (1998), pp. 37–62; Jeffrey K. Olick and Joyce Robbins, "Social memory studies: from 'collective memory' to the historical sociology of mnemonic practices," *American Review of Sociology,* xxiv (1998), pp. 105–40.

46. Peter Novick. *The Holocaust in American life.* Boston: Houghton Mifflin, 1999.

47. See Marita Sturken. *Tangled memories: The Vietnam war, the AIDS epidemic, and the politics of remembering.* Berkeley: University of California Press, 1997.

48. Dolores Hayden, "The Japanese-American monument in Los Angeles."

In *War and remembrance in the twentieth century,* edited by Jay Winter and Emmanuel Sivan. Cambridge: Cambridge University Press, 1999, pp. 142–60.

49. Doris Sommer. *Proceed with caution, when engaged by minority writing in the Americas.* Cambridge, Mass.: Harvard University Press, 1999, p. 115.

50. The citation is to the words of Werner Sollors, taken from the introduction to Gweneviere Fabre and Robert O'Meally (eds). *History and memory in African-American culture.* Oxford: Oxford University Press, 1994, pp. 7–8.

51. OECD. *Educational statistics yearbook, vol. 1 International tables.* Paris: OECD, 1974, Table 7, p. 20; *Eurostat yearbook 98/99; a statistical eye on Europe 1987–1997.* Brussels: European Community, 1999, Table 12, p. 123.

52. On "patrimoine," see Pierre Nora (ed). *Science et conscience du patrimoine: entretiens du patrimoine, theatre national de Chaillot, Paris, 28, 29 et 30 novembre 1994.* Paris: Fayard, Editions du patrimoine, c1997.

53. Alan S. Milward, "Bad memories," *The Times Literary Supplement,* 14 April 2000, p. 8.

54. Pierre Nora (ed). *Essais d'égo-histoire.* Paris: Gallimard, 1987.

55. Julian Barnes. *England, England.* London: Jonathan Cape, 1998.

56. Jean Rouaud. *Champs d'honneur.* Paris: Editions de Minuit, 1990.

57. Sébastien Japrisot. *Un long dimanche de fiançailles: roman.* Paris: Denöel, 1991.

58. Pat Barker. *Regeneration.* New York: Viking, 1991; *The eye in the door.* New York: Viking, 1993; *The ghost road.* New York: Viking, 1995.

59. Sebastian Faulks. *Birdsong.* London: Hutchinson, 1993.

60. Pat Barker. *Another world.* London: Viking, 1998.

61. Sebastian Faulks. *Charlotte Gray.* London: Hutchinson, 1998.

62. Dominick LaCapra. *History and memory after Auschwitz.* Ithaca: Cornell University Press, 1998, p. 8.

63. Laurence J. Kirmayer, "Landscapes of memory: trauma, narrative, and dissociation," in Paul Antze and Michael Lambek (eds). *Tense past: cultural essays in trauma and memory.* London: Routledge, 1996, pp. 173–98.

64. See Allen Young. *The harmony of illusions.* Princeton: Princeton University Press, 1995; and Steve Southwick's work, cited in Winter and Sivan, *War and remembrance,* p. 15n. On this field see Daniel Schachter (ed). *Memory distortion: how minds, brains and societies reconstruct the past.* Cambridge, Mass.: Harvard University Press, 1995.

65. Roger Chartier, "Intellectual history or sociocultural history? The French trajectories," in Dominick LaCapra and Steven L. Kaplan (eds). *Modern European intellectual history: reappraisals and new perspectives.* Ithaca, N.Y.: Cornell University Press, 1982, p. 30.

66. Gareth Stedman Jones. *Languages of class: studies in English working class history, 1832–1982.* Cambridge: Cambridge University Press, 1983.

67. For Koselleck's work, see among others: von Otto Brunner, Werner

Conze, Reinhart Koselleck (eds). *Geschichtliche grundbegriffe: historisches lexikon zur politisch-sozialen sprache in deutschland.* Stuttgart: E. Klett, 1972–1997; Reinhart Koselleck and Klaus Schreiner. *Burgerschaft: rezeption und innovation der begrifflichkeit vom hohen mittelalter bis ins 19. jahrhundert.* Stuttgart: Klett-Cotta, c1994; Hartmut Lehmann and Melvin Richter (eds). *The meaning of historical terms and concepts: new studies on Begriffsgeschichte.* Washington, D.C.: German Historical Institute, c1996.

68. For Assmann's work, see among others: *Das kulturelle gedachtnis: schrift, erinnerung und politische identität in fruhen hochkulturen.* Munich: Beck, c1992. See also, from a different perspective, the work of Aleida Assmann. *Erinnerungsraeume. Formen und wandel des kulturellen gedaechtnisses.* Munich: Beck, 1999.

69. See the interesting collection Christiane Caemmerer, Walter Delabar, and Marion Schulz (eds). *Die totale erinnerung. Sicherung und zerstoerung kulturhistorischer vergangenheit und gegenwart in den modernen industriegesellschaften.* Bern: Jahrbuch fuer Internationale Germanistik, Reihe A, 45, 1997, and in particular the article therein of Marianne Vogel, "Cherchez la femme, strategische ueberlegungen zur integration von schriftstellerinnen ins kulturelle gedaechtnis."

70. On this and other points, see Lynn Hunt's introductory essay to her edition of essays in the field, *The new cultural history.* Berkeley: University of California Press, 1989.

71. A good place to start on Lyotard's ideas is: *La condition postmoderne: rapport sur le savoir.* Paris: Editions de Minuit, c1979. For Kristeva, see *Soleil noir: dépression et mélancolie.* Paris: Gallimard, 1987.

72. See: (pro) Centre d'étude de l'Europe médiane. *(Post)modernisme en Europe centrale: La crise des idéologies,* sous la direction de Maria Delaperrière. Paris: Harmattan, c1999; and (con) Ernest Gellner. *Postmodernism, reason and religion.* London: Routledge, 1992.

73. Kerwin Lee Klein, "On the emergence of *memory* in historical discourse," *Representations,* 69 (Winter 2000), pp. 127–50, esp. pp. 130, 136.

Chapter 2. Shell Shock, Memory, and Identity

1. Paul John Eakin, "Autobiography, identity, and the fictions of memory." In *Memory, brain, and belief,* edited by Daniel L. Schacter and Elaine Scarry. Cambridge: Harvard University Press, 2000, pp. 290–306.

2. Paul F. Lerner. *Hysterical men: war, psychiatry, and the politics of trauma in Germany, 1890–1930.* Ithaca, N.Y.: Cornell University Press, 1993.

3. Stephen Garton, "Freud versus the rat: understanding shell shock in world war I," *Australian cultural history,* no. 16 (1997/98), pp. 45–59.

4. For instance, see Public Record Office, London, PIN 77 files of disabled First World War veterans, the series of which I established with the help of Professor Bill Nasson of the University of Capetown.

5. On Myers and others, see Ben Shephard. *A war of nerves. Soldiers and psychiatrists 1914–1994.* London: Jonathan Cape, 2000, pp. 21ff.

6. T. Bogacz, "War neurosis and cultural change in England, 1914–22," *Journal of contemporary history* (1989), pp. 18–25.

7. On embodied memory see A. M. Glenberg, "What memory is for," *Behavioral and Brain Sciences, xx,* 1 (1997), pp. 1–55; Thomas J. Csordas (ed). *Embodiment and experience: the existential ground of culture and self.* Cambridge: Cambridge University Press, 1994; Andrew Strathern. *Body thoughts.* Ann Arbor, Michigan: University of Michigan Press, 1996.

8. John Talbott, "Shell shock and the second world war," paper presented to international conference on the comparative history of shell shock, Historial de la grande guerre, Péronne, Somme, France, July 1998.

9. K. R. Eissler. *Freud sur le front des névroses de guerre.* Translated by Madeleine Drouin. Paris: Presses Universitaires de France, 1992.

10. Lewis R. Yealland. *Hysterical disorders of warfare.* London: Macmillan, 1918; Peter Leese, *Shell shock: traumatic neurosis and the British soldiers of the first world war.* New York: Palgrave, 2002. Eric Leed. *No man's land: combat and identity in world war I.* Cambridge: Cambridge University Press, 1979.

11. See Daniel L. Schacter and Elaine Scarry (eds). *Memory, brain, and belief.* Cambridge, Mass.: Harvard University Press, 2000; Glenberg, "What memory is for"; Martin A. Conway. "The inventory of experience: memory and identity." In *Collective memory of political events: social psychological perspectives,* edited by James W. Pennebaker, Dario Paez, and Bernard Rimé. Mahwah, N.J.: Lawrence Erlbaum Associates, 1997, pp. 21–45.

12. Samuel Hynes. *The soldiers' tale: bearing witness to modern war.* New York: A. Lane, 1997.

13. Archives Nationales, Paris, 382AP/1, Guerre 14–18, Souvenirs de la campagne 1914–1915.

14. See Jay Winter. *Against the grain: utopian moments in the twentieth century.* Forthcoming.

15. Marc Agi. *De l'idée d'universalité comme fondatrice du concept des droits de l'homme d'après la vie et l'oeuvre de René Cassin.* Thèse pour le doctorat d'État, Université de Nice, 10 December 1979. Antibes: Éditions Alp'azur, 1980.

16. Louis Ferdinand Céline. *Bagatelles pour un massacre.* Paris: Denoël, 1937.

17. Frederic Vitoux. *La vie de Céline.* Paris: B. Grasset, 1988; Jay Winter, "Céline and the cultivation of hatred." In *Enlightenment, passion, modernity: historical essays in European culture and thought,* edited by Mark Micale and Robert Dietle. Palo Alto: Stanford University Press, 2000, pp. 230–48.

18. Winter, "Céline."

19. Winter and Baggett, *14–18,* ch. 5.

20. E. E. Southard. *Shell-shock and other neuropsychiatric problems presented in five hundred and eighty-nine case histories from the war literature, 1914–1918.* Boston: W. M. Leonard, 1919.

21. Southard, *Shell-shock*, pp. 882–83.

22. Southard, *Shell-shock*, p. 903.

23. Southard, *Shell-shock*, p. 732.

24. All these references are from Southard, *Shell-shock*, pp. 332ff.

25. Jeremy Wilson. *Lawrence of Arabia*. London, Heinemann, 1989, p. 460 (hereafter cited as Lawrence).

26. Lawrence, p. 666.

27. Lawrence, p. 668.

28. Lawrence, p. 696.

29. Lawrence, p. 710.

30. Lawrence to Lionel Curtis, 19 March 1923, in D. Garnett (ed). *The letters of T. E. Lawrence*. London, Jonathan Cape, 1938, p. 412 (hereafter cited as Lawrence letters).

31. Lawrence to Curtis, 14 May 1923, in Lawrence letters, pp. 416–17.

32. Lawrence, p. 739.

33. Lawrence, p. 789.

34. As a start, see Paul S. Appelbaum, Lisa A. Uyehara, Mark R. Elin (eds). *Trauma and memory: clinical and legal controversies*. New York: Oxford University Press, 1997; Cathy Caruth (ed). *Trauma: explorations in memory*. Baltimore: Johns Hopkins University Press, 1995.

35. See the special issue of *Journal of contemporary history*, xxx, 1 (January 2001), on the comparative history of shell shock; and Mardi J. Horowitz (ed). *Essential papers on posttraumatic stress disorder*. New York: New York University Press, 1999; Horowitz. *Stress response syndromes. PTSD, grief, and adjustment disorders*. Northvale, N.J.: Jason Aronson, 1997; Paul Antze and Michael Lambek (eds). *Tense past. Cultural essays in trauma and memory*. New York: Routledge, 1996; Yoram Bilu and Eliezer Witztum, "War-related loss and suffering in Israeli society: an historical perspective," *Israel Studies*, v.2 (1999), pp. 1–31.

Chapter 3. All Quiet on the Eastern Front

1. See Jay Winter. *Sites of memory, sites of mourning*. Cambridge: Cambridge University Press, 1995, ch. 3.

2. George Mosse. *Fallen soldiers. Reshaping the memory of the world wars*. New York: Oxford University Press, 1990.

3. Daniel Goldhagen. *Hitler's willing executioners: ordinary Germans and the Holocaust*. New York: Knopf, 1996.

4. Werner T. Angress, "The German army's *Judenzählung* of 1916: genesis, consequences, significance," *Leo Baeck Institute Yearbook*, vol. xxiii (1978), p. 117.

5. Marsha Rozenblit. *Reconstructing a national identity: the Jews of Habsburg Austria during world war*. Oxford: Oxford University Press, 2001, p. 9; David Rechter. *The Jews of Vienna and the first world war*. London: Littman Library of Jewish Civilization, 2001.

6. Marion Kaplan. *The making of the Jewish middle class.* New York: Oxford University Press, 1991, pp. 219–26.

7. Jacob R. Marcus. *The Rise and destiny of the German Jew.* New York: Ktav Publishing House, 1973, p. 82.

8. As cited in Donald L. Niewyk. *The Jews in Weimar Germany.* Baton Rouge: Louisiana State University Press, 1980, p. 48.

9. Leo Baeck Institute, New York. Bardach papers, AR 6632, Bardach Tagebuch, entry for 13 August 1914.

10. See Roman Wishniac. *A vanished world.* Oxford: Oxford University Press, 1988.

11. Isaac Bashevis Singer. *Nobel lecture.* New York: Farrar, Straus, Giroux, 1979, p. 7.

12. Thanks are due to Richard Stites for this story.

13. I owe this reference to Peter Gatrell.

14. Steven E. Aschheim, "Eastern Jews, German Jews and Germany's Ostpolitik in the first world war," *Leo Baeck Institute Yearbook,* vol. xxvii (1983), p. 352.

15. Ibid., p. 363.

16. See Vejas Liulevicius. *War land on the eastern front: culture, national identity and German occupation in world war I.* Cambridge: Cambridge University Press, 1999.

17. Walter Benjamin. *Illuminations.* Translated by Harry Zorn. Theses on the philosophy of history, Thesis V. Boston: Schocken, 1990.

Chapter 4. War Letters

1. Samuel Hynes. *A war imagined: the first world war and English culture.* London: Bodley Head, 1990, p. 209.

2. See a replica in Paul Fussell. *The great war and modern memory.* Oxford: Oxford University Press, 1975, p. 11.

3. For some pioneering work along different lines from those adopted here, see Bernd Ulrich. *Die Augenzeugen. Deutsche Feldpostbriefe in Kriuegs- un Nachkriegzeit 1914–1933.* Essen: Klartext, 1997; see also Ulrich, "Feldpostbriefe des Ersten Weltkrieges B Möglichkeiten und Grenzen einer alltagsgeschichtlichen Quelle," *Militärgeschichtliche Mitteilungen,* 53 (1994); and Ulrich and Benjamin Ziemann (eds). *Frontalltag im Ersten Weltkrieg: Wahn und Wirklichkeit: Quellen und* Dokumente. Frankfurt am Main: Fischer Taschenbuch Verlag, 1997.

4. The sole comparative study to date is that of Aribert Reimann. *Der grosse Krieg der Sprachen: Untersuchungen zur historischen Semantik in Deutschland und England zur Zeit des Ersten Weltkriegs.* Essen: Klartext, 2000.

5. Jan Assmann. *Das kulturelle Gedächtnis: Schrift, Erinnerung und politische Identität in frühen Hochkulturen.* Munich: C. H. Beck, c1992; Aleida

Assmann (ed). *Mnemosyne: Formen und Funktionen der kulturellen Erinnerung.* Frankfurt: Fischer-Taschenbuch-Verlag, 1991; Aleida Assmann. *Erinnerungsräume: Formen und Wandlungen des kulturellen Gedächtnisses.* Munich: C. H. Beck, c1999.

6. *Kriegsbriefe deutscher studenten,* hrsg. von Professor Dr. Philipp Witkop. Gotha: F. A. Perthes, 1916; *Kriegsbriefe gefallener Studenten* / herausgegeben in Verbindung mit den Deutschen Kultusministerien von Philipp Witkop. Leipzig, Berlin: B. G. Teubner, 1918; *Kriegsbriefe gefallener Studenten* / in Verbindung mit den Deutschen Unterrichts-Ministerien herausgegeben von Philipp Witkop. Munich: Georg Müller, 1928. All present citations are from the 1929 English edition of *German student war letters.* Translated by A. F. Wedd. London: Methuen, 1929.

7. Jeffrey Verhey. *The spirit of 1914: militarism, myth, and mobilization in Germany.* Cambridge: Cambridge University Press, 2000.

8. Wolfgang G. Natter. *Literature at war 1914–1940. Representing the "time of greatness" in Germany.* New Haven: Yale University Press, 1999, p. 111.

9. Philipp Witkop. *Die Anfange der neueren deutschen Lyrik.* Leipzig: Teubner, 1908; Philipp Witkop. *Die neuere deutsche lyrik.* Leipzig, Berlin: B. G. Teubner, 1910–13; Philipp Witkop. *Gottfried Keller als lyriker.* Freiburg: C. Troemer's universitäts—buchahndlung, 1911. See also the patriotic defense of the German war effort he put together with others, *Der Weltkrieg im Unterricht; Vorschläge und Anregungen zur Behandlung der weltpolitischen Vorgänge in der Schule.* Gotha: F. A. Perthes, 1915.

10. Natter, *Literature at war,* pp. 92ff.

11. On Dix, see Linda F. McGreevy. *Bitter witness. Otto Dix and the great war.* New York: Peter Lang, 2001, pp. 163–65.

12. On Marc, see Klaus Lankheit (ed). *Franz Marc im Urteil seiner Zeit. Einfuhrung und erlauterende.* Köln: M. DuMont Schauberg, [1960]; and in general Roland N. Stromberg. *Redemption by war: the intellectuals and 1914.* Lawrence, Kansas: Regents Press of Kansas, c1982.

13. Natter, *Literature at war,* p. 94.

14. The finest collection of these newspapers is in the Bibliothek für Zeitgeschichte in Stuttgart.

15. On these newspapers, see Nelson, "German soldiers' newspapers of the great war," Ph.D. diss., Cambridge, 2002; for an alternative view see Anne Lipp, "Friedenssehnsucht und durchhaltebereitschaft. Wahrnehmungen und Erfahrungen deutscher Soldaten im Ersten Weltkrieg," *Archiv für Sozialgeschichte,* xxxvi (1996), pp. 279–92, and Anne Lipp, "Heimatwahrnehmung und soldatisches 'Kriegserlebnis,' " in *Kriegserfahrungen. Studien zur Sozial- und Mentalitätsgeschichte des Erste Weltkrieges,* edited by Gerhard Hirschfeld, Gerd Krumeich, Dieter Langewiesche, and Hans Peter Ullmann. Essen: Klartext, 1997, pp. 225–42. On trench journalism in British and French forces respectively, see J. G. Fuller. *Troop morale and popular culture in the British and Dominion armies*

1914–1918. Oxford: Clarendon Press, 1990, and Stéphane Audoin-Rouzeau. *Men at war, 1914–1918: national sentiment and trench journalism in France during the first world war* Translated by Helen McPhail. Providence, R.I.: Berg, 1992.

16. Alex Watson, " 'For kaiser and reich.' The identity and fate of the German volunteers, 1914–1918," *War in History* xii, 1 (January 2005), p. 51.

17. Manfred Hertlin and Michael Jeismann, "Der Weltkrieg als Epos. Philipp Witkops 'Kriegsbriefe gefallener Studenten.' " In *Keiner fühlt sich hier mehr als Mensch,* edited by Hirshfeld, Krumeich, and Rens, pp. 175–98. Essen: Klartext, 1993.

18. Laurence Housman. *War letters of fallen Englishmen.* London: Gollancz, 1930.

19. On the two collections, see Neil Jacob, "Representation and commemoration of the great war: a comparative study of Philipp Witkop's *Kriegsbriefe gefallener Studenten* (1928) and Laurence Housman's *War letters of fallen Englishmen* (1930)," *Irish History* (2002).

20. As cited in Natter, *Literature at war,* pp. 108–9.

21. See Ernst Jünger's version of this sense of "inner experience" in Richard Winter (ed). *Der Krieg als inneres Erlebnis; Auszuge aus den Schriften Ernst Jungers.* Bielefeld: Velhagen and Klasing, 1941.

22. Joan W. Scott, "The evidence of experience," *Critical Inquiry,* xvii (Summer 1991), pp. 780ff.

23. Ibid., p. 793.

24. Samuel Hynes. *The soldiers' tale: bearing witness to modern war.* New York: Penguin Books, 1997.

25. For some examples, see Margaret R. Higonnet (ed). *Nurses at the front: writing the wounds of the great war.* Boston: Northeastern University Press, c2001; and Margaret R. Higonnet. *Lines of fire: women writers of world war I.* New York: Plume, c1999.

Chapter 5. Ironies of War

Thanks are due to Fritz Stern, Annette Becker, and Sarah Cole for their comments on this chapter.

1. I am grateful to Helen MacPhail for her advice on this matter.

2. Bernard Le Floch has kindly provided me with his edition of these poems. Siegfried Sassoon. *Poèmes de guerre.* Translated from English by Bernard Le Floch. Paris: Caractères, 1987.

3. Siegfried Sassoon. *Mémoires d'un chasseur de renards.* Translated from English by Antoinette Sémeziès and Jacques Elsey. Paris: Gallimard, 1938.

4. Paul Fussell. *The great war and modern memory.* New York: Oxford, 1985.

5. Samuel Hynes. *A war imagined: the first world war and English culture.* New York: Atheneum, 1991.

6. Modris Eksteins. *Le sacre du printemps: la grande guerre et la naissance de la modern.* Paris: Plon, 1991.

7. Raymond Williams. *The Long Revolution.* New York: Columbia University Press, 1961.

8. Samuel Hynes. *The Edwardian turn of mind.* London: Jonathan Cape, 1970.

9. For a survey of some of this vast literature, see D. C. Muecke. *Irony.* London: Methuen, 1970; Cleanth Brooks. *Modern poetry and the tradition.* Chapel Hill: University of North Carolina Press, 1939; Wayne Booth. *A rhetoric of irony.* Chicago: University of Chicago Press, 1974; and more recently, Birgit Baldwin, "Irony, that 'little invisible personage,' a reading of Kierkegaard's Ghosts," *MLN,* civ, 5, (1989), pp. 124–41, and Alan Wilde. *Horizons of assent: modernism, postmodernism, and the ironic imagination.* Philadelphia: University of Pennsylvania Press, 1987. I am grateful to Sarah Cole for her guidance in this literature.

10. Eleanor N. Hutchens, "The identification of irony," *ELH,* xxvii, 4 (December 1960), pp. 363.

11. Ibid., p. 358 (her italics).

12. Martin Middlebrook. *The first day on the Somme.* London: Fontana, 1975, pp. 124, 254.

13. Robert Graves. *Goodbye to all that.* London: Penguin, 1930, p. 79.

14. As cited in Paul Fussell. *The great war and modern memory.* New York: Oxford, 1975, p. 203.

15. Charles Carrington. *Soldiers from the wars returning.* London: Methuen, 1965, pp. 252–53.

16. Guy Chapman. *A passionate prodigality.* London: Heinemann, 1933, p. 277.

17. Maurice Genevoix. *Ceux de 14.* Paris: le Seuil, 1984.

18. Antoine Prost, "Combattants et politiciens: Le discours mythologiques sur la politique entre les deux guerre," *Mouvement social* (1973), pp. 117–49. I am grateful to Antoine Prost for many discussions of this theme. For an English version of this essay see Prost. *Republican identities in war and peace: representations of France in the nineteenth and twentieth centuries.* Translated by Jay Winter and Helen McPhail. Oxford: Berg, 2002.

19. Antoine Prost. *Les Anciens combattants et la société française,* 3 vols. Paris: Publications de la Fondation nationale des sciences politique, 1977.

20. On the play, see Roy Lewis. *Giraudoux: la guerre de Troie n'aura pas lieu.* London: Edward Arnold, 1971; Gunnar Graumann. *"La Guerre de Troie" aura lieu: la préparation de la pièce de Giraudoux.* Lund: C. W. K. Gleerup, 1979; Michel Maillard. *Giraudoux: des repères pour situer l'auteur.* Paris: Nathan, 1997; Chris Marker. *Giraudoux.* Paris: Seuil, 1978.

21. See Jean Giraudoux. *Campaigns and intervals.* Translated by Elizabeth S. Sergeant. Boston: Houghton Mifflin, 1918.

22. On Giraudoux, among many other works, see Jacques Body. *Giraudoux et l'Allemagne.* Paris: Publications de la Sorbonne. *Littératures* 7, 1978; Jacques Body. *Jean Giraudoux. La légende et le secret.* Paris: PUF, 1986; Chris Marker. *Giraudoux par lui-même.* Paris: Editions du Seuil, 1980.

Chapter 6. War Memorials

1. Thanks are due to Carol Gluck for discussions on these issues.

2. Avishai Margalit. *The ethics of memory.* Cambridge, Mass.: Harvard University Press, 2002.

3. Jay Winter and Emmanuel Sivan (eds). *War and remembrance in the twentieth century.* Cambridge: Cambridge University Press, 1999, ch. 2.

4. As cited by Coser in his introduction to Maurice Halbwachs. *On collective memory.* Translated by Lewis A. Coser. Chicago: University of Chicago Press, 1992, p. 13.

5. See Adrian Gregory. *The silence of memory: Armistice Day 1919–1946.* Oxford: Berg Publishers, 1994.

6. For the full story, see Jay Winter and Blaine Baggett. *The great war and the shaping of the twentieth century.* New York: Viking Studio, 1996, ch. 8.

7. Jay Winter. *Sites of memory, sites of mourning. The great war in European cultural history.* Cambridge: Cambridge University Press, 1995, ch. 4.

8. Gregory, *Silence of memory,* pp. 164–72.

9. Sophie Delaporte. *Les gueules cassées: les blessés de la face de la Grande Guerre.* Paris: Noësis, 1996.

10. For details see Winter, *Sites of memory,* ch. 3.

11. Winter, *Sites of memory,* ch. 4.

12. Jeffrey Verhey. *The myth of the "Spirit of 1914" in Germany, 1914–1945.* Cambridge: Cambridge University Press, forthcoming, ch. 3.

13. Winter, *Sites of memory,* ch. 4.

14. See Regina Schulte, "Käthe Kollwitz's sacrifice," *History Workshop Journal,* no. 41 (1996), pp. 193–221.

15. Käthe Kollwitz. *Die Tagebücher,* edited by Jutta Bohnke-Kollwitz. Berlin: Siedler, 1989, pp. 368–69.

16. Julia Kristeva. *Black Sun. Depression and melancholy.* Translated by L. S. Roudiez. New York: Columbia University Press, 1989.

17. Kollwitz, *Die Tagebücher,* p. 278.

18. Kollwitz, *Die Tagebücher,* p. 428.

19. Kollwitz, *Die Tagebücher,* p. 603.

20. See Winter and Sivan (eds), *War and remembrance,* ch. 1.

21. For a powerful discussion of the contrast between abstract and figurative forms of commemorative art, see R. Koselleck, "Bilderverbot. Welches Totengedenken?" *Frankfurter Allgemeine Zeitung,* 8 April 1993.

22. See Jacques Derrida, "Jacques Derrida zu 'between the lines,'" *Radix—*

Matrix (1991), pp. 115–17, as cited in Andreas Huyssen, "The voids of Berlin," *Critical Inquiry*, vol. 24, no. 1 (1997), pp. 57–81.

Chapter 7. War, Migration, and Remembrance

1. Annette Becker. *Maurice Halbwachs. Un intellectuel en guerres mondiales 1914–1945.* Paris: Agnès Viénot Editions, 2003.

2. Stephen Constantine (ed). *Emigrants and Empire: British settlement in the dominions between the wars.* Manchester: Manchester University Press, 1990, p. 2.

3. W. A. Carrothers. *Emigration from the British Isles.* London: Oxford University Press, 1929, pp. 308–9.

4. J. M. Winter. *The great war and the British people.* London: Macmillan, 1985, p. 267.

5. Thomas Brinley. *Migration and economic development: a study of Great Britain and the Atlantic economy.* Cambridge: Cambridge University Press, 1973.

6. Neil Tranter. *British population in the twentieth century.* Basingstoke: Macmillan, 1996, pp. 30ff.

7. See Jay Winter and Emmanuel Sivan. "Framework." In *War and remembrance in the twentieth century,* edited by Jay Winter and Emmanuel Sivan. Cambridge: Cambridge University Press, 1999.

8. J. M. Winter. *The experience of world war one.* London: Macmillan, 1988, p. 132.

9. Pierre Nora, "Between memory and history: Les lieux de mémoire," *Representations,* no. 26 (1989), pp. 7–25.

10. J. A. Mangan, "The grit of our forefathers: invented traditions, propaganda and imperialism"; John MacKenzie, " 'In touch with the infinite': the BBC and the Empire"; and Stephen Constantine, " 'Bringing the Empire alive': the Empire Marketing Board and imperial propaganda, 1926–33." All in *Imperialism and popular culture,* edited by John MacKenzie. Manchester: Manchester University Press, 1986, pp. 113–40, 165–91, and 192–231.

11. K. S. Inglis. *Sacred places: war memorials in the Australian Landscape.* Melbourne: Melbourne University Press, 1998.

12. Susan Thorne. *Congregational missions and the making of an imperial culture in nineteenth-century England.* Stanford, Calif.: Stanford University Press, 1999.

13. As cited in Inglis, *Sacred places,* p. 287.

14. Thomas W. Laqueur, "Names, bodies, and the anxiety of erasure." In *The social and political body,* edited by Theodore R. Schatzki and Wolfgang Natter. New York: Guilford Press, 1996, pp. 123–44.

15. Jay Winter and Jean-Louis Robert. *Capital cities at war: Paris, London, Berlin 1914–1919.* Cambridge: Cambridge University Press, 1997, p. 6.

Chapter 8. Grand Illusions

1. Walter Benjamin, "A Berlin chronicle." In *One-way street and other writings.* Translated by Edmund Jephcott and Kingsley Shorter. London, Verso, 1979, p. 314.

2. Benjamin, "A Berlin chronicle," p. 314.

3. All references are to the American Historical Review Forum on film and war, published in volume 106, number 3, of the *American Historical Review* in 2001. The articles discussed here are Geoff Eley, "Finding the people's war: film, British collective memory, and world war I," pp. 818–38; Denise Youngblood, "A war remembered: Soviet films of the great patriotic war," pp. 839–56; and John Bodnar, "*Saving private Ryan* and postwar memory in America," pp. 805–17. Page references in the text are to the on-line edition.

4. Pieter Lagrou. *The legacy of Nazi occupation: patriotic memory and national recovery in western Europe, 1945–1965.* Cambridge: Cambridge University Press, 2000.

5. Pierre Sorlin, "Children as victims in postwar European cinema." In *War and remembrance in the twentieth century,* edited by Jay Winter and Emmanuel Sivan. Cambridge: Cambridge University Press, 1999, pp. 104–24.

6. See Mark Mikale's penetrating discussion of the subject in his review in *The Times Literary Supplement* of 14 September 2000 of Ruth Leys. *Trauma: a genealogy.* Baltimore: Johns Hopkins University Press, 2000.

7. See Samuel Hynes. *The soldiers' tale.* New York: Penguin, 1997.

8. See Catherine Merridale. *Nights of stone: death and memory in twentieth-century Russia.* London: Jonathan Cape, 2000.

9. See for some suggestive remarks, Samuel Hynes. *A war imagined,* London: Bodley Head, 1993.

10. See the stimulating essays in D. L. Schacter and E. Scarry (eds). *Memory, brain, and belief.* Cambridge, Mass.: Harvard University Press, 2000.

11. Alon Confino, "Collective memory and cultural history: problems of method," *American Historical Review* (December 1997), pp. 1386–1403.

12. See the discussion in Roger Chartier. *On the edges of the cliff.* Baltimore: Johns Hopkins University Press, 1999.

13. See for instance Roger Bastide, "Mémoire collective et sociologie de bricolage," *Année sociologique,* 21 (1970), pp. 65–108.

14. See Maurice Halbwachs. *On collective memory.* Translated by Lewis A. Coser. Chicago: University of Chicago Press, 1992, pp. 172ff. On the genesis of these ideas, see Patrick Hutton. *History as an art of memory.* Hanover, N.H.: University of New England Press, 1993, ch. 4. See Annette Becker's definitive study of Halbwachs's work, *Maurice Halbwachs: Un Intellectuel en guerres mondiales 1914–1945.* Paris: Agnès Viénot, 1993.

Chapter 9. Between History and Memory

1. See the Australian journal *Public history review;* and David Glassberg. *Sense of history: the place of the past in American life,* Amherst: University of Massachusetts Press, 2001; Susan Porter Benson, Stephen Brier, and Roy Rosenzweig (eds). *Presenting the past: essays on history and the public.* Philadelphia: Temple University Press, 1986; Phyllis K. Leffler and Joseph Brent. *Public and academic history: a philosophy and paradigm.* Malabar, Fla.: R. E. Krieger, c1990; David F. Trask and Robert W. Pomeroy III (eds). *The craft of public history: an annotated select bibliography.* Westport, Conn.: Greenwood Press, 1983; Simone Rauthe. *Public History in den USA und der Bundesrepublik Deutschland.* Essen: Klartex, 2001; James B. Gardner and Peter S. LaPaglia (eds). *Public history: essays from the field.* Malabar, Fla.: Krieger, 1999.

2. Paul Fussell. *The great war and modern memory.* New York: Oxford University Press, 1975; John Keegan. *The face of battle.* London: Penguin Books, 1976; Eric Leed. *No man's land: combat and identity in world war I.* Cambridge: Cambridge University Press, 1979.

3. Modris Ekstein. *Rites of spring: the great war and the birth of the modern age.* Boston: Houghton Mifflin, 1989; Samuel Hynes. *A war imagined: the first world war and English culture.* London: Bodley Head, 1990.

4. See Jay Winter and Antoine Prost. *The great war in history: debates and controversies 1914 to the present.* Cambridge: Cambridge University Press, 2005.

Chapter 10. War Museums

1. Jay Winter. *Sites of memory, sites of mourning.* Cambridge: Cambridge University Press, 1995, ch. 4.

2. Roger Chartier. *On the edge of the cliff. History, language, and practices.* Translated by Lydia Cochrane. Baltimore: Johns Hopkins, 1997, pp.23ff.

3. Louis Marin. *On Representation.* Translated by Catherine Porter. Stanford: Stanford University Press, 2001.

4. Michel de Certeau. *La prise de la parole.* Paris: Desclée de Brouwer, 1968.

5. Ernst Jünger. *Storm of Steel.* New York: Howard Fertig, 2002.

6. Georges Duhamel. *Civilization 1914–1917.* Paris: Mercure de France, 1920.

7. Stéphane Audoin-Rouzeau. *Cinq deuils de guerre.* Paris: Noësis, 2001.

8. Annette Becker. *Maurice Halbwachs. Un intellectuel en guerres mondiales 1914–1945.* Paris: Agnès Viénot, 2003.

9. Becker Jean-Jacques et al. (eds). *Guerre et cultures 1914–1918.* Paris: A. Colin, 1994.

10. For a fuller elaboration, see Jay Winter. "George Mosse's comparative cultural history." In *What history tells: George L. Mosse and the culture of modern*

Europe, edited by Stanley G. Payne, David Jan Sorkin and John S. Tortorice. Madison: University of Wisconsin Press, 2003, pp. 48–60.

11. Stéphane Audoin-Rouzeau. *14–18, les combattants des tranchées* Paris: A. Colin, 1986; J. G. Fuller. *Troop morale and popular culture in the British and Dominion armies 1914–1918.* Oxford: Clarendon Press, 1990; Rob Nelson, "German soldiers' newspapers of the great war." Ph.D. diss., Cambridge, 2002.

12. Laura Lee Downs. *Manufacturing inequality: gender division in the French and British metalworking industries, 1914–1939.* Ithaca: Cornell University Press, 1995.

13. Charles Rearick. *The French in love and war: popular culture in the era of the world wars.* New Haven: Yale University Press, 1997.

14. See Antoine Prost and Jay Winter. *Penser la grande guerre.* Paris: Le Seuil, 2004.

15. Gerhard Hirschfeld, Gerd Krumeich, and Irina Renz (eds). *Keiner fühlt sich hier mehr als Mensch. Erlebnis und Wirkung des Ersten Weltkriegs.* Essen: Klartext, 1993; Gerhard Hirschfeld, Gerd Krumeich, Dieter Langewiesche, and Hans-Peter Ullmann (eds). *Kriegserfahrungen. Studien zur Sozial une Mentalitätsgeschichte des Ersten Weltrkriegs.* Essen: Klartext, 1997.

16. Dan Todman, *The great war. Myth and memory.* London: Hambledon and London, 2005.

17. Michael Howard. *The continental commitment: the dilemma of British defense policy in the era of the two world wars.* London: Maurice Temple Smith, 1972; Niall Ferguson. *The pity of war.* New York: Basic Books, 1999.

Chapter 11. "Witness to a Time"

1. Joan W. Scott, "The evidence of experience," *Critical inquiry,* xvii (Summer 1991), pp. 780ff.

2. Immanuel Kant. *Religion within the limits of reason alone.* Translated by Theodore M. Greene and Hoyt H. Hudson New York: Harper and Row, 1960, pp. 28ff.

3. Avishai Margalit. *The ethics of memory.* Cambridge, Mass.: Harvard University Press, 2002, pp. 147ff.

4. Margalit, *Ethics,* pp. 148–49.

5. Margalit, *Ethics,* p. 151.

6. Margalit, *Ethics,* p. 154.

7. Margalit, *Ethics,* p. 155.

8. Margalit, *Ethics,* p. 157.

9. Margalit, *Ethics,* p. 163.

10. Margalit, *Ethics,* p. 167.

11. Margalit, *Ethics,* p. 174.

12. Margalit, *Ethics,* p. 168.

13. Margalit, *Ethics*, p. 182.

14. Scott, "The evidence of experience," p. 780.

15. One of the most popular Great War music hall songs in Britain makes a point which bears on this matter. "They'll never believe us" was the reprise that veterans sang, and meant. Still, they continued to sing the song.

16. Antoine Prost. "The French contempt for politics: the case of veterans in the inter-war period. In his collected essays, *Republican identities in war and peace. Representations of France in the 19th and 20th centuries.* Berg: Oxford, 2002, p. 285.

17. Prost, *Republican identities*, pp. 302–3.

18. Prost, *Republican identities*, p. 297.

19. See chapter 4.

20. Jean Norton Cru. *Témoins. Essai d'analyse et de critique des couvenirs de combattants édités en français de 1915 à 1928.* Paris: Les Étincelles, 1929.

21. Jean Norton Cru. *Du Témoignage.* Paris: Librairie Gallimard (NRD), 1931.

22. An English translation of 1967 sidestepped the problem completely by entitling the work *War books. A study in historical criticism,* edited and annotated by Ernest Marchand and Stanley J. Picetl, Jr. San Diego: San Diego State University Press, 1976.

23. Norton Cru, *War books,* pp. 169–75.

24. Norton Cru, *War books,* p. 178.

25. Norton Cru, *War books,* p. 2.

26. Norton Cru, *War books,* p. 4.

27. Norton Cru, *War books,* pp. 7–8.

28. On this theme, see Christophe Prochasson, "Les mots pour le dire: Jean Norton Cru, du témoignage à l'histoire," *Revue d'histoire moderne et contemporaine,* xlviii, 4 (October–December 2001), pp. 160–89.

29. Norton Cru, *War books,* p. 19.

30. As cited in Len Smith, "Jean Norton Cru, lecteur des livres de guerre," Dossier pour les *Annales du Midi,* "La France méridionale dans la Grande Guerre," cxii, No. 232 (2000), pp. 510–19.

31. Victor Klemperer. *I will bear witness: the diaries of Victor Klemperer.* 2 vols. New York: Random House, 1998–2000.

32. Annette Wieviorka. *L'Ère du témoin.* Paris: Plon, 1998.

33. The literature by and on Levi is gigantic. The starting point for any discussion is his *Survival in Auschwitz: the Nazi assault on humanity.* Translated by Stuart Woolf. New York: Summit Books, 1986.

34. Leon Weliczker took the surname Wells when he came to the United States. His publications and his testimony to the Eichmann trial use the surname "Weliczker Wells." I use "Weliczker" to describe his life in Lvov, and "Weliczker Wells" to deal with his later narratives of it.

35. Leon Weliczker Wells. *The death brigade (the Janowska road)*. New York: Holocaust Library, 1963.

36. Weliczker Wells, *Death brigade*, p. 135.

37. Yale University Library, Fortunoff Video Archives, Cassette T 0778, 1:13. Hereafter referred to as "Wells testimony."

38. Weliczker Wells, *Death brigade*, p. 174.

39. Weliczker Wells, *Death brigade*, p. 162.

40. Weliczker Wells, *Death brigade*, p. 183.

41. Weliczker Wells, *Death brigade*, p. 169.

42. Weliczker Wells, *Death brigade*, p. 178.

43. Levi, *Survival in Auschwitz*, p. 100.

44. Weliczker Wells, *Death brigade*, p. 95.

45. Weliczker Wells, *Death brigade*, p. 217.

46. Weliczker Wells, *Death brigade*, p. 224.

47. They were fed by a Polish woman who took terrifying risks to do so. Why did she do it? She said simply that this was the first time she made a decision for herself. Instead of working for the men in her family, she did this act because she wanted to do so. Wells testimony, 1:26.

48. Wells testimony, 1:34.

49. Weliczker Wells, *Death brigade*, p. 239.

50. Wells testimony, 1:38.

51. Wells testimony, 1:37. My italics.

52. Wells testimony, 1:35; Weliczker Wells, *Death brigade*, p. 282.

53. Leon Weliczker. *Brygada śmierci: (Sonderkommando 1005): pamiętnik*. Łódz: Wydawn. Centralnej Żydowskiej Komisji Historycznej przy Centralnym Komitecie Żydów Polskich, 1946.

54. Weliczker Wells, *Death brigade*, pp. 297–305.

55. The full transcript of Wells's testimony may be found at http://www.nizkor.org/hweb/people/e/eichmann-adolf/transcripts/. All references are to this source.

56. This is how the prosecutor put it during Wells's testimony: "I have to prove this operation of removing the traces—for when a murderer wishes to cover up his tracks, this proves his guilt and his intention."

57. Wells testimony, 1:16.

58. Leon W. Wells. *Shattered faith: a Holocaust legacy*. Lexington, Ky.: University Press of Kentucky, 1995; Leon Weliczker Wells. *Who speaks for the vanquished?: American Jewish leaders and the Holocaust*, edited by Michael Ryan. New York: P. Lang, c1987.

59. Wells testimony, 57:30.

60. Wells testimony, 1:17.

61. Wells testimony, 1:16.

62. For a start, see Robert Jay Lifton. *Death in life; survivors of Hiroshima*. New York: Random House, 1968.

63. Wells testimony, 1:05.

64. Wells, *Who speaks for the vanquished?*, p. ix.

65. Wells, *Shattered faith*, p. 92.

66. Wells, *Shattered faith*, p. 95.

67. Wells, *Shattered faith*, p. 100.

68. Wells, *Shattered faith*, p. 141.

69. Renaud Dulong. *Le Témoin oculaire. Le conditions sociales de l'attestation personnelle.* Paris: Éditions de l'École des Hautes Études en Sciences Sociales, 1998. I am grateful to Len Smith for drawing this book to my attention.

70. Wells, *Who speaks for the vanquished?*, p. 270.

71. Peter Balakian. *The black dog of fate.* New York: Basic Books, 1997.

72. David Grossman. *See under love.* Translated by Betsy Rosenberg. New York: Farrar, Strauss and Giroux, 1989.

73. Margalit, *The ethics of memory*, p. 147.

74. Scott, "The evidence of experience," pp. 780ff.

75. See chapter 2.

Chapter 12. Controversies and Conclusions

1. Walter Benjamin, "A Berlin chronicle." In *One-way street and other writings.* Translated by Edmund Jephcott and Kingsley Shorter. London: Verso, 1979, p. 314.

2. Paul Ricoeur. *La Mémoire, l'histoire, l'oubli.* Paris: Seuil, 2000, p. 4.

3. Jay Winter and Emmanuel Sivan (eds). *War and remembrance in the twentieth century.* Cambridge: Cambridge University Press, 1999, ch. 1.

4. Ibid.

5. http//memory.loc.gov/ammem/amhome.html.

6. Robert Pinsky, "Poetry and American memory," *Atlantic monthly* (October 1999), pp. 60–70.

7. On this point, see Antoine Prost and Jay Winter. *Penser la grande guerre.* Paris: Le Seuil, 2004.

8. Kerwin Lee Klein, "On the emergence of memory in historical discourse," *Representations* (Winter 2000), pp. 127ff.

9. Pierre Nora, "The era of commemoration." In *Realms of memory, iii, symbols.* Paris: Gallimard, 1992, p. 618.

10. Nora, "The era of commemoration," p. 632.

11. Nora, "The era of commemoration," p. 634.

12. Pierre Nora (ed). *Realms of memory. the construction of the French past. I. Conflicts and divisions.* Translated by Arthur Goldhammer. New York: Columbia University Press, 1996, p. 1. This essay was published originally as Pierre Nora, "Between memory and history. Les lieux de mémoire," *Representations*, no. 26, Special Issue: Memory and Counter-Memory (Spring 1989), pp. 7–24.

13. Nora, *Realms*, p. 6.

14. Nora, *Realms,* p. 9.

15. Charles S. Maier, "A surfeit of memory? Reflections on history, melancholy and denial," *History & memory* (1993), pp. 136–51; see also Charles S. Maier, "Hot memory . . . cold memory: on the political half-life of fascist and communist memory," paper delivered to conference on "The memory of the century," Institut für die Wissenschaften vom Menschen, Vienna, 9–11 March 2001.

16. Peter Burke, "History and social memory." In his *Facets of cultural history.* Cambridge: Polity Press, 2003.

Bibliography

Agi, Marc, *De l'idée d'universalité comme fondatrice du concept des droits de l'homme d'après la vie et l'oeuvre de René Cassin*. Thèse pour le doctorat d'État, Université de Nice, 10 Dec. 1979. (Antibes: Éditions Alp'azur, 1980).

Agulhon, Maurice, "Le statumanie au xixè siècle," *Le romantisme*, xxx (1981), pp. 20–30.

——, *Marianne au combat: l'imagerie et la symbolique républicaines de 1789 à 1880*. (Paris: Flammarion, c1979).

Angress, Werner T., "The German army's *Judenzählung:* of 1916: genesis; consequences; significance," *Leo Baeck Institute Yearbook*, xxiii (1978).

Anissimov, Myriam, *Primo Levi: tragedy of an optimist*, trans. by Steve Cox. (London: Aurum, 1998).

Antze, Paul, and Michael Lambek (eds), *Tense past. Cultural essays in trauma and memory*. (New York: Routledge, 1996).

Appelbaum, Paul S., Lisa A. Uyehara, and Mark R. Elin (eds), *Trauma and memory: clinical and legal controversies*. (New York: Oxford University Press, 1997).

Archives Nationales, Paris, 382AP/1.

Aschheim, Steven E., "Eastern Jews, German Jews and Germany's Ostpolitik in the First World War," *Leo Baeck Institute Year Book*, xxvii (1983), p. 352.

Assmann, Aleida, *Erinnerungsraeume. Formen und Wandel des kulturellen Gedaechtnisses*. (München: C. H. Beck, 1999).

——, "Gedächtnis als Leitbegriff der Kulturwissenschaften." Unpublished paper.

Assmann, Jan, *Das kulturelle Gedachtnis: Schrift, Erinnerung und politische Identität in fruhen Hochkulturen*. (Munich: Beck, c1992).

Assmann, Jan, and Tonio Holscher (eds), *Kultur und Gedachtnis*. Frankfurt: Suhrkamp, 1988.

Audoin-Rouzeau, Stéphane, *Cinq deuils de guerre*. (Paris: Noesis, 2001).

——, *14–18. Les combatants des tranchées a travers leurs journeaux*. (Paris: A. Colin, 1986).

——, *Men at war, 1914–1918: national sentiment and trench journalism in France during the First World War*, trans. by Helen McPhail. (Providence, R.I.: Berg, 1992).

Balakian, Peter, *The black dog of fate*. (New York: Basic Books, 1997).

Baldwin, Birgit, "Irony, that 'little invisible personnage': a reading of Kierkegaard's Ghosts," *MLN*, civ, 5, Comparative literature (1989), pp. 124–41.

Barker, Pat, *Another world*. (London: Viking, 1998).

——, *Regeneration*. (New York: Viking, 1991).

——, *The eye in the door*. (New York: Viking, 1993).

——, *The ghost road*. (New York: Viking, 1995).

Barnes, Julian, *England, England*. (London: Jonathan Cape, 1998).

Bastide, Roger, "Mémoire collective et sociologie de bricolage," *Année sociologique*, xxi (1970), pp. 65–108.

Beausoleil, Jeanne, "La collection Albert Kahn," in *Autochromes 1901/1928*. (Paris: Tresors de la photographie, 1978).

Beausoleil, Jeanne, and Pascal Ory (eds), *Albert Kahn 1860–1940. Realites d'une utopie*. (Boulogne-Billancourt: Musée Albert Kahn-Departement des Hauts-de-Seine, 1995).

Becker, Annette, *Maurice Halbwachs, intellectuel en guerres mondiales 1914–1945*. (Paris: Agnès Viénot Editions, 2003).

Becker, Jean-Jacques, *1914: comment les Français sont entrés dans la guerre: contribution à l'étude de l'opinion publique, printemps–été 1914*. (Paris: Presses de la fondation nationale des sciences politiques, 1977).

Becker, Jean-Jacques et al. (eds), *Guerre et cultures, 1914–1918*. (Paris: A. Colin, 1994).

Benjamin, Walter, *Illuminations*, trans. by Harry Zorn. (Boston: Schocken, 1990).

——, *One-way street and other writings*, trans. by Edmund Jephcott and Kingsley Shorter. (London: Verso, 1979).

Bhabha, Homi K., *The location of culture*. (London: Routledge, 1994).

Bilu, Yoram, and Eliezer Witztum, "War-related loss and suffering in Israeli society: an historical perspective," *Israel Studies*, v.2 (1999), pp. 1–31.

Body, Jacques, *Giraudoux et l'Allemagne*. (Paris: Publications de la Sorbonne. Littératures 7, 1989).

——, *Jean Giraudoux. La légende et le secret*. (Paris: PUF, 1986).

Boemeke, Manfred F., Roger Chickering, and Stig Forster (eds), *Anticipating total war: the German and American experiences, 1871–1914*. (Cambridge: Cambridge University Press, 1999).

Bogacz, Ted, "War neurosis and cultural change in England, 1914–22," *Journal of contemporary history* (1989), pp. 18–25.

Bonnell, Victoria E. (ed), *Identities in transition: Eastern Europe and Russia after the collapse of communism*. (Berkeley: Center for Slavic and East European Studies, University of California at Berkeley, c1996).

Booth, Wayne, *A rhetoric of irony*. (Chicago: University of Chicago Press, 1974).

Bouwsma, William James, *A usable past: essays in European cultural history*. (Berkeley: University of California Press, c1990).

Brah, Avtar, and Annie E. Coombes (eds), *Hybridity and its discontents: politics, science, culture*. (London: Routledge, 2000).

Brooks, Cleanth, *Modern poetry and the tradition*. (Chapel Hill: University of North Carolina Press, 1939).

Brunner, Otto, Werner Conze, and Reinhart Koselleck (eds), *Geschichtliche Grundbegriffe: historisches Lexikon zur politisch-sozialen Sprache in Deutschland*. (Stuttgart: E. Klett, 1972–1997).

Burke, Peter, his *Facets of cultural history*. (Cambridge: Polity Press, 2003).

Butler, Thomas (ed), *Memory: history, culture and the mind*. (Oxford: Basil Blackwell, 1990).

Caemmerer, Christiane, Walter Delabar, and Marion Schulz (eds), *Die totale Erinnerung. Sicherung und Zerstoerung Kulturhistorischer Vergangenheit und Gegenwart in den modernen Industriegesellschaften*. (Bern: Jahrbuch fuer Internationale Germanistik, Reihe A. 45, 1997).

Cannadine, David, "The context, performance and meaning of ritual: the British monarchy and the invention of tradition, c. 1820–1977," in *The invention of tradition*, edited by Hobsbawm and Ranger, pp. 98–132.

Carrington, Charles, *Soldiers from the wars returning*. (London: Methuen, 1965).

Carrothers, W. A., *Emigration from the British Isles*. (London: Oxford University Press, 1929).

Caruth, Cathy (ed), *Trauma: explorations in memory*. (Baltimore: Johns Hopkins University Press, 1995).

Céline, Louis Ferdinand, *Bagatelles pour un massacre*. (Paris: Denoël, 1937).

Certeau, Michel de, *La prise de la parole*. (Paris: Desclée de Brouwer, 1968).

Chapman, Guy, *A passionate prodigality*. (London: Heinemann, 1933).

Chartier, Roger, "Intellectual history or sociocultural history? The French trajectories," in *Modern European intellectual history: reappraisals and new perspectives*, edited by Dominick LaCapra and Steven L. Kaplan. (Ithaca: Cornell University Press, 1982).

——, *On the edge of the cliff. History, language, and practices*, trans. by Lydia Cochrane. (Baltimore: Johns Hopkins, 1997).

Clendinnen, Olga, *Reading the Holocaust*. (Cambridge: Cambridge University Press, 1994).

Conan, Eric, and Henry Rousso, *Vichy: an ever-present past*, trans. and annotated by Nathan Bracher; foreword by Robert O. Paxton. (Hanover: University Press of New England, c1998).

Confino, Alon, "Collective memory and cultural history: problems of method," *American Historical Review vol.* (December 1997), pp. 1386–1403.

Constantine, Stephen, " 'Bringing the Empire alive': the Empire Marketing Board and imperial propaganda, 1926–33," in *Imperialism and popular culture*, edited by John MacKenzie. (Manchester: Manchester University Press, 1986), pp. 192–231.

—— (ed), *Emigrants and Empire: British settlement in the dominions between the wars*. (Manchester: Manchester University Press, 1990).

Conway, Martin A., "The inventory of experience: memory and identity," in *Collective memory of political events: Social psychological perspectives*, edited by James W. Pennebaker, Dario Paez, and Bernard Rimé. (Mahwah, N.J.: Lawrence Erlbaum Associates, 1997), pp. 21–45.

Cru, Jean Norton, *Du Témoignage* (Paris: Librairie Gallimard [NRD], 1931).

——, *Témoins. Essai d'analyse et de critique des souvenirs de combattants édités en français de 1915 à 1928*. (Paris: Les Étincelles, 1929).

——, *War books. A study in historical criticism*, edited and annotated by Ernest Marchand and Stanley J. Pictel, Jr. (San Diego: San Diego State University Press, 1976).

Csordas, Thomas J. (ed), *Embodiment and experience: the existential ground of culture and self.* (Cambridge: Cambridge University Press, 1994).

Damousi, Joy, *Languages of loss.* (Cambridge: Cambridge University Press, 1998).

De Grandis, Rita, and Zila Bernd, *Unforeseeable Americas: questioning cultural hybridity in the Americas.* (Amsterdam: Rodopi, 2000).

Delaperrière, Maria (ed), *Centre d'étude de l'Europe médiane. (Post)-modernisme en Europe centrale: La crise des idéologies* (Paris: Harmattan, c1999).

Delaporte, Sophie, *Les gueules cassées: les blessés de la face de la Grande Guerre.* (Paris: Noësis, 1996).

Derrida, Jacques, "Jacques Derrida zu 'Between the Lines,'" *Radix—Matrix* (1991), pp. 115–17.

Downs, Laura Lee, *Manufacturing inequality: Gender division in the French and British metalworking industries, 1914–1939.* (Ithaca: Cornell University Press, 1995).

Duhamel, George L., *Civilization 1914–1917* (Paris: Mercure de France, 1920).

Dulong, Renaud, *Le Témoin oculaire. Le conditions sociales de l'attestation personnelle.* (Paris: Éditions de l'École des Hautes Études en Sciences Sociales, 1998).

Eakin, Paul John, "Autobiography, identity, and the fictions of memory," in *Memory, brain, and belief,* edited by Daniel L. Schacter and Elaine Scarry. (Cambridge: Harvard University Press, 2000), pp. 290–306.

Ehrenbourg, Ilya, and Vassili Grossman (eds), *Le livre noir: sur l'extermination scélérate des Juifs par les envahisseurs fascistes allemands dans les régions provisoirement occupées de l'URSS et dans les camps d'extermination en Pologne pendant la guerre de 1941–1945, textes et témoignages,* trans. from Russia by Yves Gauthier et al. (Arles: Actes Sud, 1995).

Eissler, K. R., *Freud sur le front des névroses de guerre,* trans. by Madeleine Drouin. (Paris: Presses Universitaires de France, 1992).

Ekstein, Modris, *Rites of spring: The great war and the birth of the modern age.* (Boston: Houghton Mifflin, 1989).

Eurostat Yearbook 98/99; a statistical eye on Europe 1987–1997. (Brussels: European Community, 1999).

Fabre, Gweneviere, and Robert O'Meally (eds), *History and memory in African-American culture.* (Oxford: Oxford University Press, 1994).

Faulks, Sebastian, *Birdsong*. (London: Hutchinson, 1993).

——, *Charlotte Gray*. (London: Hutchinson, 1998).

Felstiner, John, *Paul Celan: poet, survivor, Jew*. (New Haven: Yale University Press, 2001).

Ferguson, Niall, *The pity of war*. (London: Penguin Press, 1998).

Ferro, Marc, *La Révolution de 1917*. (Paris: Aubier, 1967).

Forster, Stig (ed), *Moltke: von Kabinettskrieg zum Volkskrieg: eine Werkauswahl*. (Bonn: Bouvier, 1992).

Fortunoff Video Archive, Yale University Library, Cassette T 0778, 1:13. Wells testimony.

Frassica, Pietro (ed), *Primo Levi as witness: proceedings of a symposium held at Princeton University, April 30–May 2, 1989*. (Fiesole: Casalini, 1990).

Fuller, J. G., *Troop morale and popular culture in the British and Dominion armies 1914–1918*. (Oxford: Clarendon Press, 1990).

Fussell, Paul, *The great war and modern memory*. (Oxford: Oxford University Press, 1975).

Garnett, D. (ed), *The Letters of T. E. Lawrence*. (London: Jonathan Cape, 1938).

Garton, Stephen, "Freud versus the rate: understanding shell shock in World War I," *Australian cultural history*, no. 16 (1997/98), pp. 45–59.

Gellner, Ernest, *Postmodernism, reason and religion*. (London: Routledge, 1992).

Genevoix, Maurice, *Ceux de 14*. (Paris: le Seuil, 1984).

Giraudoux, Jean, *Campaigns and intervals*, trans. by Elizabeth S. Sergeant. (Boston: Houghton Mifflin, 1918).

Girouard, Mark, *Life in the English country house: a social and architectural history*. (New Haven: Yale University Press, 1978).

Glenberg, A. M., "What memory is for," *Behavioral and Brain Sciences*, xx, 1 (1997), pp. 1–55.

Goldhagen, Daniel, *Hitler's willing executioners: ordinary Germans and the Holocaust* (New York: Knopf, 1996).

Gombrich, E. H., *Aby Warburg. An intellectual biography. With a memoir on the history of the library by F. Saxl*. (Oxford: Phaidon, 1970).

Graumann, Gunnar, *"La Guerre de Troie" aura lieu: la préparation de la pièce de Giraudoux*. (Lund: C. W. K. Gleerup, 1979).

Graves, Robert, *Goodbye to all that*. (London: Penguin, 1930).

Gregory, Adrian, *The silence of memory: Armistice Day 1919–1946*. (Oxford: Berg, 1994).

Grossman, David, *See under love,* trans. by Betsy Rosenberg. (New York: Farrar, Strauss and Giroux, 1989).

Halbwachs, Maurice, *Les cadres sociaux de la memoire.* (Paris: F. Alcan, 1925).

——, *On collective memory,* trans. by Lewis A. Coser. (Chicago: University of Chicago Press, 1992).

Hayden, Dolores, "The Japanese-American monument in Los Angeles," in *War and remembrance in the twentieth century,* edited by Jay Winter and Emmanuel Sivan. (Cambridge: Cambridge University Press, 1999), pp. 142–60.

Hertlin, Manfred, and Michael Jeismann, "Der Weltkrieg als Epos. Philipp Witkops "Kriegsbriefe gefallener Studenten," in *Keiner fühlt sich hier mehr als Mensch,* edited by Hirshfeld, Krumeich, and Rens, pp. 175–98.

Higonnet, Margaret R., *Lines of fire: women writers of World War I.* (New York: Plume, c1999).

—— (ed), *Nurses at the front: writing the wounds of the great war.* (Boston: Northeastern University Press, c2001).

Hirschfeld, Gerhard, and Gerd Krumeich, with Irina Renz, *Keiner fühlt sich hier mehr als Mensch: Erlebnis und Wirkung des Ersten Weltkriegs.* (Essen: Klartext, 1993).

Hirschfeld, Gerhard, Gerd Krumeich, Dieter Langewiesche, and Hans-Peter Ullmann (eds), *Kriegserfahrungen. Studien zur Sozial une Mentalitätsgeschichte des Ersten Weltrkriegs,* (Essen: Klartext, 1997).

Hobsbawm, Eric, and Terence Ranger (eds), *The invention of tradition.* Cambridge: Cambridge University Press, 1983.

Homer, Frederic D., *Primo Levi and the politics of survival.* (Columbia: University of Missouri Press, c2001).

Horkheimer, Max, and Theodor W. Adorno, *Dialectic of enlightenment,* trans. by John Cumming. (New York: Continuum, 1972).

Horowitz, Mardi J. (ed), *Essential papers on posttraumatic stress disorder.* (New York: New York University Press, 1999).

——, *Stress response syndromes. PTSD, grief, and adjustment disorders.* (Northvale, N.J.: Jason Aronson, 1997).

Howard, Sir Michael, *The continental commitment: the dilemma of British defence policy in the era of the two world wars.* (London: Maurice Temple Smith, 1972).

Hunt, Lynn (ed), *The new cultural history.* (Berkeley: University of California Press, 1989).

Hutchens, Eleanor N., "The identification of irony," *ELH*, xxvii, 4 (December 1960), pp. 363–75.

Hutton, Patrick, *History as an art of memory*. (Hanover, N.H.: University of New England Press, 1993).

Huyssen, Andreas, "The voids of Berlin," *Critical Inquiry*, vol. 24, no. 1 (1997), pp. 57–81.

Hynes, Samuel, *A war imagined: the First World War and English culture.* (New York: Atheneum, 1991).

——, *The Edwardian turn of mind.* (London: Jonathan Cape, 1970).

——, *The soldiers' tale: bearing witness to modern war.* (New York: A. Lane, 1997).

Inglis, K. S., *Sacred places: war memorials in the Australian Landscape.* (Melbourne: Melbourne University Press, 1998).

Irwin-Zarecki, Iwona, *Frames of remembrance: the dynamics of collective memory.* (New Brunswick, N.J.: Transaction, 1994).

Jacob, Neil, "Representation and commemoration of the Great War: A comparative study of Philipp Witkop's *Kriegsbriefe gefallener Studenten* (1928) and Laurence Housman's *War letters of fallen Englishmen* (1930)," *Irish History* (2002).

Japrisot, Sébastien, *Un long dimanche de fiançailles: roman.* (Paris: Denöel, 1991).

Jones, Gareth Stedman, *Languages of class: studies in English working class history, 1832–1982.* (Cambridge: Cambridge University Press, 1983).

Joyce, James, *Portrait of the artist as a young man.* (London: The Egoist Ltd., c1916).

Junger, Ernst, *Storm of Steel.* (New York: Howard Fertig, 2002).

Kant, Immanuel, *Religion within the limits of reason alone,* trans. by Theodore M. Greene and Hoyt H. Hudson. (New York: Harper and Row, 1960).

Kaplan, Marion, *The making of the Jewish middle class.* (New York: Oxford University Press, 1991).

Keegan, John, *The face of battle.* (London: Allen Lane, 1976).

Kirmayer, Laurence J., "Landscapes of memory: trauma, narrative, and dissociation," in *Tense past: cultural essays in trauma and memory,* edited by Paul Antze and Michael Lambek. (London: Routledge, 1996), pp. 173–98.

Klein, Kerwin Lee, "On the emergence of *memory* in historical discourse," *Representations,* 69 (Winter 2000), pp. 127–50.

Klemperer, Victor, *I will bear witness: the diaries of Victor Klemperer,* 2 vols. (New York: Random House, 1998–2000).

Kollwitz, Käthe, *Die Tagebücher,* edited by Jutta Bohnke-Kollwitz. (Berlin: Siedler, 1989).

Koselleck, Reinhart, "Bilderverbot. Welches Totengedenken?," *Frankfurter Allgemeine Zeitung,* 8 April 1993.

Koselleck, Reinhart, and Klaus Schreiner, *Burgerschaft: Rezeption und Innovation der Begrifflichkeit vom Hohen Mittelalter bis ins 19. Jahrhundert.* (Stuttgart: Klett-Cotta, c1994).

Kristeva, Julia, *Black sun. Depression and melancholy,* trans. by L. S. Roudiez. (New York: Columbia University Press, 1989).

LaCapra, Dominick, *History and memory after Auschwitz.* (Ithaca: Cornell University Press, 1998).

Lagrou, Pieter, *The legacy of Nazi occupation: patriotic memory and national recovery in western Europe, 1945–1965.* (Cambridge: Cambridge University Press, 2000).

Lankheit, Klaus (ed), *Franz Marc im Urteil seiner Zeit. Einfuhrung und erlauterende.* (Köln: M. DuMont Schauberg, 1960).

Laqueur, Thomas W., "Names, bodies, and the anxiety of erasure," in *The social and political body,* edited by Theodore R. Schatzki and Wolfgang Natter. (New York: Guilford Press, 1996), pp. 123–44.

Leed, Eric, *No man's land: combat and identity in World War I.* (Cambridge: Cambridge University Press, 1979).

Leese, Peter, *Shell shock: traumatic neurosis and the British soldiers of the first world war.* (New York: Palgrave, 2002).

Lees-Milne, James (ed), *The National Trust, a record of fifty years' achievement,* with an introduction by G. M. Trevelyan and contributions by Ivor Brown et al. (London: B. T. Batsford, 1946).

Lehmann, Hartmut, and Melvin Richter (eds), *The meaning of historical terms and concepts: new studies on Begriffsgeschichte.* (Washington, D.C.: German Historical Institute, c1996).

Levi, Primo, *Survival in Auschwitz: the Nazi assault on humanity,* trans. by Stuart Woolf. (New York: Summit Books, 1986).

Levinas, Emmanuel, *God, death, and time,* trans. by Bettina Bergo. (Palo Alto: Stanford University Press, c2000).

Lewis, Roy, *Giraudoux: La guerre de Troie n'aura pas lieu.* (London: Edward Arnold, 1971).

Leys, Ruth, *Trauma: a genealogy.* (Baltimore: Johns Hopkins University Press, 2000).

Library of Congress American Memory Web site: http://memory.loc .gov/ammem/amhome.html.

Lifton, Robert Jay, *Death in life; survivors of Hiroshima.* (New York: Random House, 1968).

Lipp, Anne, "Friedenssehnsucht und Durchhaltebereitschaft. Wahrnehmungen und Erfahrungen deutscher Soldaten im Ersten Weltkrieg," *Archiv für Sozialgeschichte,* xxxvi (1996), pp. 279–92.

——, "Heimatwahrnehmung und soldatisches 'Kriegserlebnis,'" in *Kriegserfahrungen. Studien zur Sozial- und Mentalitätsgeschichte des Erste Weltkrieges,* edited by Gerhard Hirschfeld, Gerd Krumeich, Dieter Langewiesche, and Hans Peter Ullmann. (Essen: Klartext, 1997), pp. 225–42.

Liulevicius, Vejas, *War land on the Eastern Front: culture, national identity and German occupation in World War I.* (Cambridge: Cambridge University Press, 1999).

Lyotard, Jean-François, *La condition postmoderne: rapport sur le savoir.* (Paris: Editions de Minuit, c1979).

MacKenzie, John (ed), *Imperialism and popular culture.* (Manchester: Manchester University Press, 1986).

——, "'In touch with the infinite': the BBC and the Empire," in *Imperialism and popular culture,* edited by John MacKenzie. (Manchester: Manchester University Press, 1986), pp. 165–91.

Maier, Charles S., "A surfeit of memory? Reflections on history, melancholy and denial," *History & memory* (1993), pp. 136–51.

——, "Hot memory . . . cold memory: on the political half-life of fascist and communist memory," paper delivered at conference on "The Memory of the Century," Institut für die Wissenschaften vom Menschen, Vienna, 9–11 March 2001.

——, "Lines of force: territoriality, technologies, and the production of world order in the modern era," lecture, Yale University, 11 February 2000.

——, *The unmasterable past: history, holocaust, and German national identity.* (Cambridge, Mass.: Harvard University Press, c1988).

Maillard, Michel, *Giraudoux: des repères pour situer l'auteur.* Paris: Nathan, 1997.

Mangan, J. A., "'The grit of our forefathers': invented traditions, propaganda and imperialism," in *Imperialism and popular culture,* edited by John MacKenzie. (Manchester: Manchester University Press, 1986), pp. 113–40.

Marcus, Jacob R., *The rise and destiny of the German Jew*. (New York: Ktav Publishing House, 1973).

Margalit, Avishai, *The ethics of memory*. (Cambridge, Mass.: Harvard University Press, 2002).

Marin, Louis, *On representation*, trans. by Catherine Porter. (Palo Alto: Stanford University Press, 2001).

Marker, Chris, *Giraudoux*. (Paris: Seuil, 1978).

——, *Giraudoux par lui-même*. (Paris: Editions du Seuil, 1980).

McGreevy, Linda F., *Bitter witness. Otto Dix and the great war*. (New York: Peter Lang, 2001).

McNally, Richard, *Remembering trauma*. (Cambridge, Mass.: Harvard University Press, 2003).

Megill, Allen, "History, memory, identity," *History of the human sciences*, xi, 3 (1998), pp. 37–62.

Merridale, Catherine, *Nights of stone: death and memory in twentieth-century Russia*. (London: Jonathan Cape, 2000).

Micale, Mark, and Robert Dietle (eds), *Enlightenment, passion, modernity: historical essays in European culture and thought*. (Palo Alto: Stanford University Press, 2000).

Middlebrook, Martin, *The first day on the Somme*. (London: Fontana, 1975).

Milward, Alan S., "Bad memories," *The Times Literary Supplement*, 14 April 2000, p. 8.

Mosse, George L., *Fallen soldiers: reshaping the memory of the world wars*. (New York: Oxford University Press, 1990).

Muecke, D. C., *Irony*. (London: Methuen, 1970).

Natter, Wolfgang G., *Literature at war 1914–1940: representing the "time of greatness" in Germany*. (New Haven: Yale University Press, 1999).

Nelson, Rob, "German soldiers newspapers of the Great War," Ph.D. diss., Cambridge, 2002.

Niewyk, Donald L., *The Jews in Weimar Germany*. (Baton Rouge: Louisiana State University Press, 1980).

Nora, Pierre, "Between memory and history. Les Lieux de mémoire," *Representations*, no. 26 (Special Issue: Memory and Counter-Memory) (Spring 1989), pp. 7–24.

—— (ed), *Essais d'égo-histoire*. (Paris: Gallimard, 1987).

——, *Les Lieux de mémoire*, 7 vols. (Paris: Gallimard, c1984–c1992).

——, *Realms of memory. The construction of the French past. I. Conflicts and divisions*, trans. by Arthur Goldhammer. (New York: Columbia University Press, 1996).

——, *Science et conscience du patrimoine: Entretiens du patrimoine, Théâtre national de Chaillot, Paris, 28, 29 et 30 novembre 1994*. (Paris: Fayard, Editions du patrimoine, c1997).

——, "The era of commemoration," in *Realms of memory, iii, symbols*. (Paris: Gallimard, 1992).

Novick, Peter, *The Holocaust in American life*. (Boston: Houghton Mifflin, 1999).

OECD, *Educational statistics yearbook, vol. 1: international tables*. (Paris: OECD, 1974).

Olick, Jeffrey K., and Joyce Robbins, "Social memory studies: from collective memory to the historical sociology of mnemonic practices," *American Review of Sociology*, xxiv (1998), pp. 105–40.

Ophuls, Marcel, *The sorrow and the pity: a film*, introduction by Stanley Hoffmann, filmscript translated by Mireille Johnston, biographical and appendix material by Mireille Johnston. (New York: Outerbridge and Lazard; distributed by Dutton, 1972).

Painter, George D., *Marcel Proust: a biography*. (London: Penguin, 1990).

Payne, Stanley G., David Jan Sorkin, and John S. Tortorice (eds), *What history tells: George L. Mosse and the culture of modern Europe*. (Madison: University of Wisconsin Press, 2003).

Pennebaker, James W., Dario Paez, and Bernard Rimé (eds), *Collective memory of political events: social psychological perspectives*. (Mahwah, N.J.: Lawrence Erlbaum Associates, 1997).

Perez Firmat, Gustavo, *Life on the hyphen: the Cuban-American way*. (Austin: University of Texas Press, 1994).

Pinsky, Robert, "Poetry and American memory," *Atlantic Monthly* (October 1999), pp. 60–70.

Prochasson, Christophe, "Les mots pour le dire: Jean Norton Cru, du témoignage à l'histoire," *Revue d'Histoire Moderne et Contemporaine*, 48–4, (October–December 2001), pp. 160–89.

Prost, Antoine, "Combattants et politiciens: Le discours mythologiques sur la politique entre les deux guerre," *Mouvement social* (1973), pp. 117–49.

——, *Les anciens combattants et la société française 1914–1939*, 3 vols. (Paris: Presse de la Fondation Nationale des sciences politiques, 1977).

——, *Republican identities in war and peace: representations of France in the nineteenth and twentieth centuries,* trans. by Jay Winter and Helen McPhail, (Oxford: Berg, 2002).

Prost, Antoine, and Jay Winter, *Penser la grande guerre.* (Paris: Le Seuil, 2004).

Public Record Office, London, PIN 77 files of disabled First World War veterans.

Rearick, Charles, *The French in love and war: popular culture in the era of the World Wars.* (New Haven: Yale University Press, 1997).

Rébérioux, Madeleine, "La mur des Fédérées," in Nora, *Les lieux de mémoire,* vol. 2, pp. 220–62.

Reimann, Aribert, *Der grosse Krieg der Sprachen: Untersuchungen zur historischen Semantik in Deutschland und England zur Zeit des Ersten Weltkriegs.* (Essen: Klartext, 2000).

Renan, Ernest, *Qu'est-ce qu'une nation?: conférence faite en Sorbonne, le 11 mars 1882.* (Paris: Calmann Lévy, 1882).

Ricoeur, Paul, *La Mémoire, l'histoire, l'oubli.* (Paris: Seuil, 2000).

Rouaud, Jean, *Champs d'honneur.* (Paris: Editions de Minuit, 1990).

Rousso, Henry, *The Vichy syndrome: history and memory in France since 1944,* trans. by Arthur Goldhammer. (Cambridge, Mass.: Harvard University Press, 1991).

Sassoon, Siegfried, *Mémoires d'un chasseur de renards,* trans. from English by Antoinette Sémeziès and Jacques Elsey. (Paris: Gallimard, 1938).

——, *Poèmes de guerre,* trans. from English by Bernard Le Floch. (Paris: Caractères, 1987).

Schachter, Daniel L. (ed), *Memory distortion: how minds, brains and societies reconstruct the past.* (Cambridge, Mass.: Harvard University Press, 1995).

——, *The seven sins of memory. (How the mind forgets and remembers).* (Boston: Houghton Mifflin, 2000).

Schacter, Daniel L., and Elaine Scarry (eds), *Memory, brain and belief.* (Cambridge, Mass.: Harvard University Press, 2000).

Schatzki, Theodore R., and Wolfgang Natter (eds), *The social and political body.* (New York: Guilford Press, 1996).

Schulte, Regina, "Käthe Kollwitz's sacrifice," *History Workshop Journal,* no. 41 (1996), pp. 193–221.

Scott, Joan W., "The evidence of experience," *Critical Inquiry,* xvii (Summer 1991), pp. 780–808.

Shephard, Ben, *A war of nerves. Soldiers and psychiatrists 1914–1994.* (London: Jonathan Cape, 2000).

Singer, Isaac Bashevis, *Nobel Lecture.* (New York: Farrar, Straus, Giroux, 1979).

Slobodin, Richard. *W. H. R. Rivers: pioneer anthropologist, psychiatrist of the ghost road.* (Stroud: Sutton, 1997).

Smith, Len, "Jean Norton Cru, lecteur des livres de guerre," Dossier pour les *Annales du Midi*, "La France méridionale dans la Grande Guerre," cxii, no. 232 (2000), pp. 510–19.

Sommer, Doris, *Proceed with caution, when engaged by minority writing in the Americas.* (Cambridge, Mass.: Harvard University Press, 1999).

Sorlin, Pierre, "Children as victims in postwar European cinema," in *War and remembrance in the twentieth century,* edited by Jay Winter and Emmanuel Sivan. (Cambridge: Cambridge University Press, 1999), pp. 104–24.

Soulez, Philippe, *Henri Bergson. Un biographie,* begun by Philippe Soulez and completed by Frederic Worms. (Paris: Flammarion, c1997).

Southard, E. E., *Shell-shock and other neuropsychiatric problems presented in five hundred and eighty-nine case histories from the war literature, 1914–1918.* (Boston: W. M. Leonard, 1919).

Spence, Jonathan D., *The memory palace of Matteo Ricci.* (New York: Viking, 1984).

Strathern, Andrew, *Body thoughts.* (Ann Arbor: University of Michigan Press, 1996).

Stromberg, Roland N., *Redemption by war: the intellectuals and 1914.* (Lawrence, Kans.: Regents Press of Kansas, c1982).

Sturken, Marita, *Tangled memories: the Vietnam war, the AIDS epidemic, and the politics of remembering.* (Berkeley: University of California Press, 1997).

Talbott, John, "Shell shock and the Second World War," paper presented at international conference on the comparative history of shell shock, Historial de la grande guerre, Péronne, Somme, France, July 1998.

Theweleit, Klaus, *Male fantasies,* trans. by Stephen Conway in collaboration with Erica Carter and Chris Turner, foreword by Barbara Ehrenreich, 2 vols. (Minneapolis: University of Minnesota Press, 1987–89).

Thomas, Brinley, *Migration and economic development: a study of Great Britain and the Atlantic economy.* (Cambridge: Cambridge University Press, 1973).

Thorne, Susan, *Congregational missions and the making of an imperial culture in nineteenth-century England*. (Palo Alto: Stanford University Press, 1999).

Thum, Bernd, and Thomas Keller (eds), *Interkulturelle Lebenslaufe*. (Tubingen: Stauffenburg, c1998).

Todman, Dan, *The great war. Myth and memory*. (London: Hambledon and London, 2005).

Tranter, Neil, *British population in the twentieth century*. (Basingstoke: Macmillan, 1996).

Tuleja, Tad (ed), *Usable pasts: traditions and group expressions in North America*. (Logan, Utah: Utah State University Press, 1997).

Tulving, Endel, and Martin Lepage, "Where in the brain is the awareness of one's past," in *Memory, brain and belief*, edited by Daniel L. Schacter and Elaine Scarry. (Cambridge, Mass.: Harvard University Press, 2000).

Ulrich, Bernd, *Die Augenzeugen. Deutsche Feldpostbriefe in Kriegs- und Nachkriegszeit 1914–1933*. (Essen: Klartext, 1997).

——, "Feldpostbriefe des Ersten Weltkrieges—Möglichkeiten und Grenzen einer alltagsgeschichtlichen Quelle," *Militärgeschichtliche Mitteilungen*, 53 (1994).

——, *Krieg im Frieden: die umkampfte Erinnerung an den Ersten Weltkrieg: Quellen und Dokumente*. (Frankfurt am Main: Fischer Taschenbuch Verlag, 1997).

Ulrich, Bernd, and Benjamin Ziemann (eds), *Frontalltag im Ersten Weltkrieg: Wahn und Wirklichkeit: Quellen und Dokumente*. (Frankfurt: Fischer, 1994).

Vergara, Benito M., *Displaying Filipinos: photography and colonialism in early 20th century Philippines*. (Quezon City: University of the Philippines Press, 1995).

Verhey, Jeffrey, *The spirit of 1914: militarism, myth, and mobilization in Germany*. (Cambridge: Cambridge University Press, 1996).

Vitoux, Frederic, *La vie de Céline*. (Paris: B. Grasset, 1988).

Vogel, Marianne, "Cherchez la femme, Strategische Ueberlegungen zur Integration von Schriftstellerinnen ins kulturelle Gedaechtnis," in *Die totale Erinnerung. Sicherung und Zerstoerung Kulturhistorischer Vergangenheit und Gegenwart in den modernen Industriegesellschaften*, edited by Christiane Caemmerer, Walter Delabar, and Marion Schulz. (Bern: Jahrbuch fuer Internationale Germanistik, Reihe A. 45, 1997).

Watson, Alex, " 'For kaiser and reich.' The identity and fate of the

German volunteers, 1914–1918," *War in History* xii, 1 (January 2005), pp. 49–74.

Wells, Leon W., *Shattered faith: a Holocaust legacy.* (Lexington, Ky.: University Press of Kentucky, 1995).

Wells, Leon Weliczker, *The death brigade (the Janowska Road).* (New York: Holocaust Library, 1963).

——, *Who speaks for the vanquished?: American Jewish leaders and the Holocaust,* edited by Michael Ryan. (New York: P. Lang, c1987).

Wieviorka, Annette, "From survivor to witness: voices from the Shoah," in *War and remembrance in the twentieth century,* edited by Jay Winter and Emmanuel Sivan. (Cambridge: Cambridge University Press, 1999), pp. 101–29.

——, *L'Ère du témoin.* (Paris: Plon, 1998).

Wilde, Alan, *Horizons of assent: modernism, postmodernism, and the ironic imagination.* (Philadelphia: University of Pennsylvania Press, 1987).

Williams, Raymond, *The country and the city.* (New York: Oxford University Press, 1973).

——, *The long revolution.* (New York: Columbia University Press, 1961).

Wilson, Jeremy, *Lawrence of Arabia.* (London: Heinemann, 1989).

Winter, J. M., *Sites of memory, sites of mourning. The great war in European cultural history.* (Cambridge: Cambridge University Press, 1995).

——, *The experience of World War One.* (London: Macmillan, 1988).

——, *The great war and the British people.* (London: Macmillan, 1985).

Winter, Jay, "Céline and the cultivation of hatred," in *Enlightenment, passion, modernity: historical essays in European culture and thought,* edited by Mark Micale and Robert Dietle. (Palo Alto: Stanford University Press, 2000), pp. 230–48.

——, "George Mosse's comparative cultural history," in *What history tells: George L. Mosse and the culture of modern Europe,* edited by Stanley G. Payne, David Jan Sorkin, and John S. Tortorice. (Madison: University of Wisconsin Press, 2003), pp. 48–60.

——, "Remembrance and redemption: a social interpretation of war memorials," *Harvard Design Magazine* (Fall 1999), pp. 71–77.

——, *Visions and violence: imagining the twentieth century.* (New Haven: Yale University Press, 2004).

Winter, Jay, and Blaine Baggett, *14–18. The great war and the shaping of the twentieth century.* (London: BBC Books, 1996; New York: Viking Studio, 1996).

Winter, Jay, and Jean-Louis Robert, *Capital cities at war: Paris, London, Berlin 1914–1919*. (Cambridge: Cambridge University Press, 1997).

Winter, Jay, and Emmanuel Sivan (eds), "Framework," in *War and remembrance in the twentieth century*. (Cambridge: Cambridge University Press, 1999), pp. 1–39.

——, *War and remembrance in the twentieth century*. (Cambridge: Cambridge University Press, 1999).

Winter, Richard (ed), *Der Krieg als inneres Erlebnis; Auszuge aus den Schriften Ernst Jungers*. (Bielefeld, Velhagen and Klasing, 1941).

Witkop, Philipp, *Die Anfange der neueren deutschen Lyrik*. (Leipzig: Teubner, 1908).

——, *Die neuere deutsche lyrik*. (Leipzig, Berlin: B. G. Teubner, 1910–13).

——, *Gottfried Keller als lyriker*. (Freiburg: C. Troemer's universitäts— buchhandlung, 1911).

Yates, Frances A., *The art of memory*. (London: Routledge and K. Paul, 1966).

Yealland, Lewis R., *Hysterical disorders of warfare*. (London: Macmillan, 1918).

Young, Allen, *The harmony of illusions*. (Princeton: Princeton University Press, 1995).

Zamora, Lois Parkinson, *The usable past: the imagination of history in recent fiction of the Americas*. (Cambridge: Cambridge University Press, 1997).

Index